DISCOVERING GENEALOGICAL ROOTS IN SUWANEE COUNTY, FLORIDA

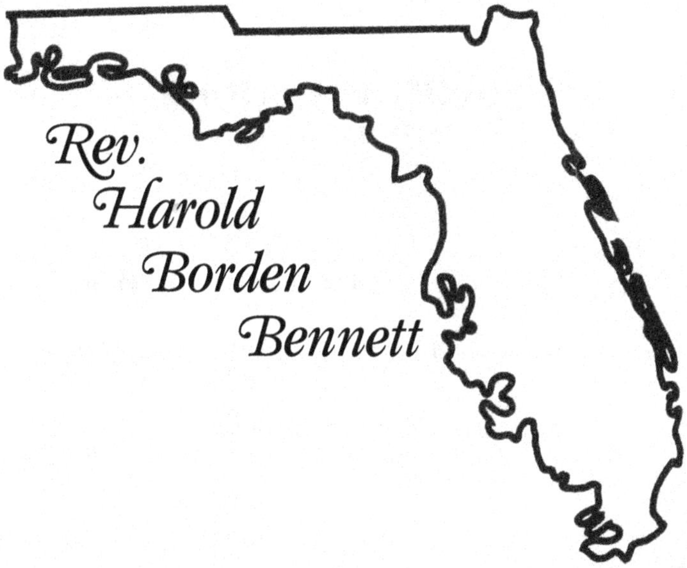

Rev. Harold Borden Bennett

(LATE 1700'S TO EARLY 1900'S)

HERITAGE BOOKS
2010

HERITAGE BOOKS
AN IMPRINT OF HERITAGE BOOKS, INC.

Books, CDs, and more—Worldwide

For our listing of thousands of titles see our website
at
www.HeritageBooks.com

Published 2010 by
HERITAGE BOOKS, INC.
Publishing Division
100 Railroad Ave. #104
Westminster, Maryland 21157

Copyright © 1997 Rev. Harold Borden Bennett

All rights reserved. No part of this book may be reproduced or transmitted in any form or by any means, electronic or mechanical, including photocopying, recording or by any information storage and retrieval system without written permission from the author, except for the inclusion of brief quotations in a review.

International Standard Book Numbers
Paperbound: 978-0-7884-0731-4
Clothbound: 978-0-7884-8490-2

INTRODUCTION

Allow me to introduce myself. My name is Harold Borden Bennett and I am a retired minister. I originally came from Brooklyn, N.Y. and am very new to Suwannee County, Florida. Due to my interest in genealogy, on August 4, 1992 I began writing a column entitled "What's In A Name" for the Suwannee Democrat of Live Oak, Florida. I have always been interested in genealogy and enjoyed doing it. It seemed that very little area history and family research had ever been done on the early settlers of the county and even though Suwannee County was not formed as a county until December 21, 1858, I discovered a great deal of information predating that time.

I discovered several record books of early vintage including a will book dating back to 1850 and an old land grant book with Suwannee County area land grants/purchases dating back to 1828...well before Suwannee County became a county. As I wrote my column week after week I kept finding other early records which I recorded on my computer. Later I was asked if I would publish these findings in book form. The answer is found in the remaining pages of this book. It is our sincere wish that this publication will prove fruitful to those interested in locating their family origins in the Suwannee County, Fl. region.

                                           Rev. Harold B. Bennett,
                                           Founder & Director of the
                                           Suwannee County Genealogical Society

The following "table of contents" show the breakdown of the sections whereas the "index" at the end of the book shows the location of the surnames and places spoken of in the book.

TABLE OF CONTENTS

```
Introduction.....................................1
Table of Contents................................2

Chapter 1 - Basics of Genealogical Research......3
     Name Origins................................3
     Vital Statistics............................7
     Researching Basics..........................9

Chapter 2 - Early Settlers......................17
     Suwannee County Roots......................18
     Timetable of Important Events..............19
     Early Suwannee County Families.............21

Chapter 3 - Early Land Grants...................33
Chapter 4 - Voter Lists.........................41

Chapter 5 - Wills, Probates, & Inventories......49
     Wills......................................49
     Inventories................................69
     Probate Records............................81

Chapter 6 - Military & Pension Records..........83
     Pension Records............................87

Chapter 7 - Tax Lists...........................89
Chapter 8 - Court Cases.........................93
Chapter 9 - Early County Officers...............95

Chapter 10 - Early Suwannee County Marriages...97

Chapter 11 - Columbus Area Cemeteries..........103
     Suwannee County Burials Born Pre-1850.....105

Chapter 12 - Miscellaneous Articles............117
     State & County Changes....................117
     Helpful Information...............117 & 124
     Notes from "The American Siberian".......118
     Carolina Gleanings........................120
     Columbia Cty & Wellborn Gleanings..121 & 123
     Early Passports from Georgia..............121
     Scottish Immigrants.......................122
     Convicts & Rebels.........................124

Index..........................................127
```

Basics of Genealogical Research
(Chapter One)

Have you ever wondered where you came from...originally??? None of our family lines began in this country...not even the Indians. Have you ever wondered where your line began? I did and so I began a very exciting journey into my past and I not only found where my "roots" were but much, much, more! For example, I discovered that even though I was born in Brooklyn, New York, my father and the three generations before him were all born in Long Branch, New Jersey. In further research I discovered that Adrianese BENNETT, who had migrated to this country from Holland was the ancestral father of most New Jersey Bennett's. He had purchased land from an Indian tribe in the early 1600's in what later became known as that part of New York City known as Brooklyn...just a few miles from where I was born. Further research showed my roots to be in Ireland (on my mother's side), and Holland and England (on my father's side). I have discovered hundreds of bits of interesting information which have helped me understand more about myself. Its truly an exciting pilgrimage...one I hope I can encourage each of you to take... even as I did.

NAME ORIGINS

Do you know where your name originated? As I have stated earlier, none of us have our true "roots" in this country. We all have our origins in another part of the world. Actually 82% of all Americans can be traced back to England. The earliest settlers (Jamestown, Va. 1607) were English. The Pilgrims (Plymouth Rock, MA. 1620) were separatists from the Church of England. These were the first of over 5 million English people to settle this land. From then until late in the 1700's this country was predominantly English. In his book entitled "English Surnames", Charles BARDSLEY lists over 600 pages of English names, many of which found their way to America.

During the late 1700's and throughout the 1800's Germans and Scotch-Irish (along with other nationalities) migrated to America in large numbers. Before the Revolutionary War (1775-1783) over 200,000 Germans had settled in New York and Pennsylvania. These, like the early English settlers, came to this country to be free to worship God according to their own consciences.

During this same period, the Scotch-Irish (about 250,000 of them) migrated to America as a consequence of Irish agitation and "hard times". They settled primarily in the Shenendoah Valley of Virginia and the Appalachian regions. By the time the Declaration of Independence was written (1776), 10% of America's population consisted of the Scotch-Irish people. Jeane WESTIN, author of the popular book "Finding Your Roots", said "When the first census was taken in 1790, there were a little under 5 million people in the United States and except for 750,000 black African slaves, most were descended from these three groups...the English, German, and Scotch-Irish".

The Irish, not to be confused with the Scotch-Irish, began their migration to this country during the time of the great potato famine in 1845. Their crops had failed and rather than face the prospect of starvation they chose to come to America. Since then more than 4 million Irish people have migrated to this country...many settling in New York City.

Recently I was asked how to discover family roots in Ireland. It was a good question because most of the library and archive information in Ireland was not collected and recorded until the late 1800's. HOWEVER, there is a better way to discover one's Irish roots. Most Irish families came from a small number of Irish chiefs, which later developed into over 150 kingdoms, and because of this it can be said that every one of Irish descent has a king or queen in their family tree. Because of this each family member was required to know his/her heritage, thus, good records were kept. Where are the records today? In the county of family origin!! THIS IS THE KEY! If the county is known then the town of the individual's ancestral origin can be determined..and by checking the local libraries in Ireland, many family histories can be discovered. However, one MUST know the county in Ireland that the family originated from.

In the United States today there are over 50 million people with "some" Irish blood. That means that one out of every five Americans are of Irish descent. I have a set of books in my library entitled "Irish Ancestors In America" by O'Brien which lists about 1300 pages of Irish immigrants. As I stated earlier, Irish records do not date very far back. For example, vital records such as birth, marriage, and death records can be found in the office of the Registrar-General, the Custom House in Dublin, Ireland...BUT these records only go back to 1864 and unfortunately they are written in Latin. Church records, primarily Roman Catholic registers, are generally kept by the local parish priest. They go back to 1800 and the National Library in Dublin has many of these records on microfilm. Census records are also available in this same library but they only go back to 1901. Property records can prove highly valuable since they go back as far as 1708. These are housed at the Registry of Deeds, Henrietta Street, Dublin, Ireland.

You mustn't forget certain publications and genealogical societies. Among the more important publications, the "Irish Genealogical Helper" can be secured from the Augustan Society, 1617 West 261st Street, Harbor City, CA 90710. Another publication entitled "Irish Ancestors - An Illustrated Journal" is available from Miss Rosemary Folliott, Pirton House, Sydenham Villass, Dundrum, Dublin 14, Ireland. There are two very important books on the market that should prove quite helpful. They are "A Handbook on Irish Genealogy" which is published by Heraldic Artists, Ltd., Trinity College, College Green, Dublin 2, Ireland and "Irish Family Names" by Captain Patrick Kell which is published by Gale Research Company, Book Tower, Detroit, Michigan, 48226. Finally, one might write to the Irish Genealogical Research Society, 82 Eaton Square, London SW1, England

The French has been migrating to this country since the early 1600's as fur traders, planters, etc. Many came to this country directly from France during the 1700's by way of Canada. Over the years they followed the Missouri & Mississippi rivers south, finally settling in great numbers in Louisianna. They are, for the most part, those which are called "Cajuns" today.

The Chinese first came to the west coat in 1850 earning a meager living by re-working gold mines which were worked out during the famed "gold rush days" in the mid 1800's. Until the Exclusion Act of 1882 which prohibited the importation of Chinese workers as "cheap labor", they helped build our nation's railroads. In the 1900's Chinese immigrants who could pay their own way to America were permitted to become American citizens...settling chiefly in Hawaii and California. The Japanese had been refused visas to this country by their own emperor until 1890. Since that time a limited number of Japanese people have immigrated to America to escape the poverty in their own land. Today, due to these circumstances, Orientals are comparatively few in number here.

Since 1820 only slightly more than 100,000 Africans have chosen to migrate to this country. For the most part their American names are assumed names taken after they were given their freedom after the Civil War. Sometimes they took their "master's" names, but mostly they chose arbitrary Americanized names such as JOHNSON, JACKSON, ROBINSON, etc. Before the emancipation, surnames for "blacks" were forbidden by law. This makes tracing an African-American's heritage difficult.

Most names are easy to discern. "Carpenter" or "Sawyer" are both derived from those who work in wood. In earlier days, men were known by their first names only. Suppose someone wanted to direct someone else to John's house...and their were two Johns living in the area. They would be identified as John the carpenter, or John who lives by the lake. Later, as populations grew, identification became much harder, so men began using first AND last names. So, John the carpenter became John Carpenter, and John who lived by the lake became John Lake. Simple, isn't it?

Let's examine how the name "Boatright" or "Boatwright" came into being. A "wright" is in effect a "carpenter". Boatrights were builders of boats...thus the attachment of that name to these folks. This would also hold true to the names "Cartwright" (a builder of carts), or "Wheelwright" (a builder of wheels), etc.

The name "Bailey" (in England) and "Bailiss" (in Scotland) both were derived from a government office...specifically, the name signified a chief magistrate of a barony (or part of a county), sometimes a chief officer of a shire which housed 100 families.

An interesting variation to all names is the different spellings of the same name in different countries. For example, Smith in England would be Schmitt in Germany. The name Smith in different languages is as follows: Dutch: Schmidt, Irish; Gowan/Goff, French: Ferris/LeFevre, Italy: Ferraro, Spain: Ferrer/Herrera, Syria: Haddad, Finland: Seppanen, Hungary: Kovacs.

In the early days spelling was done phonetically. Since most immigrants could not read or write, many names were misspelled and no one knew the difference. When an immigrant's name was asked for, it would be written just the way the recorder heard it...and the unlearned immigrant, not knowing how to read, was unable to correct him. Recently I had a phone call from an individual researching the name "BIRD"...and it was made very clear that only THAT spelling would do...not "BYRD" but "BIRD". I am confident that "BIRD" is the spelling used in this family for possibly the past 100 years...but when one goes further back, it could have been spelled any number of ways. For example, my wife's mother's name is YATES. She insisted that the folks that spelled the name YEATES were a completely different line. However, in tracing her line I discovered her grandfather, Tilmon YEATES, and his father both spelled it YEATES! As a matter of fact, in the early days it was spelled several ways. One will find most names, were spelled many different ways in the early days.

Another problem is that appendages such as "son" or "O" and "Mc" are often dropped by members of the same family...so McNeil become Neil, Robertson becomes Roberts, O'Malley becomes Malley, etc. As people learned to read they chose the spelling that suited them best and used it. Keep these things in mind as you look at names in your research.

On other occasions, names were shortened. I recently received a letter from a young man of Russian lineage whose name had been BRODOWSKY...but it had been changed to BRODY. Then there was a client whose research was at a standstill. Her name was HOWARD and the trail seemed to end. We took up the search and almost accidentally I discovered that a few generations back it originally was HAYWARD. Just a matter of pronunciation made all the difference in her lineage. ALWAYS be sure to check all possible spellings. You may be surprised how your name was spelled originally. In 1754, a gentleman named WILCOX found in viewing several documents containing his name that it was spelled WILCOX, WILCOCKS, WELLCOX, WELLCOCKS, and WELCOCKS. One of my ancestral lines, BORDEN, I found later was often spelled BURDIN.

When dealing with a common name, a problem with a signature written by using an "X" can make it difficult to discern who the individual really was...especially in his relationship to you... if indeed he was related to you at all. In these instances, other proofs must be found, or else you may end up connecting a totally different family line to yours.

In a will, this isn't as much of a problem as it could be...especially if some of the children mentioned in the will have unusual names. Names like William, John, Thomas, Mary, Susan, etc. were commonly used and it isn't unusual for several John Smiths to have children with the same first names. In any event prove that you have the right ancestor. One mistake can take you a long way from the truth.

VITAL STATISTICS

What are they and when did they begin? According to historical records they were (and are) records of births, christenings, baptisms, marriages, deaths, and burials. They began shortly after the Church of England and the Church of Rome separated in 1538. Ministers were required to keep a record of these events and to present these records to the court at least once a year. This law was enacted in this country in Virginia in 1632. By 1639 this law was adopted by the Massachusetts Bay Colony. Connecticut and other colonies began the practice soon thereafter. By the year 1644 Massachusetts added a penalty against those who failed to comply, and by 1692 town clerks were empowered to collect three pence for each event (birth, marriage, death, etc.) that was registered and to assess fines against those who did not report these events. Unfortunately this registration fee became a deterrent to good reporting and more and more the law and the reporting became less effective.

By 1833 only 1/10 of the world was registering vital statistics, and in America only five cities were keeping any kind of registration records. However, it was not until 1875 that death record registration was truly enforced. For most of these early years, census records were the best source of information concerning birth dates and family relationships. In the 1850 census records a line was added which identified those who had become married within the census year. By 1860 the month of birth was added to those who were born within the census year. Little by little census records added information that was difficult to find anywhere else.

The greatest boon for the genealogist was the creation (by an act of Congress) of the National Board of Health in 1879. From its outset it began receiving and publishing vital statistics for all cities who would report them. In its initial year 24 cities cooperated and by 1880 over 90 cities were participating. For the most part, birth and death records are a recent innovation. However, a great deal of information may be gleaned from these records. For example, if you have an ancestor who died at age 90 in 1930, he would have been born in 1840. A death certificate will usually tell the place and cause of death...and sometimes even the place of burial. It may also show the names and places of birth of the decedent and his/her parents.

Birth certificates are of less value in that they are quite

recent and do not take one back far enough to be of any great value (with some exceptions). Marriage certificates have the greatest degree of antiquity and list the marriage partners, date of the marriage, the officials (minister, witnesses, etc.) and sometimes the parents of both parties.

Church records are a source of genealogical information often overlooked by many researchers. Records may have been lost in a "courthouse fire" or some other tragedy...but church records are usually kept intact. The reason many people never take advantage of this important source of information when researching their family line is their lack of knowledge in this field of inquiry. Church records are important in that they list many vital statistics. They usually keep accurate records on births...although sometimes just the christening date is used, but this usually takes place within days of the actual birth. They also keep records on marriages, deaths, and other useful bits of information. For example, those who are researching in the Middlesex County area of Virginia (a county which had its beginnings in 1669), would do well to research the parish register of Middlesex County. It has 341 pages of vital information. It also has a large section naming slaves and their owners. Many parishes have these important records in book form. Another example is the Friends (or Quaker) Church. They kept accurate records of the major events in the lives of their people...births, marriages, deaths, and much more. Even if you don't know if they were part of that group...and many were...you would be wise to spend some time researching these possibilities. REMEMBER too that most churches have graveyards and they provide a great deal of information on relatives.

Even if you're not sure whether your ancestor was part of a particular church group, it would pay to inquire concerning the churches that were in a given area during your ancestor's lifetime. You never know what will turn up! Most people were involved in some church in the early days. In pre-colonial days, church membership in the Church of England was required. Church minutes also are an important source of information. If you can discover these you will find many important pieces of genealogical data in them. And don't forget the itinerant minister's records. People were often scattered over wide areas in pioneer areas and as the minister would travel from home to home, he would do christenings, marriages, and burials...and he would keep records. Later, he would turn this information in to whatever denomination he represented. Go to the library and ask for the addresses of various church headquarters. Write to their archival department for information on the records they maintain. Many churches keep copies or originals of their own proceedings. Find the churches that have been in an area the longest and write to them.

MOST OFTEN USED GUIDES IN TRACING A FAMILY TREE

- A. Census & Indexes
- B. Vital Statistics - Birth, Death, & Marriages
- C. Newspapers
- D. County Histories, Biographies
- E. Cemeteries
- F. Atlases, Maps, City Directories
- G. Libraries
- H. Church Records
- I. Adjutant General, Grave Registration, Military Records
- J. Wills, Probate Records, Guardianships
- K. Land Grants, Deeds
- L. Pensions
- M. National Archives

IF YOU WANT TO FIND:

Birth Dates or Ages: A-B-C-E-G-H-I-J-L
Marriage Dates: B-C-D-E-H-I-J-L
Death Dates: B-C-D-E-G-H-I-J-K-L
Parent of a Person: A-B-C-D-E-G-H
Wife's Maiden Name: B-C-D-G-H-L
Nativity: A-B-C-F-G-I-J-K-L
Locale: B-D-F-G-J-K
Children's Names: A-C-D-G-J-K
Military Records: C-D-E-G-I-L-M

RESEARCHING BASICS

Where should one start if one wants to start a "family tree"? Allow me to share some insights in this matter. First BE SURE to check to see if someone else may have already prepared a printed record of your family line. Most state archives have a listing of family lines that have been printed. You might also check out the local branch library of the Church of the Latter Day Saints (Mormon) Church.

Secondly, there are some rules one must be aware of. Rule #1 is "ONE MUST BEGIN WITH WHAT ONE KNOWS!!!" The simplest way to begin is to search your own documents and especially elderly relatives. Old letters, certificates of birth, marriage, and death that may be held by you or close relatives, and photos (especially when names, dates, and places are written on the back). If one has older relatives (grandfather, grandmother, etc) take time to visit (or write to) these folks. If they are close by, tape your conversation. Plan questions ahead of time.

Old obituaries are quite helpful as are cemetery records. Town histories (found in the library where the individual lived) is usually helpful especially for the earlier years when most people had a part in the activities of the community. Don't forget to look for "last wills and testaments". These come in two forms. A will made by the one who has died or a probate record. The latter is a court procedure used when an individual does NOT make out a valid will. Either of these contains much useful information.

Deeds and land records also are very useful and predate most recorded records. Courthouses generally house land records as well as probate, tax, marriage, and other valuable records.

A major contributor to the genealogist is the census record....state or federal. These can be found in larger libraries and archives. They can also be rented through the Church of the Latter Day Saints Branch Library and sometimes borrowed through local libraries. Records of people's lives are voluminous.

One can always find enough information to make a family history. However, a word of advice! Whatever source you research, be sure to list the source you searched and the information found (if any). This will save a lot of lost time duplicating search patterns later. Keep a notebook for this and when you enter information on your "pedigree charts" and your "family group sheets" (we'll discuss these later), SHOW THE SOURCE!!! Incidentally most genealogical computer programs have a means by which you can list the source in a hidden file.

When researching your ancestry the most important record in your file is the pedigree chart. This chart numbers each ancestor, shows the basic vital statistics, and shows the relationships to other members of the family. Here's how it works. Let's suppose to want to research your family. You would put information about yourself on line #1 (simply fill in the blanks as the chart is self-explanatory). Line #2 would be for your father and line #3 would be for your mother. Another rule to remember is that the male ancestors are always even numbers, whereas the females are always identified with odd numbers. You might consider purchasing a book entitled "The Researcher's Guide to American Genealogy" by Val D. Greenwood. Most libraries have a copy on their shelves...or they can get it for you on inter-library loan. The second most important record is the family chart. This groups all the statistical information about each individual family and is also self-explanatory.

Let me share some important information concerning some of the writing differences between modern and older documents. It has proved confusing to some...and well it should. Have you ever tried to read a will for someone in the year 1750? Its truly an adventure! Allow me to take the time to share some of the problems. For example, before 1752 (the year the calendar was changed to what we have today) New Year's Day fell on March 25th. Let us suppose you noticed that a will you have an interest in reveals that an individual draws up his will in October of 1692...and then goes on to say that he died in February of 1692. It would appear that he made his will AFTER he died. BUT since the year 1692 runs from March to March, the entry is found to be correct. The man died 4 months AFTER he made up his will. In order to avoid confusion, we would simply write the dates as follows...dates from March 25 through December 31 would be written as 1692. However, dates from January 1 through March 24 should be written 1692/1693. Remember this dating system is valid only on dates before 1752.

Many older documents are literally overrun with ABBREVIATIONS. Notice...church is written as "chh"; ditto is "do" or "d^o" namely is written as "vis"... (for Latin "videlicet"); receipt is "rec^t"; the is written as "y^e"; testament is "teste"; said is "s^d"; etc. It might also be remembered that capitalization is arbitrary and many abbreviations are made by simply shortening a word at the writer's discretion. A shortened word with a line through it or a word written in superscript is a signal that the word was shortened. This practice was quite common in the writing of names.

Certain letters also cause problems in deciphering some writings. For example, the double "s" was usually written as an "f"...which in turn could easily be confused with the actual "f" or "p". Curlecues on letters which have below the line appendages such as "g" or "y" or above the line appendages such as "d" can also prove troublesome as they tend to run into other letters on adjacent lines. The small "e" was often written as an "o" which presents another problem. These are the more common problems. A careful study of the document will help one understand the particular characteristics of the writer's style.

Another area of difficulty are Latin terms which make interpretation difficult. For example...Circa = about, et al = and others, liber = book, nepes = grandson, obiit = he or she died, sic = so or thus, testes = witnesses, ultimo = last, uxor = wife, item = likewise...and so it goes.

We have been dealing with certain problems that every researcher faces having to do with abbreviations, names, arbitrary capitalization, punctuation, look-alike letters, and Latin terms. Now I would like to discuss spelling, marks\signatures, relationships, and naming practices.

A major trouble spot is the use of terms of relationships. For example, "Jr." and "Sr." are normally taken for a father-son relationship...however, in early documents "uncle" and "nephew" relationships were often identified using these same terms. The terms "cousin", "brother", and "sister" also can be confusing. "Cousin" usually denoted a nephew or niece, but not always! Sometimes it applied to a relative outside of the immediate family circle..e.i. 2nd, 3rd, and 4th cousins. Many times the terms "brother" and "sister" had nothing to do with a blood relative...but rather they denoted church relationships...but sometimes they did relate to blood kin. Proving it one way or another is sometimes nearly impossible. Take time to prove relationships.

Another very important issue that needs to be dealt with is in the area of "organizing and evaluating" what you have discovered. Without this, the rest is confusion. The above sources already discussed will help you construct the outline or skeleton of your family history. However, one needs to put meat on those dry bones to make your family history appealing and interesting. Many have heard the news commentator Paul Harvey speak of "the rest of the story"...well, to the genealogist, organizing and evaluating what you have discovered IS the rest of the family history story. Remember the good old days when your English teacher would assign a "book report" for homework? You could only accomplish this by really understanding what you read. Then you had to outline the book, think the material through, and then you had to write it down in an interesting manner. Basically one does the same thing with a family history...the only difference is that you start with the outline which reveals three important facts...names, places, and dates. From this you develop the family history.

For example, suppose you discovered that your grandfather was born in 1920, married in 1940, had his first child in 1941, his second child in 1942, his third child in 1947, and his fourth child in 1949. What could you deduce from this? Realizing that World War 2 happened from 1941 through 1946, it would be very likely he enlisted or was drafted into service seeing that no children were born between 1943-1946. You could write for possible military records for more details of his life. Let's explore another example. Your great-great-great grandfather was born in Richmond, Virginia in 1870. He was married in 1895 in Martinsville, Va. Their first two children were born in Martinsville, Va. in 1897 and 1899. The third child was born in Atlanta, Ga. in 1901, and their fourth child was born in Lake City, FL in 1903. He died in Lake City, FL. in 1950, and his wife died in Richmond, Va. in 1960. What could you learn from this? You could get his birth certificate from Richmond, Va. From this you could discover a number of pieces of information...possibly including his parents names. The fact that he was married in Martinsville, Va. would give you the source for their marriage certificate which holds more information. Their first two childrens' birth certificates would also be found here. You have learned that sometime between 1899 and 1900 they moved to Atlanta. Considering the years of his children's births, it is not likely he served in the Spanish-American War...nor is it likely that he served in World War 1 since he would have been in his forties. Sometime between 1901 and 1903 they moved to Lake City, FL. From the fact that his wife died in Richmond, Va. (her deceased husband's birthplace) we might deduce that her parents had died and that she lived near her husband's kinfolk after he died. This is the idea. One must think about the happenstances of life and try to see how one's ancestors fit into those events. That is the basis for a family history.

It seems appropo to speak to you about the steps involved in "organization and evaluation". During the initial research, one will usually discover information beyond the customary names, dates, and places. Keep this information in a notebook or file. An index card serves this purpose well. It keeps the information with the individual researched, and it is concise enough to make the information easily accessible. For example, if you use the index card system, have the primary name card list name #1 on the pedigree chart. You will want to show the names of parents, wife, and children on the first card. **You will need to maintain a separate card for each member of each family.**

On the second card you should list all pertinent information regarding the birth (date, time, place, hospital (if any), doctor, personal characteristics, etc. This type of information can be added as found. A third card can be used exclusively for marriage particulars while a fourth card might be used for death particulars. Additional cards might be added for military service, education, occupation, miscellaneous, etc. Each individual can be set up in this way. Tabs can be added to show the category of each card. A different color for each type of card would add to the system's efficiency. ALWAYS be sure to list sources with the information you find. Those using computers can accomplish the same thing by using a database.

When listing a book or microfilm/microfiche source, be sure to list 1) the compiler, author, or editor, 2) title & edition, 3) place & date of publication, 4) publisher, 5) page numbers. This will make it possible for others to find this information in later years. By putting the names of parents, grandparents, and children on one card, relationships are shown and one is sure to get the correct cross-reference card. A final tip would be to always CAPITALIZE the primary name to avoid confusing it with secondary names (names on card they relate to).

Research notes must be complete and simple enough for others to understand them. Another important tool is the RESEARCH CHART/CALENDAR. This is a sheet (or index card) used to list areas researched or to be researched. One may have to search several different areas in order to secure one piece of information. As the list grows, it is easy to forget where one has searched, therefore this RESEARCH CHART becomes an important tool to prevent duplicating searches. Headings may include 1) a description of source...a book, a courthouse record, a cemetery, etc. 2) purpose of the search, 3) date of search, 4) identifying number of microfilm/microfiche, and/or volume and page of book, etc., 5) place of search (this may be entered in description of source column...e.g. Jackson County, Miss. Court House, or, Cemetery at Pine Grove Methodist Church, Suwannee Cty, FL., 6) report of findings...if any. If nothing was found, list it that way. I trust this will prove useful and will aid you in your organization.

We would like to conclude our thoughts on "organization" with some important remarks on the keeping of research notes. There are several hard and fast rules that must be observed lest we find ourselves in a quagmire of confusion. In the earlier phase of our research, source notes seem of little importance, but when one gets deeper in one's research, one will begin to get confused about which research sources have been done and which haven't been done...unless good research practices are followed.

It may prove helpful to maintain a cross-file for both location AND surname...especially when several lines converge in one locale. Identify what your research purpose was!!! An example might look like this...1) Date: July 1, 1992, 2) Place: Suwannee County Courthouse, 3) Purpose: Marriage records for John Smith and Mary Jones, 4) Result: No record found...or possibly, Marriage record dated January 2, 1900 found. If no record is found then one must reanalyze the facts and look in other directions.

The following are some ideas gleaned from years of genealogical research. Maybe they will help you in your research.

1) Area histories sometimes prove quite helpful. For example, I was looking for a branch of my wife's mother's family named LINKOUS. For many years I scoured the records in county and state without finding anything of any real value. I had gotten back to my wife's mother's great grandfather on her mother's side. I had learned that Abraham Linkous (b.1811) was married to Emmaline Simpson (b.1819) and they lived in Bluefield, W.Virginia. Nothing more was to be found...UNTIL I happened to mention my plight to a librarian in the genealogical section of a library I researched on a number of occasions. She suggested-gested I look at a book having to do with a German settlement of the New River area in Virginia. Her reasoning was, the name was German and this area in Virginia had been developed by German immigrants. I looked and...BINGO!!!...I found Abraham and his family line all the way back to his ancestry to the 1500's. I never even knew this book existed...and I would have thought by the title that it was simply a history of the area. It gave a number of genealogies of several families. Quite a bonanza. Sometimes it pays to find the books that are for a certain locale and go through the indices of each book checking out the names you think be there.

2) Another interesting idea is to organize an individual you are having trouble with in a chronological order of events. Take the earliest event you have and list it in a column with the next earliest event...etc. until you arrive at the most recent event. List year, event, place, etc. For example, let's organize the life of Richard Borden in this way. 1601..born Hedcorn, Kent Cty, England. 1625..married Joan Fowler, 1626..son Thomas born in England 1627..son Francis born in England 1630..dau. Mary born in England 1635..migrated to America to Boston Neck, Ma. 1638..son Matthew born in Portsmouth, R.I. 1638..received 5 acres of land at Portsmouth....other dates & events....1671..died at Portsmouth, R.I. 1688..wife died same place. Reviewing an individual's life in this manner will make it easier to see when and where the events of one's life unfolds. Another good idea is to have a parallel column showing historical events that took place during the individual's life...wars, political things, etc. They often give clues which help you discover new areas to research. In due course of time, the life of the ancestor becomes fuller.

3) Another tip is in writing dates. Be SURE to use a three or four letter abbreviation for the month. Some people write the date for June 9, 1825 as 6/9/1825. Someone else might write June 9, 1825 as 9/6/1825. Someone later sees the date of an ancestor's birth as 6/9/1825. Depending on how the original author was thinking, it could be June 9th or Sept. 6th. Which is correct? You will need other evidence to learn the answer to that question. When you write a date, spell out the month with letters, not numbers. That way June will always be June and September will always be September.

4) It only takes 5 or 6 generations to accumulate hundreds of names. Sometimes you may find it difficult...at least time-consuming, to find an ancestor. Help yourself out by developing an index card file. Store your names alphabetically. On the primary card (in capitol letters) list the family name...ex. BENNETT. List the remainder of the pertinent information in regular lettering..ex. Harold Borden. Show the pedigree chart and person number of the individual. In my genealogy I am found on Chart #1, Line #1. My great-great grandfather will be found on Chart #2, Line #1. As long as you know the name, you'll know where to find them in your records. You can also add the number of the family sheet (devise a numbering system) Put the Chart 1, Line 1 person on Family Sheet #1. Put the father's family on sheet #2, the grandfather's family on sheet #3, etc. Use your ingenuity to its best advantage.

5) When writing your family history in book form, be sure to show your ancestor's and their relationships. One needs a simple, yet definitive system. One possibility is as follows; If my genealogy starts with me, then I am #1. My first child would #11, my second child would be #12, my third #13 etc. If I had (and thank God I don't) 12 children, the twelfth would be numbered 112. My father is #2, therefore I, as his first child would be #21, the second would be #22, etc. Since wives are related to their husband, they would not have a number. However, if my grandfather was married twice and had 3 children by each marriage, they would be numbered 31a for the first child of the first wife and 31b for the first child of the second wife. They would show more than one marriage with their respective children. This works fine for pedigree chart #1...but what happens when you get to your g-g-g-grandfather who is number 1 on chart #2? The answer is simple. Use a superscript number 2 before his number and subsequent children. For ex. the number of his 3rd child would be a superscript 2 before his number 13. It would be the same as the first pedigree chart but with a superscript 2...and if you were to get to the third pedigree chart you would use the superscript 3 before the number of the individual,etc. OR, you could opt to simply change the #1 on the second sheet to the last number on the first sheet. Another problem arises. When you arrive at the 3rd generation, you would have a paternal side AND a maternal side. The third generation paternal would be identified as follows...31p (3=3rd generation head, 1=1st child, and p=paternal or father's side). On the maternal side the number

might be 31m (3=3rd generation, 1=1st child, and m=maternal or mother's side). The fourth generation would be as follows..41p1 would be 4=4th generation, 1=1st child, p=paternal side, and 1=1st head of house on paternal side. If it were 41p2 it would be the same excepting the final 2=2nd head of house on paternal side. Follow the same procedure for the maternal side. Regarding the earlier generations, follow the same procedure except for the final number (head of house) which would be 1,2,3, & 4 on either side. The 6th generation would have no less than 8 heads on either side. It sounds confusing but it is a sure-fire numbering system. One can always identify the individuals relationship to the other members of the family.

Early Settlers
Chapter 2

What do names like CHARLES, DYALL, HAWKINS, ROUSSEAU, STAPLETON, VICKERS, SHARP, BONNELL, BREWER, WHITTON, or HERRINGTON mean to us today? They are some of the first recorded settlers of Suwannee County and they were here long before Suwannee County became a county. According to military and census records these men and their families settled here as early as 1818. They braved the rigors of taming the land and of overcoming the dangers posed by threatened Indians.

In my research I have found very little information about these early settlers. There are, however, no less than 80 of their descendants living in Suwannee, Lafayette, Columbia, Madison, Hamilton, and Taylor counties today.

It always amazes me at how quickly people migrated from one place to another in the middle 1800's. Suwannee County inhabitants should never overlook searching adjoining counties when doing research. We are joined to the following counties: Madison, Hamilton, Columbia, and LaFayette. Recently I received several books concerning LaFayette County and was happily surprised to find a number of names of early Suwannee County people. For example, Samuel BARBER owned land in Suwannee County in 1852, but is missing in the census records for Suwannee County after that. However I found him and his wife Mary in the LaFayette County census of 1860. Other names that are prevalent in Suwannee and LaFayette counties are: BEVAN, BOATRIGHT, BYNUM, CANNON, CARAWAY, CASON, DEAN, DEAS, FUTCH, GRANT, HEWITT, HURST, JOHNSON, LEE, McALPIN, McCULLERS, MICKLER, McQUEEN, O'STEEN, PARKER, PEACOCK, PONCHIER, SEARS, SISTRUNK, SUGGS, TILLIS, WILLIAMS, and WILSON. There are others but these stand out. For those of you interested in LaFayette County, I will list 4 books and where you can purchase them..."1860 Federal Census of LaFayette County", "History of New Troy" (Capitol of LaFayette County in early 1800's), "LaFayette County Veterans Grave Registration and Confederate Pension Applications for Dixie, LaFayette, Madison, Suwannee, and Taylor Counties", and "Lafayette County and the Anaconda" (this is a record of the Union Naval Blockade of LaFayette County during Civil War). At the time of this writing, the cost of these books was $2.00 each (plus postage) from Wilburn P. Bell, P.O. Box 575, Day, Fl. 32013.

So often we find ourselves wondering where our families fit into our area history. I would like to begin a two-fold history of Suwannee County...a history of events and a history of the people that made the events happen. Much has been written concerning the early development of Florida and even of Suwannee County, but we have no interest in rehashing history that has been worked "to death". Our intention is to highlight the obvious and expand that which has not been dealt with to any great degree.

Suwannee County Roots

As early as the 1500's the Timucuan Indians were the primary caretakers of this part of the country. Throughout this period of time the Timucuan Indians were the predominant tribe in north and central Florida. Their life style was pretty much the same as other "farming" tribes. They lived off the land by way of hunting and farming. They lived in circular structures comparable in size to the white man's log cabins. As early as 1513, Ponce de Leon had contact with the Timucuan Indians in Florida, and in 1539 Hernando DeSoto led a party of Spaniards across our county following a trail from what is now Ichetucknee Springs to Charles Springs. By the late 1600's the Timucuans were extinct.

By the early 1700's, most of north central Florida became almost without human inhabitant. This condition continued until the late 1700's when refugees and renegades from the Creek nation took up residence in northern Florida. These were the beginnings of the Seminole tribes. The word "seminole" means "renegade", or "runaway". By 1815 there were approximately 5000 Seminoles living in North Florida. We'll speak more on the Seminoles later.

Most of north Florida's immigrant settlers migrated from the Carolina's and Georgia. Many south Georgians crossed what is now Jefferson County on their way to the Gulf to boil water for its salt content (this was the shortest route). During these migrations, some of the settlers decided to stay. Over the years they expanded and settled Madison, Hamilton, Suwannee and other nearby counties. Immigrants also came from the eastern part of Georgia along the coast, down the St.Mary's River and into areas now occupied by Jacksonville and St. Augustine. These overflowed into adjacent counties such as Columbia County. One of the enticements for our Suwannee County area was the Suwannee River. It provided transportation, good farmland, and more.

From the early years of the Timucuan Indians to the early 1800's, Florida was controlled by Spain, England, France, and finally, the United States. Through the efforts of Gen. Andrew Jackson, the United States was enabled to purchase Florida from Spain in 1821. An interesting sidelight is found in the census records for 1820 and 1830. In the 1820 census almost all the listed names were of Spanish origin...but one would be hard-pressed to find Spanish names in the 1830 census. They moved out quickly wherver they went. General Jackson was appointed Florida's first governor in 1821. Jacksonville (formerly Cowford) was named for Andrew Jackson. In 1819 a fort was built near White Springs for the protection of the early settlers from the Indians of the area. Later, the fort was used for church revivals and camp meetings.

The Suwannee River played an important role in the formation of Florida's counties in the early years. Initially Florida was divided into two counties. All the land in the Florida territory that was west of the Suwannee River became Escambia County whereas all the land east of the Suwannee River became St. John's County. The counties that were established afterwards were all derived from these two counties.

TIMELINE OF IMPORTANT EVENTS

The following dates constitute the important events leading up to the formation of Suwannee County. I trust these dates and their events will prove helpful in your study of this part of our Suwannee County history.

@1500 - Timucuan Indian country.

@1800 - Trails across the county were formed by the earlier travels of Spanish, English, French, Americans, and Indians in and around our county area.

1812 - After the War of 1812 many veterans received land grants to this area. Not all settled here but some "brave souls" did.

@1818 - Reuben & Rebecca CHARLES established a trade route between St.Augustine and Pensacola. Later they established a ferry service and a trading post at Charles Springs.

1819 - A fort was built in the area of the Pine Grove Camp Meeting (near White Springs) to protect the early settlers from Indian attacks. Judge DYALL, along with others, spent several months there during the Seminole Indian uprisings.

1820 - The first census was taken (mostly Spaniards since this was their land at that time).

1821 - The U.S. purchased the land from Spain.

1822 - The Pine Grove Methodist Church was established. It was the first church built in this area.

1822 - Duval County was formed.

1824 - Alachua County was formed.

1830 - As far as can be accurately determined, only 10 families were living in our area...but there were probably many more.

1832 - Columbia County was formed.

1835-1842 - Seminole Indian War raged. Capt. George E. McClellan organized a home militia to protect the settlers.

1841 - Columbus township (now extinct) was formed and thrived for 60+ years.

1845 - Florida became a state.

1858 - Suwannee County was formed.

1868 - Live Oak became the County Seat of Suwannee County. Prior to that the town of Houston had been the County Seat.

This outline is limited but it may help. An individual could have lived in the Suwannee County area during 1800-1860 and be counted a resident of 5 counties during that time.

The "Land Acts" of our governing bodies also had a great deal to do with settling of Florida. You may find these useful so I will list them by date order...

1607-1776 - The British Crown granted all lands to the colonies. Each colony was then responsible as to how and to whom land was sold or granted to.

1776 - The Federal Government of the United States was formed. All land OTHER than that of the 13 original colonies...Vermont, Kentucky, Tennessee, Maine, West Virginia, Hawaii, and Texas, were "State Land States"...all other lands were "Public Land States". State Land States could sell/grant land within their boundaries...but the Public Land States original land was sold/granted by the Federal Government.

1785 - The transfer of Public Land States land (hereafter called Public Domain) began with the Land Act of 1785. The Federal Government sold "public domain" land in 36 section townships (23,040 acres) and in single sections (640 acres) at $1.00 per acre payable within a year.

1796 - A new Federal Government Land Act raised the selling price to $2.00 per acre.

1800 - An ordinance was passed reducing the minimum land purchase to 320 acres. This could be paid for in 4 payments over a five year period.

1812 - This was the first act passed regarding military bounty land grants (commonly called "bonus land"). It was for privates and non-commissioned officers who served in the Revolutionary War. It consisted of 50 acre grants for land in Arkansas, Illinois, and Missouri districts and was non-tranferable.

1820 - A new ordinace was passed which eliminated "credit sales". It also reduced minimum land purchases to 80 acres at $1.25 per acre.

1830 - This ordinace allowed settlers, including squatters (people living on land that was not theirs), who had lived on and cultivated public domain land in 1829, to purchase up to 160 acres for $1.25 per acre.

1838 - This ordinance allowed any head of household OR anyone over 21 years of age, who had been living on public domain land up to 4 months before passage of the act to purchase up to 160 acres for $1.25 per acre. There was an influx of over 70 heads of house that purchased land in Suwannee County as a result of the passage of this "act".

1841 - A permament "preemption act" was passed, allowing any United States citizen (including those who had declared their intention to become a citizen) who was either a head of household or over 21 years of age to stake a claim on any public domain land up to 160 acres for $1.25 an acre.

1842 - East Florida granted any man over 18 or any head of house who took up permament residence in the area, 160 acres of FREE LAND.

1847 - An act was passed to grant bounty lands (free land for services rendered in the military) to those who served in the Mexican War (1846-48) for a minimum of one year.

1850 - An act was passed to grant bounty lands to those who served in the War of 1812 (1812-14), and the Indian Wars (1675 to 1776). Another act was passed giving FREE LAND in the Oregon Territory to any settler who would homestead there before December 1, 1850 and pledge to live there for 4 years. A single man qualified for 320 acres, whereas a married man qualified for 640 acres.

1852 - Bounty land grants were extended to include officers as well as enlisted men.

1853 - Residency requirements for those living in Oregon was reduced to 2 years.

1854 - An "act" was passed stating that public domain lands that had been on the market for 30 years could be sold for 12 and 1/2 cents per acre. Over 80 settlers in Suwannee County took advantage of this offer.

1855 - The FREE LAND acts for Oregon and Washington expired. Another act passed which awarded bounty lands to every military personnel including heirs who served at least 14 days in any war.

1862 - The Homestead Act passed. Settlers (over the age of 21 and being citzens or having declared intention of becoming a citizen) could have up to 160 acres of FREE PUBLIC DOMAIN LAND simply by living on the land and cultivating it for 5 years.

1863 - The FREE LAND act for settlers of New Mexico territory expired.

1872 - Civil War veterans became eligible for Homestead Act rights.

EARLY FAMILIES

Note: Most of the genealogies of many of the following families are kept by the Suwannee County Genealogical Society.

NATHANIEL BRYAN

In 1860 Nathaniel (b.1808 in N.C.) and his wife (b.1816 in Ga.) were living in Suwannee Cty, Fl. Their children, all Florida born were, Nathaniel Jr. (b.1844), Sarah (b.1850), William (b.1853), Joshua (b.1855), and Charles (b.1859).

On April 27, 1835 he was the treasurer at the Hamilton County Court House. He was also a Justice of the Peace in 1833,

1835, and 1837. He was also postmaster (1833-1836, possibly again in 1842) in Swift Creek area of Hamilton County, Fl. In 1837 he served as representative of Hamilton County to the Legislative Council of the Florida Territory.

An inventory of Nathaniel's goods was published on June 16, 1862. One negro boy, Amos, and some monies owed him are all that are mentioned.

ARCHBALD CARRAWAY

Archibald CARRAWAY was born in Darlington County, South Carolina around 1814. He moved to Florida in the late 1840's, being listed in the 1848 Mineral Springs District voting list. He purchased land in that area in 1850 and lived there til he died in 1871. His first wife was Susan Ann ????? of Sampson County, North Carolina. They were married in 1835. Their children were as follows: Joseph (b.1836 in S.C., d.1907 in FL. He married Maniza A. HILL), William F. (b.1838 in S.C. d. ????. He married Miniza KING), Susannah (b.1840 in S.C., d. 1875 in FL. She married C.W.P. HOWELL), Elizabeth (b.1842 in S.C., d. ????. She married Thomas S. HILL), Caroline (b.1842 in S.C., d. 1875 in FL. She married William H. FIELDS), Frances (b.1848, d. 1922 in FL. She married Benjamin ALEXANDER), Charles (b.1853 in FL. d.1919 in FL. Never married), and John W. (b.1855 in FL., d.1925 in FL. He married Martha BENNETT. Susan, Archibald's first wife died in 1855. Later Archibald married Clarky S. ???? from Georgia.

A number of CARRAWAY's had purchased or were granted land here. They are as follows: Martin (1852), Joshua (1852), Elijah (1854), and Archibald (1855). Mr. Carraway lists his line as follows: Thomas (1704), Elijah (1741), Ezekiel (1774), Archibald (1814), John Wesley (1855), Arthur Jackson (1882), Carl Francis (1911), and Glenn Byron...our contributor (1938).

CATESWORTH LOGAN CARRUTH

Catesworth Logan CARRUTH Sr. was one of the early settlers. He was born in North Carolina on October 14, 1802. He married Caroline White LIVINGSTON on March 26, 1833 in South Carolina. Their first son, Thomas Alexander CARRUTH was born in South Carolina on Sept.7, 1835. William S. CARRUTH was born in Madison County, Florida in 1839, as was James L. CARRUTH (b.1842), and Catesworth L. CARRUTH Jr. (1844). Catesworth Logan CARRUTH Sr. was serving as clerk of the Madison County Circuit Court when the 1850 census was taken. His wife Caroline died in December of 1847 in the general vicinity of the present day Antioch Baptist Church. He died in January of 1865. Their son, Thomas Alexander, married Mary Ann HERRING on October 29, 1854.

In the 1860 Suwannee County census, Catesworth Sr. was married to Rhoda HINSON (b.1802 in S.C.). His son William S. was still living with them as was a daughter of Rhoda from an earlier marriage. Her name was also Rhoda Hinson (b.1843 in Fl.).

REUBEN CHARLES

One of the first settlers in northern Florida was Reuben CHARLES. In order for Mr. Charles to be eligible for a rather large tract of land (350 acres) situated about 12 miles north of St. Augustine, he needed affirmation that he was homesteading a portion of the land. Andrew STORRS verified the fact by declaring, "that in 1818, Reuben Charles and his family were upon the land, having a large log house with 3 or 4 cleared acres. He planted rice in 1819." Mr. Storrs also stated that in 1922 he found them in possession of the land...Mr. Charles appearing to be 50 to 60 years of age. They had arrived in Florida sometime after 1814 since their first born son, Andrew J. Charles, was born in 1814 in South Carolina. Sometime during this period, Reuben established a trade route between St. Augustine and Pensacola. He served both the Indians and the Spanish before the United States took possession of the Florida Territory in 1821.

Due to continued Indian uprisings throughout north Florida congress saw the need for a military road to be constructed linking St.Augustine, Tallahassee, and Pensacola, therefore a bill was passed to ensure its development. In 1819 a fort was built in the area of the Pine Grove Camp Meeting (near White Springs) to protect the early settlers from Indian attacks.

Mr. Charles, knowing where the trail crossed the Suwannee River, secured a charter to build a trading post and operate a ferry at what is now Charles Springs (just south of Dowling Park on the western border of Suwannee County). Later a fort was built at Charles Springs as a protection from the Indians during the Seminole Indian War (1835-1842). Incidentally it has been reported that a Franciscan monk had established the mission of San Juan De Guacara in 1655 in the same land area that Charles Springs evolved on.

In the 1830 Alachua County Census, Reuben CHARLES is listed as head of house in a household of 11 occupants as follows: Reuben was between 40-50 years of age...indicating his birth was somewhere between 1780 & 1790. Rebecca, his wife, was 36 (her birth was on May 1, 1794 according to her tombstone). At this census they had 1 boy named Andrew J. (bet.15-20 yrs), 1 unnamed boy (bet.10-15 yrs...probably Reuben H.), 1 girl named Drucilla (bet.10-15 yrs), and a girl named Mary A. (under 5). They also had 1 male adult (bet.50-60)...possibly one of their parents or a hired hand. In addition to these, they had 3 slaves...1 man (bet.24-36 yrs), 1 girl (bet. 36-55 yrs), and 1 girl (bet.10-24 yrs). They lived on the Suwannee River. The census record below gives more exact dates of birth. (NOTE: Other than the head of house, the 1830 census does not show names. Those that I have included above have been proven to be correct from other records).

The 1850 Florida Census (coupled with other records) reveals the following: Reuben was not shown since he died in 1840. This is proven by a legal document housed at Tallahassee showing his wife received authority to operate the ferry at Charles Springs crossing in lieu of Reuben's death. The document was dated 1840. Rebecca was 56 years of age, having been born in North Carolina. According to her tombstone, she was born on May 1, 1794. She died on January 25, 1852. Notice...she was buried in the Charles Cemetery (hers is the only stone there) which is located near Charles Springs. To view this stone, take highway 51 south out of Live Oak and go to Charles Springs Road. Turn right (west), and go to River Road, then turn south on River Road and go 2/10ths of a mile. Walk east 300 feet and you're there. The inscription reads as follows:

Rebecca CHARLES - b. May 1, 1794, d. Jan.25, 1852.
Poem on marker reads...
"In hope I rest beneath the ground though mingled with the dust,
Yet when the angel's trump shall sound, I will rise in Christ I trust,
Thou art laid in the grave, we no longer behold thee, nor tread the rough paths of this world by thy side,
But the wide arms of mercy are spread to enfold thee, and sinners may hope since the Saviour has died".

Andrew J. Charles was listed as head of house in Madison County, Florida. He had moved to Madison County before 1847. We know this because he is listed on the 1847 Madison County tax listing. Andrew and his wife Lania were both born in South Carolina, he in 1814 and she in 1816. At this time the census shows they had 2 daughters...Francis (b.1846), Emily (b.1848), and 1 son Benjamin (b.1844). Their children were all born in Florida as were...Drucilla Charles (b.1823), Mary A. Charles (b.1828), and Reuben H. Charles (b.1832).

Reuben H. born in 1832 in Florida. Records show that he was appointed to serve as Captain of Columbia County's 1st Militia in 1859 in anticipation of an expected "slave uprising". Reuben H. was living in Lake City when the 1860 Columbia County census was taken. The record lists himself (b.1832), his wife Mary V. (b.1840), and a son named Garrett V. (b.1857). Reuben's wife was born in Georgia whereas his son was born in Florida.

He also served as a First Lieutenant in the Civil War in the First Florida Calvary through 1864. It is not known exactly when Reuben H. died but it was before 1870. I know this because "Reuben Charles, deceased" had his land sold for taxes in that year. Reuben died sometime between 1864-1870 and is probably buried in Columbia County.

The following are early lands received by the CHARLES family listed by exact location and date.

```
Reuben  -   80 acres T4,R11,S4 - W1/2 of SW1/4 on Apr.28,1828
Andrew J.- ? acres T4,R11,S5 - Applic 7619 on Aug.31,1838
   "       40 a. T3,R11,S20 - N1/2 of Lot 7 on NE1/4 of SE1/4
                              on Aug.1, 1837
Rebecca - 148.5 a. T3,R11,S20 - Lot 5 on Jan.20, 1849
   "     -  40 a. T4,R11,S23 - NW1/4 of SE1/4 on May 12,1847
   "     - 113 a. T4,R11,S21 - Lot 2 on Nov.14,1848
   "     -  80 a. T4,R11,S21 - Lot 1 on Oct.26, 1848
   "     -  80 a. T4,R11,S20 - Lot 6 on W1/2 of SE1/4. No date
```
All of these sites were within a few miles of each other and they were near Charles Springs.

Finally, I have found a Rebecca CHARLES who had married Robert Allen on May 6, 1866 in Suwannee County. She also received a land grant from the United States in 1891. This may be a relative of the CHARLES family we have been discussing...only further research will tell.

BENJAMIN G. CURRY

Presently this man is something of a mystery. Upon checking the 1840 and 1850 Florida census records I found three mentions of Benjamin Curry...none of Benjamin G. Curry. In all three instances he is shown to be living in Key West, Florida and to have been born in the Bahama Islands. There is a Benjamin Curry (b.1788) who was married to Catherine (b.1793 in the Bahamas). No children were listed...however their children were probably on their own by this time. Another Benjamin Curry (b.1793) was married to Martha (b.1800 in the Bahamas). Three children were listed: Benjamin (b.1834), Samuel (b.1837), and Mary E. (b.1842). Benjamin and Samuel were also born in the Bahamas, but Mary was born in Florida (probably in Key West).

In a book entitled "Homeward Bound" by Sandra Riley, which is a history of the settlement of the Bahama Islands, there are a large number of "Curry/Currie" families...some of which migrated to Florida and other places in the continental United States land area. Over 65 members of this surname are mentioned...all before 1850. By now you may be wondering why Benjamin G. Curry is mentioned in a history of Suwannee County. There are two deed records in Suwannee County where he is mentioned. On Sept.10, 1831, Benjamin received 160 acres of land from the Federal Government in Township 2, Range 14, and Section 23. However, in 1838 Benjamin sold this land and that's the last we hear of him.

JOSEPH DYALL

Joseph DYALL was born in the Darlington District of South Carolina in 1790 (Wiregrass Records) or 1787 (1860 Florida Census). Mr. Dyall came to Appling County, Ga. soon after it was created and is shown there in the 1820 census. He served there as a Justice of the peace of the 451st District from 1821-25. This district was known as the Waresboro District becoming part of Ware County when it was formed in 1825. At the first election in Ware County, Joseph was elected State Senator, serving in the 1826 session.

In 1827 he moved to Alachua County (land that would become Suwannee County later). During the time that his residency was listed as Columbia County (formed in 1832), he served 4 years as a judge. The tour of duty began February 11, 1835. He had two known brothers, John and George, and he was the son of John Dyall. He was married 3 times. His first wife is unknown, however, in 1815 she bore him a son which they named James R. Dyal. James married Caroline GOODBREAD (dau.of John S. GOODBREAD). Interestingly enough, James and his father Joseph both bought land in 1838 here in the Suwannee County area of Florida, both voted in the election of 1845, and both paid taxes in Suwannee County in 1860. His second wife was Jane ????. She was born in Georgia in 1813 (1809 in the 1860 Florida census). As far as we know she only bore him one son named William A. He was born in 1839 and he married Theresa A. ????. On August 14, 1866 Joseph married Martha NEWSOME. This marriage record identifies Joseph as William Joseph. According to the Deed Records, they had separated by January 23, 1867 so the marriage was short-lived. Joseph died in March of the same year.

As shown above, Joseph A. (Judge) DYALL migrated from Ware County, Ga. to the Pine Grove section of what was to become Suwannee County in 1827. He built a home about one mile from the Suwannee River near the present day Pine Grove Methodist Church on Route 136A. He and another earlarly settler from Georgia, a Mr. Howell HAWKINS, both of whom were staunch Methodists, built a log building near their homes and called it the Pine Grove Church. The church was organized in 1827 and is one of the first organized churches in the Florida territory.

In 1833 Governor Duval appointed Joseph DYALL as justice of the peace for part of what was to become Columbia County and later Suwannee County. During the Indian Wars (1835-1842) Judge DYALL had to leave his home, taking refuge in the fort at White Springs. Later, when he returned to his home, he held court at the old camp meeting grounds on the old White Springs road...located about 1 1/2 miles from the Pine Grove Church. In 1838 Joseph purchased 120 acres of land. In 1852 he purchased an additional 160 acres...all in the Pine Grove area.

Judge DYALL died in March of 1867 and was reportedly buried in the Pine Grove Methodist Church Cemetery although there is no marker.

ISAIAH D. HART

Isaiah D. HART bought 448 acres of land here on Sept. 29, 1836 in Township 2, Range 11E, Section 3 (extreme western part of county). According to the 1850 census Isaiah was born in Georgia in 1793. He married a Nancy ???? (b.1800 in S.C.). They probably married in 1818. Their children Oscar (b.1819 in S.C.), Ossin (or Orsin)(b.1821 in Ga.). The rest of their children were all born in Florida. They were Laura (b.1823), Lodiska?(b.1825), Daniel (b.1830), Nancy (b.1832), and Julia?(b.1834). In 1850 they were living in Duval County, Fl.

SOME OTHER HARTS

Vincent T. & Thomas W. HART bought land here in 1864 & 1872 respectively. Thomas W. also served as a 2nd Lt. in Co.B, 5th Fl.Inf. as a Confederate soldier during the Civil War. He was born in 1840 and died in 1909. He is buried in Mt. Pleasant Cemetery. In 1870 Adeline, Jesse, John, Lucy & Robert HART all lived in Live Oak...Rany? lived in Houston. John is shown as a debtor to J.B. WOOD in 1861. John was also involved in a court case in the same year. Jesse was on a voter list in 1867-8. Nancy HART is was buried in Mimms Cemetery in 1898 at age 61. A "J." HART was a slave owner in 1859. In 1866 an Ambrose B. HART migrated from Poughkeepsie, N.Y. to Columbia County and his brother "Ed" settled in the Ichtuknee area. There are a large number of the HART family buried in Suwannee County.

THOMAS HAWKINS

Thomas HAWKINS, progenitor of the Hawkins' families of our area, was born in Georgia in 1793. He came to the Pine Grove area from Loundes County, Georgia in 1827...about the same time as Judge Joseph DYALL. As mentioned earlier, the two men worked together to establish and build the Pine Grove Methodist Church. Thomas married Nancy J. SHARPE around 1815 in Georgia. Nancy was born in 1794 in Georgia...a daughter of Joshua SHARPE (b.1760 in Virginia). Thomas purchased land in Suwannee Cty (then Columbia County) in 1833. He is buried in the Little River Cemetery, however, there are no dates on the headstone.

Thomas and Nancy brought the following children into the world...
1) Howell Sharp Hawkins was born on Aug.20,1818 in Georgia. He married Jane BARBER (b.1826, dau.of Samuel Barber) in either 1841 or 1842 in Alachua County, Fl. (our present Suwannee County area). Howell served in the Indian Wars, was involved in the 1845 state election, and purchased his first Florida land in 1848. They had no less than 11 children before they died. Howell died in 1887 and Jane died in 1883. Both are buried in the Little River Cemetery (off Rt.49 in Suwannee Cty).
2) John Wesley Hawkins was born in 1827 in Georgia (this was apparently the year they came to Florida since the next child was born the next year in Florida). John married Eliza COLLINS on Jan.27, 1848 in Alachua Cty (really in Suwannee Cty). They had 8

children. He died in Hillsborough Cty, FL. in 1878. Nothing is known of his wife's death.

3) Mary D. Hawkins was born in Florida in 1828. She married a DEES and moved to Hillsborough Cty, Fl. when her brother, John Wesley, moved there.

4) Elizabeth Hawkins was also born in Florida in 1831. This is all that is presently known of her.

5) Bethelhuge H. Hawkins was born in 1823 (probably in Georgia). He married a Lucy Brantly (b.1831, d.1893). He died in 1901 and both he and his wife are buried in the Antioch Baptist Church cemetery just north of Live Oak, Fl.

HAWKINS GRAVE LISTING - The following members of the Hawkins family who were buried at the Little River Cemetery were...Jackson B. (b.1863, d.1927), Ella (Jackson's 1st wife) (b.1856, d.1903), Julia A. (Jackson's 2nd wife) (b.1881,d.1968)...3 children of Jackson & Julia, all being born and dying during the years 1907 through 1909. In the back of the cemetery were Thomas HAWKINS (No dates. Father of Howell Sharp). Howell Sharp HAWKINS (b.1818,d.1887), Howell's wife Jane(b.1826,d.1883), Thomas HAWKINS (b.1845,d.1919), his wife Sophronia (b.1845, d.1897), This latter Thomas served in the Civil War as a Confederate Soldier (Co.H, 1st Regt.,Fl.Calvary). The remainder of the Hawkins graves are children of the above couples with one exception...that of Nancy Hawkins, the mother of Howell Sharp Hawkins. This would make her the wife of the earlier Thomas Hawkins. All in all there are 18 Hawkin's family members buried here...no less than 3 generations.

JOSEPH M. HULL

Joseph M. (b.1823 in Ga.) married Mary Elisabeth (b.1829 in Ga.) around 1846. Joseph was a farmer of some stature. By 1860 he owned over 500 acres of land valued at $5000 and had a personal wealth of $12,000. Their first child James (b.1847) was born in Georgia, however by 1849, Joseph was born in Florida indicating they came to Florida in 1848. The remainder of their children were born in Florida. They were, McQueen (b.1851), C.B.(d.in Fl. bef.1860), Mary (b.1853), Noble (b.1855), Alexander (b.1857), and William H.(b.1859). Interestingly, I found a small graveyard for 7 Hull children on the property of Thomas Hawkins on highway 49. Why they were buried their is a mystery.

LEWIS MATTAIR

In 1845 Lewis voted in the 1845 Florida Statehood election asa resident of Mineral Springs. He was an "election inspector". In 1860 Lewis (b.1802 in Fl.) and his wife Louisa (b.1812 in Fl.) were living in Suwannee Cty, Fl. The Florida born children were Downing (b.1839), Mary (b.1844), and William (b.1850). In 1845 Lewis owned 32 slaves. Douglas Dorsey, a son of "free blacks" who lived in Maryland and were "shanghied" and later sold to

Lewis, recalls that in that Lewis owned as many as 85 slaves in the early 1860's. Dorsey remembered Lewis as a "kind master" even though his wife had a reputation for whipping slaves with little provocation. The book "History of Columbia County" has more details. Lewis also served in the 2nd Seminole War.

Lewis's inventory lists several slaves, to wit, Isaiah, Peggy, Henry, Heronena & child, Delorias, Hannah, Joe Shade, Kate, Caroline, Douglas Charles, Thaddeus, Charlotte, and Jeremiah. Administrators were Louisa (his wife) and Lewis H. Mattair. Children listed were Downing, Philothea, Maxey (prob.Mary), and William. Lewis probably died before 1864???.

ANGUS McAULEY

This family had its roots in Morvin County, Ga. (according to some tombstones we found on the Mills property. However, in checking records we found there was no Morvin (maybe it was Morgan) County in Georgia). It was very difficult to get into the grave section with small trees and bushes all entwined with thorn runners. Some of the headstones were lying flat some 3"-4" underground. We recorded what we could find. The stones we did find were all from the McAULEY family. All that had dates were born and died in the mid 1800's. They were John Tickner McAULEY (Age 8), Mary McAULEY (Age 7), and Isabella McAULEY (Age 13). There were 3 other stones without dates...just initials. They were A. McAuley, J.T. McAuley, and L. McAuley.

By comparing this with the 1860 Suwannee County census I discovered that Angus (b.1808 in Ga.) was a farmer with several sizable sections of land (totalling 440 acres) just SE of Tiger Lake Estates in Suwannee County, Fl. We also learn that Angus (b.1808 in Ga.) married Margaret S. (b.1820 in Ga.), in the 1840's and that they had a large family. Isabella (b.1848 in Ga.) was their eldest living child. Their second child, Christiana, was born in 1850 in Florida. This proves the family came to Florida in 1849. John Tickner (d.at age 8) and Mary (d.at age 7) were buried in Florida. Of the remaining living children shown on the 1860 census, Alexander (b.1856 in Fl.), Aulay (b.1857 in Fl.), Angus (b.1858 in Fl.), and Ann (b.1859 in Fl.), one had died as evidenced by the tombstone inscribed "A. McAuley". The stones inscribed "J.T." and "L" were probably two other children who died in Florida before the 1860 census.

ANDREW M. McCLELLAN

Andrew (b.1810 in S.C.) married Christiana Watts (b.1815 in S.C.) on December 10, 1829 in Hamilton Cty, Fl. All their children were born in Florida. They are as follows...Joseph (b.1832), Matilda (b.1834), Charles (b.1839), Andrew (b.1841), Margaret (b.1843), George (b.1844), and Joshua (b.1849). In 1850 they were living in Columbia Cty, Fl.

On June 10, 1837 Andrew bought 80 acres (T3,R14,S3), on March 1,1839 he received an additional 80 acres (T3,R14,S3), and on February 19, 1844 he bought 180 acres (T2,R15,S19) more. He was on the 1830 Fl.Census as a resident of Hamilton Cty, Fl.

In 1845 he voted at the Columbia County voting precinct in William Carver's home at the Florida Statehood election. Andrew died in 1880 and is buried next to his wife Christiannna who died in 1890 in Friendship Cemetery, Suwannee Cty, Fl. He was a 2nd Lt. in the 2nd Regt. of the Florida militia during the Indian Wars.

GEORGE EDMOND McCLELLAN

One of Suwannee County's earliest heroes was Captain George Edmond McCLELLAN. Shortly after the Seminole Indian uprising in 1835, George McCLELLAN, a resident of our area, organized a company of 77 foot and horse soldiers to protect the settlers. He was a Captain in the Indian Wars serving the 2nd Florida Mounted Militia. It seems apparent that shortly after George organized his 77 volunteers, the group became part of Captain Martin's 2nd Brigade of the Florida Drafted Militia Mounted Company. George served 4 months as a second lieutenant. On November 28, 1840 he was mustered in at Lancaster, East Florida as a Captain in McClellan's Company associated with Dancy's 2nd Florida Mounted Militia. He was mustered out on March 6, 1841 at Lancaster, East Florida.

In the 1845 Florida Statehood election George was listed as a respresentative for Columbia County.

George was the eldest of 7 children of Rev. Charles & Elizabeth McCLELLAN. Charles was a Methodist minister. George was born on July 11, 1807 in the Barnwell District of South Carolina. In 1817 the family moved to Georgia where his father ministered to churches in Camden and Wayne counties. By 1827 the family had moved to Jefferson County, Florida...but within a year they took up residence in Hamilton County. On January 28, 1828 George was appointed clerk of the Hamilton County court.

On Sept.24, 1830 George married Isabelle Sidney TISON. She was born on March 19, 1806 to Job and Sidney Sheffield TISON in Glynn County, Georgia. She died on July 3, 1860 and is buried in the McCLELLAN cemetery just south of Wellborn, Florida. According to the 1850 census they had 10 children...C.J. (b.Aug.8,1831, d. May 20, 1833), Julia Valira (b.1833), T.T. (b.Jan.8, 1835, d. July 26, 1836), G.R. (b.Apr.15, 1836, d. Oct.30, 1845), John Webb (b.1837), Ellen Jan (b.1839), Melindale Clifford (b.1841), Isabel Sidney (b.1843), Virginia Tyler (b.1844), and William Henry (b.1845). In 1831, George and Isabelle bought 240 acres of land near Wellborn (near McClellan Lake). In 1845, George paid $7.92 in taxes for a homestead on 320 acres of land and 14 slaves. By

1852 they owned all of Section 20, Range 15E, Township 3S...altogether 640 acres.

During the 1830's, George and his family moved to Columbia County where he served (besides his military service) as justice of the peace, auctioneer, judge, Columbia County representative (in 1844) on the Legislative Council for the Territory of Fl., and he was on the Columbia Cty House of Representatives. He cast his vote at the Columbia County Precinct at William Carver's home in the 1845 Florida Statehood election. He also farmed and in 1841 he began serving as postmaster at the Little River community. In his first year he earned 76 cents, and in his last year, 1859) as postmaster, he earned $53.20. As already stated, his wife died in 1860. George married Celesta Relief HOLMAN of Suwannee County on Jan.16, 1861. They had one child...Edmonia G. (b.May 23, 1862, d.Feb.1, 1863). George and his new wife apparently moved to the land he had bought near Wellborn in 1831. In the final years of his life (1864-1865) he served as the Probate Judge of Suwannee County. He died on October 18, 1866 and was buried in the McClellan cemetery just south of Wellborn, Florida.

George's will has significant interest in that if adds significant information. The particulars are as follows. His second wife was Celestia R. McClellan. He speaks of his children, Julia, Ellen, Clifford, Bell, Virginia, and William. He also speaks of his "Piney Mount land". His wife was his executrix and the witnesses to the will were John J. TAYLOR, William P. BETHEA, and Jesse F. McLERAN. He also speaks of having advanced monies to a son named Webb for the buying of lands. He and his wife, including a number of his family are buried at the McClellan Cemetery in the Wellborn area.

MATTHEW MICKLER

In 1860 Matthew (b.1811 in Ga.) and Sarah A. Baisden (b.1817 in Ga.) were living in Suwannee Cty, Fl. with one daughter, Ellen (b.1831 in Fl.). His parents were William and Temperance (see below). In 1840 he was listed as an auctioneer in Hamilton Cty, Fl. In 1845 he was an "election inspector" and a voter in Mineral Springs at the Florida Statehood election.

He was a Captain during the Indian Wars. On August 27, 1867 he deeded 4 acres of land and all buildings thereon to the Pine Grove Methodist Church for a cemetery. He reserved a 15'x35' plot for his own use. He died on January 28, 1871 and is buried in the Pine Grove Cemetery.

MARY ANN MURDOCK

In the 1860 Florida Census there is a Mary Ann Murdock (b.1826 in N.C.) who is shown to be quite wealthy living in

Suwannee County with 4 children...Mary (b.1846 in S.C.), Margaret (b.1848 in S.C.), Neven (b.1850 in S.C.) and Donald (b.1853 in Fl.).

JOHN POWELL

The Powell family was listed in the 1830 Florida Census as being one of the early families to settle in Alachua Cty, Fl. His will was made in Suwannee Cty, Fl. in 1862. His wife name was Martha (see her will) and their children were James, Sidney (dau.), Martha, Milly Smith, Mary, John, and two unnamed sons (by this time they had their own families. He willed his wife 160 acres (T3,R15,S30). Martha's will was written on February 14, 1870. Her husband had died earlier and she names the following children as her heirs...Sidney, James Mack, Polly Grimsley, Joseph Powell, Milly Smith, and Martha Dees. Heirs of John Powell Jr. were to receive $5.00 each. 80 acres of land (T3,R15,S29...purchased from the PG&R railroad) was also mentioned. Ishom Dees (husband of Martha???) is granted 1/2 of a crop then being planted. Martha Powell died before Nov.3, 1870. John voted at the 1845 Florida Statehood election at the Columbia County Precinct at William Carver's home.

JOSHUA SHARPE

Joshua SHARPE (known as Father SHARPE) came with Howell HAWKINS Sr. from Georgia in 1827. Joshua married Matilda Nobles (dau. of Lewis S. Nobles). His father was Groves Sharpe (b.1770 in Virginia...a son of John Sharpe Sr.) His mother was Dorothy ?????? (b.1776 in Burke Cty, Ga.) His parents were married about 1793. His siblings were Hannah (b.1795 in Burke Cty, Ga....m.William Arnold on Sept.14, 1815), Groves, Jr. (b.1802 probably in Tatnall Cty, Ga..m. Anne Higgs on Sept.14, 1823, dau.of John Higgs), Littleton (b.1807in Tatnall Cty, Ga...m. Mary ?????), Rebecca (b.1818 in Tatnall Cty, Ga...never married.

He was on the 1820 census of Appling Cty, Ga. Ware Cty was created from Appling Cty. and Joshua was elected as the coroner in January 1826. Joshua SHARPE was a veteran of the Revolutionary War. Not much is known about him, however, the 1830 census indicates he was about 70 years of age. Census records tell us he died after 1850. This would have made him about 90 years of age when he was buried at the Pine Grove Methodist Church Cemetery. He had a brother named Groves Sharpe.

Early Land Grants
(Chapter 3)

Have you realized the immense value of the Land Records? This may be one of the most overlooked sources of genealogical information known to man. In the 1800's (and before) 90% of the settlers owned their own land...and of necessity, records were kept even when other records were not. As a matter of fact, it serves better as a "census record" then the official census records. For example, George W. ALLEN was a tax collector in Wellborn. As a result of his death in 1876, his land was bequeathed to his wife (Ann L.) and to his children...R.J., R.W., Eugene G., Quemora C., Leila, and John. This may be found in the 1870 census record... but in the event the census takers missed him, it is in the land records. By checking marriage, cemetery, and tax records I can fill in the rest of his life. This is not exceptional. Since almost everyone owned land, the land transactions had to be made in land grant records which show the names and relationships of individuals.

It also tells where people come from. For example...if John Jones from out of state is planning to move to Live Oak, the land transaction tells where John Jones is from. I also discovered that James M. ADAMS wife's name was Ellminor E. Be sure you check out both the "grantor" and the "grantee" index books. THEN, go to the transaction book and page to get the important details. You'll never know what you'll find. I also found transactions relative to medical licenses in the land grant books. It told where the doctor had received his training (school and place), the dates, and where he was planning to practice. There is more to a "land grant" book than just land. It is, as I have said before, a veritable genealogical information "gold mine". Check it out. You'll be glad you did. Take the time to list all the people with the same surname...they are probably related. Remember the "et.al". It tells us the transaction book will be listing others...usually family members.

Before Florida was a U.S. Territory (1800-1820) a large number of pioneers came from Virginia, the Carolinas, and Georgia. They settled, for the most part, in and around the Suwannee River. Despite the fact that these were Spanish occupied lands, they came anyway. They became the founders of such places as Bellville, Ellaville, Madison, Live Oak, Branford, Belmont, and other places near the Suwannee River. Today there are literally thousands of their descendants in Florida. Some of these early settlers lived under 5 flags...the Spanish, French, British, American, and the Confederate.

Sometimes I get questions about where someone's ancestry comes from and how they got to Florida. The simple answer to that question is "land"!! Almost everyone that came to Florida in the early days originally came from Virginia or the Carolinas. They slowly migrated south to Georgia and Florida. By 1783 the territory of Florida was claimed by Spain, France, England, and the United States. By 1810, West Florida was organized and was being settled by Americans. By 1812, the Republic of East Florida was organized. In 1819 the United States purchased Florida from Spain but it did not become official until 1822 when thousands of American settlers began migrating to this new frontier. Land acts were passed by Washington, D.C. offering land for practically nothing...and as more people moved into the Virginia and Carolina areas...others moved on to the west and the south. The larger number of modern day native Floridians will be able to trace their heritage to north Florida, then to south Georgia counties and from their to the Carolinas and Virginia.

Many Suwannee County people will find their ancestry will have come from Hamilton, Madison, and Jefferson counties...all of which had their beginnings in 1827. Most of these arrived at these counties from the early southern counties of Georgia. The early settlers of Georgia crossed over the Florida territory enroute to the Gulf of Mexico where they boiled sea water for its salt content (sorely needed for meat preservation, etc.). The shortest route for those who lived inland was through what is now Jefferson County, Florida. Many settled in this area. From there they spread to surrounding areas. Those who spread to the east settled in Madison and Hamilton Counties. From there they stayed reasonably near to the Suwannee River. In a review of the book, "History of Madison County", I found about 70 surnames common to Suwannee County. This gives us some insight as to where our ancestors came from. This will also be true for Hamilton County. A number of these same names will also be found in Jefferson County. So, for those who may be wondering where to go next...try these counties to our north...especially Jefferson County. The Wiregrass books will show the Georgia counties they came from.

Did you know that over 250 settlers were in the Suwannee County area BEFORE we became a county. They all received their land from the United States of America...the landowner by right of our purchase of Florida from Spain. Our government possesses the applications and copies of the grants/deeds with all the information they hold...which is alot. Primarily they are found in the "Cash Entry" (1820-1908), and "Donation Entry" (1842-1850) files.

I was able to find possibly the only official record that lists definite Suwannee County landowners BEFORE 1858...as far back as 1828. The discovery lists the names of 257 pre-1858 landowners. Not only does it give names and dates, but it also shows how much acreage was involved and exactly where it was located. This enables us to check these names against the census records for family information. It also tells us where these settlers came from. I will list the name of the settler in column 1 and in column 2 I will list the earliest land purchase/grant date. Many of these settlers bought multiple parcels of land, but in order to show their earliest arrival date we will only list the earliest transaction.

1. ANDREWS, Christopher 1838   2. BAISDEN, Josiah T. 1855

#	Name	Year	#	Name	Year
3.	BAKER, James M.	1855	4.	BARBER, Samuel	1852
5.	BARBER, Mary	1853	6.	BASS, Maria	1852
7.	BATES, Needham	1854	8.	BELL, Benjamin	1855
9.	BEXLEY, Augustus R.	1855	10.	BIRD, Sherrod	1855
11.	BLACKBURN, Duke	1854	12.	BLACKBURN, James C.	1846
13.	BLUE, Daniel	1845	14.	BLUE, James	1838
15.	BRINKLEY, Wiley	1854	16.	BROWN, Simon T.	1852
17.	BRUNSON, James R.	1855	18.	BRYAN, David R.	1837
19.	BRYAN, Nathaniel	1851	20.	BRYAN, Synthy	1840
21.	BRYANT, James	1855	22.	CARL, Elisha	1853
23.	CARRAWAY, Archibald	1855	24.	CARRAWAY, Elijah	1854
25.	CARRAWAY, George H.	1855	26.	CARRAWAY, Joshua	1852
27.	CARRAWAY, Martin	1852	28.	CARRUTH, Catesworth	1852
29.	CARTER, John B.	1855	30.	CARVER, Elijah	1837
31.	CARVER, Sampson	1849	32.	CARVER, Vincent J.	1854
33.	CARVER, William	1838	34.	CARVER, Wilson	1855
35.	CASON, William	1837	36.	CATO, Phillip W.	1854
37.	CHAPMAN, Benjamin	1846	38.	CHARLES, Andrew J.	1837
39.	CHARLES, Rebecca	1847	40.	CHARLES, Reuben	1828
41.	CLARKE, Lewis	1853	42.	CLAYTON, Robert B.	1835
43.	CLEMENTS, John W.	1853	44.	CLEMENTS, William J.	1838
45.	CONE, Peter	1852	46.	COOPER, Charles M.	1837
47.	COOPER, James A.	1844	48.	COOPER, James G.	1837
49.	CORBIN, Moses	1855	50.	CORBIN, William	1855
51.	COUSINS, William E.M.	1854	52.	CURRY, Benjamin G.	1831
53.	DAVIS, John H.	1838	54.	DAVIS, Lewis B.	1837
55.	DEAN, Micajah	1837	56.	DEAN, Thaddeus	1854
57.	DEAS, John S.	1854	58.	DEAS, Louis M.	1854
59.	DEES, Fleming	1852	60.	DEES, Nathaniel	1854
61.	DELEGAL, Thomas	1854	62.	DEXTER, Thomas D.	1851
63.	DORMAN, Orloff M.	1840	64.	DOZIER, John L.	1855
65.	DRIVER, George W.	1854	66.	DUERR, Christian F.	1837
67.	DYALL, James R.	1838	68.	DYALL, Joseph	1838
69.	EDWARDS, Henry	1854	70.	EDWARDS, James	1838
71.	EDWARDS, John	1854	72.	EDWARDS, Samuel	1838
73.	EDWARDS, Sarah	1852	74.	EDWARDS, Sherrod	1838
75.	EDWARDS, William	1852	76.	ELLIS, Henry V.	1840
77.	ELLIS, John B.	1840	78.	ELLIS, Thomas	1837
79.	EVANS, Thomas J.	1854	80.	EVANS, Thomas S.	1854
81.	EVERETT, Jared	1838	82.	EVERS, Jasper B.	1853
83.	FISHER, Daniel B.	1854	84.	TISON, William Hayes	1843
85.	FOSTER, Ransom S.	1852	86.	FRYAR, Simon	1841
87.	GASKINS, Asa	1845	88.	GIBBS, Henry	1854
89.	GILLESPIE, John G.W.	1855	90.	GILLET, Anderson	1838
91.	GODBOLD, James D.	1853	92.	GODWIN, Seaborn	1840
93.	GURGANUS, Moses	1854	94.	HAIR, Job	1852
95.	HAIR, John A.	1855	96.	HALL, Daniel	1852
97.	HALL, Enoch	1837	98.	HANCOCK, John W.	1855
99.	HARGRAVES, Abraham	1851	100.	HARRELL, William	1855
101.	HART, Isaiah D.	1836	102.	HAVENS, William G.	1852
103.	HAWKINS, Howell Sharp	1853	104.	HAWKINS, Thomas	1833

Note: See 145 & 146 for additional Hawkins'

#	Name	Year	#	Name	Year
105.	HILL, James A.	1855	106.	HINTON, Allen	1846
107.	HODGES, Judge R.	1854	108.	HOLLAND, Samuel	1852
109.	HOLLOMAN, Harris	1855	110.	HOLMES, William	1855

#	Name	Year	#	Name	Year
111.	HOOKER, Wm. Britton	1837	112.	HOWARD, Charles	1855
113.	HULL, Joseph M.	1851	114.	HULL, Noble A.	1850
115.	HUR(S)T, Richard	1853	116.	IRVINE, John T.	????
117.	IVES, W.W.	1852	118.	IVEY, Isabella	1857
119.	JENKINS, James	1837	120.	JOHNS, Levy	1854
121.	JOHNS, Matthew	1858	122.	JOHNSON, General P.	1854
123.	JOHNSON, Green	1854	124.	JOHNSON, Greer	1852
125.	JOHNSON, Rachel	1844	126.	JOHNSON, William E.	1852

Note: See #147 & #148 for more Johnsons

#	Name	Year	#	Name	Year
127.	JORDAN, Benjamin F.	1855	128.	KEENE, David	1855
129.	KEITH, Daniel	1855	130.	KENDRICKS, Elizabeth	1838
131.	KENDRICKS, William	1838	132.	LAMB, John J.	1851
133.	LANE, Benjamin	1845	134.	LANGFORD, William	1838

Note: See #149 & #150 for more L's

#	Name	Year	#	Name	Year
135.	LAWSON, Lewis	1853	136.	LEE, David	1852
137.	LEVINGSTON, James	1837	138.	LEVINGSTON, Thomas	1835
139.	LEWIS, John	1835	140.	LEWIS, Lion B.	1838
141.	LIVINGSTON, William	1837	142.	LOWE, John Wesley	1837
143.	MALLETT, William P.	1855	144.	MANNING, Job	1850
145.	HAWKINS, John W.	1853	146.	HAWKINS, Matthews R.	1845
147.	JOHNSON, Randall	????	148.	JOHNSON, William	1837
149.	LANIER, David Sloane	1845	150.	LAWSON, Henry	1852
151.	MARTIN, Alexander	1838	152.	MARTIN, Alexander H.	1852
153.	MATTAIR, Lewis	1837	154.	McAULEY, Angus	1851
155.	McBRIDE, Ferdinand	1854	156.	McCALL, Stephen	1837
157.	McCLELLAN, Andrew	1837	158.	McCLELLAN, George E.	1854
159.	McCLELLAN, George Edmond	1831	160.	McCLELLAN, George Reid	1837
161.	McCLELLAN, Joseph H.	1854	162.	McCORMICK, Paul	1834
163.	McINTOSH, John W.	1840	164.	McLAREN, Nevin	1853
165.	McLAREN, Rebecca	1852	166.	McLAREN, William F.	1854
167.	McNEILL, Samuel	1855	168.	MICKLER, Lawrence J.	1854
169.	MICKLER, Matthew	1854	170.	MICKLER, William	1837
171.	MILLER, Ephraim E.	1854	172.	MIMS, Julius A.	1855
173.	MITCHELL, George W.	1852	174.	MOBLEY, Elathorn	1838
175.	MORGAN, Daniel	1838	176.	MOSELEY, Robert M.	1855
177.	MOSELY, Lewis W.	1855	178.	MOTLEY, Robert	1852
179.	MURDOCK, Mary Ann	1853	180.	NEWBERN, Alfred	1854
181.	O'NEIL, Douglas	1838	182.	OSTEEN, Archibald	1855
183.	OSTEEN, William B.	1853	184.	PARKER, Owen	1855
185.	PARKER, William G.	1855	186.	PARRAMORE, Redding W.	1844
187.	PEACOCK, Robert M.D.	1853	188.	PEARSON, Meredith	1855
189.	PELOT, James C.	1837	190.	PELOT, John C.	1837
191.	PETERSON, Albert	1853	192.	PIPKIN, Margaret	1835
193.	PLATT, David	1838	194.	PLATT, William	1846
195.	POLK, James C.A.	1852	196.	PONCHIER, John C.	1851
197.	PONCHIER, Joseph	1855	198.	POWELL, John	1837
199.	POWERS, John M.	1850	200.	RAWLS, John G.	1854
201.	REDDING, William H.	1852	202.	REED, William M.	1837
203.	RENTZ, W.G.	1838	204.	ROBERTS, George W.	1838
205.	ROBERTS, William	1854	206.	ROBERTSON, John W.	1854
207.	ROBINSON, J.W.	1847	208.	ROLAND, William	1838
209.	ROSS, Francis James	1831	210.	ROWLAND, William	1846
211.	ROUSSEAU, William H.	1853	212.	SAUNDERS, Hiram	1854
213.	SEARS, Hiram	1852	214.	SELMAN, Eliza B.	1854

215.	SHARP, Joshua	1838	216.	SHEFFIELD, Bryan	1851
217.	SHEFFIELD, John W.	1855	218.	SISTRUNK, Gasper	1843
219.	SMILEY, Andrew J.	1855	220.	SMITH, Samuel	1838
221.	SMITHSON, George B.	1853	222.	SPENCER, William S.	1838
223.	STEWART, Elijah M.	1851	224.	STEWART, James M.	1855
225.	STEWART, Thomas J.	1855	226.	STOKELY, John	bef. 1840
227.	SYKES, Arthur	1831	228.	TAYLOR, John	1858
229.	THOMAS, Allen	1837	230.	THOMAS, William	1853
231.	THOMPSON, Samuel B.	1854	232.	TILLIS, Daniel	1853
233.	TILLIS, David	1854	234.	TILLIS, Richard	1846
235.	TILLIS, Sophia	1854	236.	TILLIS, Willoughby	1837
237.	TISORD, William Hayes	1845	238.	TYNER, Ephraim	1834
239.	URGUHART, Thomas	1855	240.	WADSWORTH, Samuel	1838
241.	WATTS, Joseph B.	1844	242.	WEBB, John F.	1837
243.	WEEKS, Theophilus	1838	244.	WESTBURY, Walker	1852
245.	WHITEHURST, David S.	1839	246.	WHITFIELD, Benj. M.	1853
247.	WHITFIELD, John B.	1854	248.	WILLIAMS, Elijah B.	1852
249.	WILLIAMS, James K.	1858	250.	WILLIAMS, John Sr.	1845
251.	WILLIAMS, John	1852	252.	WILLIAMS William G.	1852
253.	WOOD, Absolom	1838	254.	WOODWARD, Richard	1853
255.	ZIPPERER, Elizabeth	1853	256.	ZIPPERER, Joseph	1845
257.	ZIPPERER, Solomon	1837			

This concludes the listing. The original records also lists the location of the land, who it was received from, and other incidental data. (See Appendix A for complete listing)

The following is a listing of large land owners in 1859-1861. They are...1) J. LIPCOMB (2200 acres), 2) A. SPEAR (2000 acres), 3) T.D. DEXTER (1940 acres), 4) George McCLELLAN (1560 acres), 5) T.P. DELEGAL (1480 acres), 6) W.L. IRVIN (1400 acres), 7) J.A. IRVIN (1360 acres), 8) Green JOHNSON (1160 acres), 9) W.H. IVY (1050 acres), 10) C. PEACOCK (1040 acres), 11) Lewis MATTAIR (1000 acres).

The following land grants were also received from the United States government. They begin with the year 1863 and go through 1929. They are not in alphabetical order, so you will have to search the entire list to find names that interest you. We will list the names through 1899. We can't list all the information which includes the kind of grant, description of the land, name, and year of transaction...but we will list the name and year. If you need more information contact Suwannee County Court House in Live Oak, Florida 32060.

They are George W. BELL (1863), Solomon ZIPPERER (1863), Thomas HURST (1869), Elza B. LELMAN (1875), Philip W. CATO (1875), William S.J. BLUNT (1876), H.K. MILLS (1876), M.C. JONES (1879), Elijah BUTLER (1879), Judson O.C. JONES (1879), John E. BRINSON (1879), Jesse JACKSON (1879), Sam HOLSENDORF (1880), Seaborn GODWIN (1880), John W. ROBINSON (1880), John W. ROBERTSON (1880), Madison JOHNSON (1880), Jerry FULGUNE (1881), James HIGDEN (1882), George WASHINGTON (1883), Micajah DEAN (1883), John H. JOHNSON (1883), Jackson RAWLINS (1883) Levi D. HARVEY (1883). **The following names received land in 1884:** Green JOHN-

STON, James A. WEIGHT, George W. ALLEN, Joseph WHITE, J.O.C. BLUNT, Alexamder M. BOATRIGHT, Mary A. JOWERS, Alfred E. HIGH, Loveless PETERSON, William E. HARRELL, William INGERVILLE, A.A. HOYL, John B. CARTER, George W. DRAWDY, Richard L. HOLLOWAY, Abraham STRICKLAND, Joseph K. TAYLOR, Robert A. REID, John F. McCLELLAN, Prince STEWART, Nathaniel BRYAN, and Isham MURRAY. **1885:** Moses STANLEY, Epsy BOYD, Brighteous LANGWOOD, John R. SCOTT, J.W. HAWKINS, George E. FOSTER, William McKAY, Thomas MEEKS, Allen WILLIAMS, Prince DELEGAL, Sopater HURT, Jepthy WILLIAMS, C.K. DUTTON, George G. TELFORD, and Nathan R. GAYLORD. **1886:** Hartwell S. HARRELL, Solomon GRAHAM, Benjamin F. MEEKSK, Samuel TRIPP, Ned YOUNG, I.D. McCORMICK, William W. O'HARA, Richard R. HURST, Mary CHEEK, Caleb SIMPKINS, Handy JONES, Lacaster STEWART, James H. TAYLOR, Eliza J. SELLERS, James DAWSON, William H. HULL, Jacob D. DIVINE, John W. WINCEY, Alexander GAINOR, George PATTERSON, Thomas I. McINTOSH, George H. ROSS, Laura A.E. BYRD, Thomas G. BAXTER, and Lewis FIELDS. **1887** - Sarah L. WILLIAMS, Hiram RAUSE, John W. HURST, John GOFF, Solomon FORT, Rufus R. LIVINGSTON, Heber A. PEACOCK, Millard BOYET, John FREDERICK, John M. McINTOSH, Henry M. DAVIS, Joseph T. PEED, Dublin ROLLINS, John and Mary SKEEN (by heir), Sanford BONDS, Robert BUTLER, and Root BUTLER. **1888:** Jeremiah HURST, Mary C. BARKER, Benjamin D. HARRELL, John jACKSON, Alfred OLIVER, Leah GRAHAM, William B. HIGH, Sarah P. COATS, John H. GRANT, and James A. WIGGINS. **1889:** George W. MITCHELL, John N. HELTON, Daniel L. HIGH, Burroughs A. PEEK, William PATRICK, David H. MERCHANT, Samuel J. McINTOSH, Wilson GOODMAN, Thomas J. AMONS, Charles DEAN, William E. FLOYD, Levi A. JENNINGS, Alexander PARKER, James E. ROBERTS, Malcomb SKEEN, Riley D. TURNER, Peter GRAHAM, John H. WILLIAMS, Jeremiah S. BADEN, William JONES, Louis FULCHER, John R. SESSIONS, Alexander PATTERSON, Susan A. CANNAN, Martin BROWN, and Eliza J. SHEPARD. **1890:** Frank FORT, Richard FORT, Lelar WINBURN, Elisha WINBURN, Francis M. TOMPKINS, William R. DAUGHTRY, William WIGGINS, James W. DAUGHTRY, Tony MITCHELL, Caroline L. STOKES, Benjamin DAVIS, James H. HODGES, William O. JACKSON, William E. VANN, Andrew HARRIS, Charles THORNHILL, James G. THOMPSON, Abrom BELL, George E. PAGE, Moses HUTCHERSON, Robert A. IVEY, Henry CIVILS, Charles HUNNICUT, Violet ALLEN, Samuel L. CLARK, Emily CLARK, John M. FAULKER, Howell MEEKS, John H. DIXON, Anthony BAKER, George W. MILLS, Henry J. CANNON, Agnes J. BYRD, Raymond H.M. STARLING, and George W. CLARK. **1891:** Robert W. INGRAM, Joshua J. ALTMAN, James BROWN, Daniel KEITH, Tabitha BROWN, Rebecca CHARLES, James M. STEWART, William O. THOMAS, Allen THOMAS, John G. HUMPHRIES, Charles HOWARD, Louis M. MOSELEY, James C.A. POLK, Ashley B. PEEK, Mary R. PEACOCK, William LITTLE, William E. JOHNSON, Martha A.E. CRAWLEY, Samuel E. PINKHAM, Green JOHNSON, Sampson ZOW, Patience BRINSON, James COLLINS, Noah L. LACQUEY, Jackson THOMAS, James P. ABBOTT, Martha WASHINGTON, and Martha FULCHER. **1892:** John T. MERCER, Joseph A. McCOLLUM, John W. O'DONIEL, Roan RICKERSON, John F. BAKER, James R. MEEKS, Thomas HOWARD, Allison IVEY, Henry J. PLATT, Daniel ANDERSON, John N. ALTMAN, Charlie L. MILLS, William GALE, Seck POLITE, Rivers HANKINS, Henry FILLMORE, Thomas P. DELEGAL, John H.T. BYNUM, John H. WALKER, Joseph & Sarah L. WILLIAMS (by heir), James H. ALLEN, Benjamin DAVIS, Mack LONDON, William P.R. ALLI-

SON, Owen J. REVELS, Thomas T. NORWOOD, William M. WELLS, Simeon FAGAN, John W. BRINSON, Henry J. LAMB, David PLATT, Joshua J. GILLETT, Theophilis ZIPPERER, James McGUIRE, William SLATEN, John W. BURNETT, Sam LOTT, Eliza BIRD, and Sophia TILLIS. **1893:** John C. HILTON, John J. ROBINSON, W.B. HOUGH, Andrew McCLELLAN, Joseph S. HURST, John W. DEES, Jesse N. CONNER, William J. HURST, Joseph TYSON, John J. HORTON, James B. MILLS, George B. CASON, Scott STEWART, James MANDRELL, William BARKER, Gabriel GRAY, Alexander C. BLACKSHEAR, Joab L. BLACKMAN, Mary JOWERS, Louis A. TIDWELL, Martin BROCK, Mary A. ATWELL, John E. BRUNSON, William D.M. LEE, and Joseph HARDEE.

Another listing of settlers were found in a plat book of Suwannee County during the early years of her formation as a county. There were no transaction dates. A question mark (?) following an entry indicates an unclear entry. Over 125 settlers can be accounted for. They are Franklin BAILEY, Mary RIGGS, John JOHNSON, Matthew MICKLER, Bryant JOHNS, Levi JOHNS, John P. GOODMAN, John WILLIAMS, Sr., Miles SCARBOROUGH, J.R. HODGES, Pinkney B. COLE, W.R. FRIER, John W. SHEFFIELD, William J. BARNETT, J.B. SPENCER, George W. ALLEN, Berry A. BRANHAM, Elizabeth FIELD, James D. GODBOLD, Hanelt? BRINKLEY, Maria INGERVILLE, Daniel MICKLER, Nancy DEAKLE, William B. BRINKLEY, W.T. McLERAN, Edward J. LUTTERTON, Brantley HACKNEY, D.C. WILSON, William HERRING, Margaret A. CLEMENS, ? THOMPSON, Allen WILLIAMS, W.H. SESSIONS, Fred S. HASSTIEN, John S. TAYLOR, Mary Ann MURDOCK, Julia V. WALKER, George E. McCLELLAN, Benjamin BELL, Kinsey CHAMBERS, Rollin S. PIRTLE, Martha POWELL, H.W. CASSON, Washington HUTTON, John W. WISE, Howell Sharp HAWKINS, Andrew M. CRAWFORD, John R. EVERS, Nathan R. GILLIE, Scott HALL, T.? F. WHITE, John WATSON, William A. BRINSON, J.W. ROBERTSON, John F.J. MITCHELL, Nancy BROCK, Benjamin MORDECIA, C. BRINSON, William H. ROUSSEAU, George C. POWELL, Randall FARNELL, William ALLISON, M. LIVELY, John J. HARRELL, C.K. DUTTON, John HANCOCK, Caroline PARRAMORE, Patience C. POWELL, Julia LANGFORD, George CONEWALL?, John FRAZIER, Enoch ALLEN, William B. HARDIE, J.J. WALKER, A. Florida FINLAYSON, James S. HALL, W.S. GOFF, Wade H. REDDING, Randall JOHNSON, James K. WILLIAMS, John STOKELY, John T. IRVINE, John BRIM, John W. RICE, George L. McCONIKE, Washington L. IRWIN, C. PEACOCK, N.T. ELLIOT, Charles T. IRWIN, Z. SHEPARD, Margaret MOSELEY, Alex MOSELEY, Wilson CARVER, Rhoda LEWIS, William H. WINN, T.C. GRIFFIN, C.B. HALL, Mannah M. BURTCHALL, John LLOYD, Thomas A. CARRUTH, E.F. HENDERSON, John SKEEN, William HINES, James R. LEWIS, Archibald CARAWAY, John S. BAILEY, C.W.P. HOWELL, P.H. COATES, William J. BEVAN, John L.(or J.) HARRELL, Eliza Ann BEVAN, Joshua CARAWAY, Thomas D. DEXTER, John H. JOHNSON, Eliza OLIFF, James HENDRICKS, David CLEMENTS, Kitty BLACKMAN, David McDONNELL, James PONCHIER, Elizabeth PONCHIER, W.A. GARDNER, Samuel B. McNEAL, Elizabeth FOSTER, John S. PONCHIER, Eliza WOOD, Harris HOLLMAN, Susie M. EARNEST, C.Y. SAVAGE, Joseph PONCHIER, J.M.B. GOODBREAD, William H. WATSON, James A. HARRIS, Sarah A. HILL, R.M.D. PEACOCK, James M. HULL, B. McQUEEN.

We have found some additional land grants from the early

days in another book. I will list them by name and year. They are...James S. ANDERSON (1845), Sherrod BIRD (1860), James C. BLACKBURN (1846), Naomi BLACKBURN (1856), Daniel BLUE (1845), Cyprian BRINSON (1856), Robert BROOKINS (1891), Nathaniel BRYAN (1851), Elijah CARRAWAY (1854), Andrew J. CHARLES (1838), John S. DEAS (1854), Thomas D. DEXTER (1851), Lewis M. DEAS (1854), Micajah DEAS (1843), Thomas P. DELEGAL (1854), John ECCLES (1857), John EDWARDS (1854), Daniel B. FISHER (1854), James FOSTER (1861), James W. FRY (1880), James D. GODBOKE (or GODBOLT) (1853), Howell Sharp HAWKINS (1848), William HINES (1855), Joseph C. HOOPER (1860), Solomon ZIPPERER (1845), John LIPSCOMB (1856), Redding LONG (1854), John Wesley LOWE (1844), Alexander H. MARTIN (1848), Lewis MATTAIR (1854), Angus McAULEY (1844), George McCLELLAN (1858), John W. McCLELLAN (1858), John C. McGEHEE (1856), Matthew MICKLER (1854), Luke MOORE (1846), Henry R. HULL (1856), Joseph M. HULL (1851), Thomas HUNT (1857), Thomas HURST (1856), John A. IRVINE (of Ga.)(1856), Green JOHNSON (1846), Rachel JOHNSON (1844), William C. JOHNSON (1877), Eliza B. LEALMAN (1854), William LEE (1834), John LEE (1834), John LEWIS (1837), Henry H. MOSELEY (1858), John MURPHY (1856), Joseph OLLIFF (1855), Calvin PEACOCK (1856), John Cooper PELOT (1845), John C. POUCHIER (1851), John G. RAWLS (1854), John W. ROBINSON (1847), William H. ROSSEAU (1846), William ROWLAND (1846), Sam RUSSEN (1846), John Williams SEWN? (1845), Florida SHEFFIELD (1854), Gasper SISTRUNK (1843), George B. SMITHSON (1853), Eliza Mary STEWART (1848), Richard TILLIS (1846), William A. TISON (1888), Benjamin M. WHITFIELD (1853), Elijah Brown WILLIAMS (1852), Kindreth WILLIAMS (1857). These were all Suwannee County landowners.

VOTER LISTS
(Chapter 4)

The following are 1845 voter records, but, they serve well as census records. Florida became a state officially in 1844. The first statewide elections took place in 1845. The following listing would incorporate the then non-existent Suwannee County and its surrounding counties...at least those counties from which most of our county's early population was composed. I will list them by COUNTY, VOTING PRECINCT, and NAME OF VOTER. I trust this will add a little bit of history to your "tree".

Columbia County
(Columbus Precinct)

Columbus was located where the Suwannee County State Park is today. It existed from the early 1800's and was a thriving township of about 500 settlers. It died out by the early 1900's. The town was incorporated in 1841 and thrived as one of the areas larger towns. They continued until the early 1900's. They had at least 3 cemeteries...possibly four.

1. Felix LIVINGSTON (Election Inspector), 2. John TURNER (Election Inspector), 3. David PLATT, 4. James M. COOKE (Election Clerk) 5. William McCARTY, 6. James SWEET, 7. Benjamin SUTTON, 8. David O. RIDGWAY, 9. Joseph B. WATTS, 10. George H. SMITH, 11. George RICHARDSON, 12. Aaron DANIELS, 13. James C.A. POLK, 14. J.N. WILLIAMS, 15. Chainock SELPH, 16. Soloman ROUSE, 17. John A. SALMOND, 18. Silas OVERSTREET, 19. James WHITE, 20. Malcolm MORRISON, 21. Henry R. SADLER, 22. James R. ROBERTSON, 23. Matthew WEST, 24. Allen B. ROBERTSON, 25. John ROBERTSON, 26. John W. ROBERTSON, 27. Thomas COWART, 28. Suffen B. LAMB, 29. David PLATT, 30. Felix LIVINGSTON, 31. John TURNER, 32. John M.C. LOUD, 33. James HARVILL, 34. Simeon DIGGERS, 35. Lemuel SLADE, 36. John R. DOWANCE, 37. J.C. SIPPLE, 38. Joel REDDING, 39. Rowland ROBARTS, 40. James M. COOKE, 41. William H. DOWANCE, 42. Joseph F. ZIPPERER, 43. George W. COLE Jr., 44. James GARNEW, 45. William C. BARRS, 46. John ZIPPERER, 47. George COLT, 48. John JENKINS, 49. Ebenezer DICKERSON, 50. Solomon ZIPPERER, 51. Jordan SWINDALL.

COLUMBIA COUNTY
(Ellaville Precinct)

Ellaville was situated across the Suwannee River from Columbus...much like cities like St.Louis, St.Paul, Kansas City, and others. As Columbus died, Ellaville prospered. Unfortunately, shortly after Columbus's demise, Ellaville also died. Today, both of these once thriving towns, are remembered by road markers.

1. James OSTEEN (Election In- spector), 2. John PREVATT (Election Inspector), 3. Horace WICKHAM (Election Inspector), 4. William WRIGHT (Election Clerk), 5. Stephen SPARKMAN, 6. Cader CLARK, 7. John COMBS, 8. Richard CLARK, 9. Stephen T. DEBUSK, 10.

Elias OSTEEN, 11. William OSTEEN, 12. Ruebin OSTEEN, 13. William BARCO, 14. Silas WEEKS, 15. Edward WEEKS, 16. William PARISH, 17. Shedrick OSTEEN, 18. John PREVATT, 19. Horace WICKHAM, 20. Jacob WILLIAMS, 21. E.B. SPARKMAN.

COLUMBIA COUNTY
(Mineral Springs Precinct)

Mineral Springs was located in the northeast sector of Suwannee County...primarily in the area of Pine Grove and surrounding area.

1. John F. WEBB (Election Inspector), 2. Lewis MATTAIR (Election Inspector), 3. Matthew MICKLER (Election Inspector), 4. William F. JONES (Election Clerk), 5. William ROWLAND, 6. Jesse WALLER, 7. Albert PETERSON, 8. Simeon BROOM, 9. J.F. GARNER, 10. Joseph M. CREWS, 11. John LONGLE, 12. Isaiah D. TILLIS, 13. William JOHNSON, 14. Aldrich WILEY, 15. John WILLIAMS Jr., 16. Asa GASKINS, 17. William MICKLER, 18. Robert FEWOX, 19. John WAYNE, 20. Joseph DURRENCE, 21. Jesse H. DURRENCE, 22. John A. MAPLES?, 23. John A. WHITEHURST, 24. Charles L. WILSON, 25. William H.C. KENDRICK, 26. James C. BLACKBURN, 27. George T. DURRANCE, 28. William Z. HERNDON, 29. William PLATT, 30. John H. MAY, 31. D.T. TRYVANT, 32. William HOLMES, 33. John WILLIAMS Sr., 34. William C. SPARKMAN, 35. William H. TUTEN, 36. JOHNSON, 37. Daniel SAVAGE, 38. Blackston ELLIS, 39. James G. MADISON, 40. William T. JOHNSON, 41. John T. TAYLOR, 42. Micajah DEAN, 43. Gasper SISTRUNK, 44. Elijah CARAWAY Jr., 45. Thomas D. DEXTER, 46. Lewis MATTAIR, 47. Mathis MICKLER, 48. Edmund ROWLAN, 49. John F. WEBB, 50. Samuel MARION

William Carver's House Precinct

This precinct was located in Wellborn and the area to the south.

George W. ROBERTS, Tapley A. TULLIS, Matthew B. HAWKINS, T.B. FITZPATRICK, Andrew McCLELLAN, Thomas HAWKINS, W.G. WILLIAMS, John CLUTE, Isaac SMITH, James BRADLEY, Howell HAWKINS, John SIMONS, Duke BLACKBURN, James L. ROSS, John POWELL, John W. CLEMENTS, Elisha CURL, William CARVER, Levy JOHNS, Lawrence J. MICKLER, Jefferson WILLIAMS, George E. McCLELLAN, Absalam WOOD, Joseph TULLIS, Wilson CARVER, William MAYS, James JERKINS, Douglass O'NIEL, Sampson CARVER, William C. HAIR, Elisha WALKER, Elisha CURL, James R. DYALL, William H. ROUSSEAU, Job MANNING, Wain TULLIS.

The following precincts were located primarily in what is our present day Columbia County area, whereas those precincts listed above were located in what is the present day Suwannee County.

1845 VOTER LIST #2

State Representatives for Columbia County were, George E. McCLELLAN, Giles U. ELLIS, Arthur ROBERTS, Joseph DYALL, and Oren VICKERS. **Precinct 1 (Home of John Dryden)** included, James F.B. McKINNEY, Burrel JOHNS, Cain STRICKLAND, William JOHNS, Roman ALVEREZ, Levi PELHAM, James M. SPARKMAN, James M. PREVATT, George VARNES, Jacob GODWIN, William CROSBY, William B. COWART, Morgan PREVATT, Joseph J. PREVATT, Joseph R. PREVATT, Richard WARD, John H. MACHET, George BRITTON, Solomon GODWIN, Joseph THOMAS, Zach MOTES, A.M. ANDREW, R.P. LEWIS, Charles McKINNEY, Stephen SPARKMAN, Silas MEEKS, R.S. MOTE, Drury REDDISH, William FUTCH Jr., William FUTCH Sr., Theophilus-philus WEEKS, Onesimus FUTCH, William PREVATT, Henry VINZANT, J.W.F. PREVATT, John PLATT, George TISON, James ALVEREZ, John DRYDEN, William H. WARD, James BROOKS, John S. PARISH, Archibald JOHNS, Riley MOORE, Valentine PREVATT, Washington JOHNS, Thomas UNDERWOOD, Benjamin GREEN, Henry SAPP, Matthias MARSHALL, R.J. GODWIN, and Sol RENFROW. **Alligator Precinct (Courthouse)** included S. WORTHINGTON, J.T. WILLIAMS, Charles GOLSEBY, John IVEY, Joseph WILKINSON, Levy WRIGHT, Thomas BRYANT, John F. BRYANT, L.A. SMITH, Jonathan A. JONES, Samuel WADSWORTH, Joseph WATTERS, Daniel JONES, Shedrick HANCOCK, Reeding LONG, W.M. IVES, Ali ROBERTS, Harmon LANE, A.D. WOOD, Anderson GILLETT, Langley BRYANT, Levy H. CARTER, Henry SMITH, Rolan WILLIAMS, R. BLOUNT, George BAINS, John NIBLACK, H.G. HUNTER, W. MARKUM, Jacob DAVIS, Terry PARRISH, William PIERCE, Henry WATTERS, J.R. SALTER, Elisha SAPP, William GILLETT, Riley BLOUNT, John T. RUTLEDGE, Moses KEEN, A.A. Stewert, James KEEN, Isaac DANIEL, West WALKER, John DELENY, Alan DANIELS, Daniel BROWMAN, David KEEN, John BRYANT, Arther JONES, William LIGHT, Daniel STEWART, W.R. DANGERFIELD, T.B. HOLDER, Jesse HICKS, Larkin COWARD, Thomas TILLIS, M.H. FRIEZE, Leander OSTEEN, John PIERCE, Jacob SUMMERLIN, Streeti PARKER, W.B. ROSS, Henry HENINGTON, S.F. SLADE, J.M. CROUSE, Silvester BRYANT, David BLUE, Martin HAIR, Abener SWETT, Joel CUREY, Shed K. KEEN, Shek SAPP, Benjamin LANE, William H. KEEN, Jacob SUMMERLIN Jr., William GODFREY, Rubin COTTLE, Moses CORBIN, Asa ROBERTS, George KEEN, Jesse CARTER, John C. PETOLLE, Elisha PARKER, Jackson MORGAN, Nick RAULERSON, Cameron TIER, Daniel MORGAN, William H. ROBERTS, Ezekiel THOMAS, F.P. MORGAN, F. LOFTIN, S. SCARBOROUGH, Elias WALKER, W.A. WILLIAMS, John DAVIDSON, Rubin PREVATT, Richard TILLIS, A.J. KEEN, W.A. CARTER, J.J. CARTER, Jacob RAULERSON, L. BRYANT Sr., Samuel BARBER, Riley WRIGHT, Ansel WALKER, Stephen BARCO, Darham HANCOCK, George TATON, F.B. BROWNING, James H. JOHNSTON, A.T. ALLAN, T.H. GOLESBY, John W. LOWE. **N.Prong St.Mary's Precinct** - James DEES Sr., Thomas ELLIS, William RAULERSON, E. JOHNSTON, William MOLPHUS, William NIGGINS (or WIGGINS), William BENNETT, Hiram BENNETT, William BENNETT Sr., West RAULERSON, J.F. OSBURN, James ALLENSTON, George COMBS, J.H. MOLPHUS, A. JOHNSTON Jr., James DEES Jr., C. RAULERSON, Nat. BRYAN, Stephen HULL, Allan SURAT, Independent RAULERSON, A. COWART, J.A. SUMMERLIN, Joel ROBERTSON, A. HOGANS, J.D. WILLIAMS, D.M. DEAS, Francis MOORE, T.W. THOMPSON. **Santa Fe Precinct** - John MARCOM, Daniel BARCO, Fisher GASKINS, Joseph DOWLING, Edward WILLIAMS, Louis CLARK, Joseph PARRISH, John TOWNSEND, Green HILL,

George N. BONE, Levy LONG, William NEWTON, William PETERSON, Stephan McGOWAN, Elisha CARTER, P.A. GIBSON, William TOWNSEND, James GOFF, Hiram PARRISH, Thomas SWINNEY, Ransom PARRISH, Henry HANCOCK, B. CASON, J.B. CREWS, C.C. COLLINS, John M. PREVATT, Littleton HANCOCK, L. WEEKS, L.R. ROBERTS, W.T. NIBLACK, C.H.B. COLLINS, Samuel NIBLACK. **Fort Call Precinct** - H.C. WILSON, Richard GAINEY, Samuel JOINER, John CASON, William CASON, C.F. FITCHETT, James PEARCE, James BROOKS, Thomas IVEY, James O. BROOKS, Levy HARVEY, William H. BROOKS, Jesse E. THOMAS, Allen HASEL, Ezekiel PARRISH, Alan THOMAS, L.M. TUCKER, Bryant GLISSON, Josiah PARRISH Jr., Odum PARRISH, John MATTHEWS, E.E. MILLER, S.H. WORTHINGTON, Isaac WINEGORD, Isaac WILLIAMS, William SCOTT, G.M. ELLIS, Edmond STAFFORD, Benjamin MOODY, Ezekiel WEEKS. **Barber's Precinct (S.Prong St.Mary's)** - Ely HICKS, John S. CLIFTON, James BOYD, Joel McLENNON, Daniel J. MANN, Nathan STEPHENS, Ely HICKS Jr., Elisha GREEN Jr., John McLENNON, William UNDERHILL, William H. WILLINGHAM, John BROWN, Joseph UNDERHILL, Hilliard JONES, Moses BARBER, Lewis LANIER. **Cone's Precinct** - Rigdon BROWN, George FLETCHER, John VICKERS, R.S. PAYNE, William JOHNSON, Samuel SWETT, Peter CANNON, William THOMPSON, John PEOPLES, John C. COOK, Charles FLETCHER, R. SANDERLING, Isaac HINES, Early WIGGONS, John M. BRANNAN, James SWETT, John McCLENNAN, John GOODBREAD, Jesse LONG, Wiley HICKS, James BEAL, William SUMMERALL, P. NUNEZ, Silas McCLENNAN, Moses McCLENNAN, Corr. VOREEZS, James PARRISH, William CONE, Grandison BARBER, J.L. KING, J.T. GOODBREAD, Joseph DYALL, C. PARRISH, William FRINK, J.A. STEWART, David WILKERSON, J.W. CATHEY. **Robert Brooks Precinct** - William HAIR, John RAULERSON, John THOMAS, Littleburg WALKER, Robert BROWN, William J. WHIDDON, Christopher ZERBENDINE, Thomas R. ELLIS, Shubeal BURNS, Robert BROOKS, David MAIN, Henry M. FRIER, William T. RUSHING. **Cedar Creek Precinct** - Josiah JOHNSON, Gideon Ylventon, John CANADY (or KENADY), William WILKINSON, James POWELL, Willis SMITH, James M. BURNSED, Elisha GREEN, Martin BUTLER, John HARVEY. **Swift Creek Precinct** - William HANCOCK, Stephen HANCOCK, Alexander DOUGLAS, John COLEMAN, Benjamin GURNEY, Jordan GARTON, Benjamin COWARD, J.R. JOHNSTON, John WESTER, William PARRISH, John DIAS, Benjamin BROWN, Arthur ROBERTS, Richard HARVEY, John WIGGINS.

1867-68 VOTER REGISTRATION LISTS

The following voter lists from Suwannee County are an important contribution to our files and I will share them with you here. These are compiled from original documents at the Florida State Archives. Our thanks go to the Tallahassee Genealogical Society. These records include 67 heads of house from the Wellborn District, 162 heads from the Houston District, 252 heads from the Live Oak District, 31 heads from the Columbus District, 45 heads from the Plowden District, and 16 heads from the New Boston District. These folks registered to vote well over 100 years ago...folks that may be your ancestors.

Information includes the name of the head of house, his race, and the length of time he had been in the state. It is interesting that everyone in this listing is shown as having entered the state no more than 12 months before the registration. I know of a number of these who had been in the state for many years. This leaves us with one conclusion... that the recorders listed their time as from the last registration (1 year earlier). For those who had a lesser number than 12 months...it can be assumed that they were recently come to Florida. These short-timers may have come here because of a land grant for service in the recently ended civil war. Be that as it may, let us begin the listing. I will show the full name followed by their race in parentheses. If they are shown as having been in Florida less that 12 months, I will indicate the months in the same parentheses as the race indicator. For example...John Doe (W,9) or John Smith (B,2). This would show name, race (White or Black), and number of months when less than 12. Where no number follows the race, it will indicate they had been assigned 12 months...presumably from the last registration.

WELLBORN - Joseph ALLEN (W), George W. ALLEN (W), Henry M. BLOOM (W), Armsted BALEY (B), Robert BUTLER (B), George H. BELVIN (W), Benjamin W. BRANNAN (W), Thomas A. CARRUTH (W), Peter CANNAN (B), Kelly DEAN (B), William DUNN (B), Prince DELEGAL (B), Andrew J. DOWLESS (W), George W. DUPREE (W), Jacob ELLIS (W), James W. FLEMING (W), Nathan R. GAYLARD (W), Moses GILES (B), Joseph GOLDSMITH (B), Jesse GRAHAM (B), Alfred GREEN (B), William GREEN (B), John S. GARFIELD (W), Richard GRAHAM (B), Frederick S. HAISTEN (W), William J. HAISTEN (W,9m), Jackson HEDDING (B), Joseph A. HODGES (W,9m), Peter W. HALL (W), John W. HALL (W), John A. HARE (W), Robert KENNEDY (B), James LEE (B), January MURDOCK (B), William MOBLEY (B), Peter T. MICKLER (W), William B. MICKLER (W), Robert J. MICKLER (W), William H. McCLELLAN (W), John RIGSBEE (B), Pinkney REDMAN (B), Warren S. ROBERTS (W), Hyder D. RIGGSBEE (W), Elam SAPP (W,2m), Samuel R. SESSIONS (W), King STOCKTON (B), Gabriel SIMS (B), Ezekiel L. SELPH (W), Robert C. SMITH (W), Hardy E. STOKES (W), Frank STOCKTON (B), John J. TAYLOR (W), William THOMAS (B), Homer TYSON (B), Thomas URGUHART (W), Dubbin WELLS (B), Thomas WILLIAMS (B), William H. WILSON (W), Glisson WILLIAMS (W), Thomas J. WILLIAMS (W), Isom DEAS (W), William HOLMES (W), Jesse P. STANSIL (W), John R. WILLIAMS (W), Abraham BROWN (B), Sam ELLIOTT (B), Thomas R. TEDDER (W).

HOUSTON - Albert PRINCE (B), Isaac ALEXANDER (B), Frank ALEXANDER (B), Samuel T. AMISON (W), Thomas AMISON (W), Samson ALEXZOW (B), John BAILEY (W), Peter BATTLE (B), Richard BARTLEY (B), Earnest BENTON (B), August BAKER (B), Richard BATEY (B), Johnson BRYANT (B), Thadius S. BARCLAY (W), Alfred BROWN (B), William BERRY (B), John BALEY (B), Cezar BRYANT (B), Jacob J. BARNES (W), William S. BUGG (W), James BASS (W), Franklin BAILEY (W), Joab BLACKMON (W), Lewis BUTLER (B), Joseph BRADLER (W), Joseph CATE (B), Archibald CARAWAY (W), Samuel P. CREWS (W), James J. CHERRY (W), William F. CARAWAY (W), James R. DICKSON (W), James D. DALRYMPLE (W), Nathaniel M. DEES (W), John R. EVERS (W), Charles FLOYD (B), Watkins N. FOSTER (W), James M. FOSTER (W), David Y. GRAY (B), Augustus GREEN (B), Lewis GROSE (B), Noah GRAHAM (B), Burwell K. GREEN (W), William D. GREEN (W), Abraham GRAHAM (B), Jerry GRAHAM (B), Charles F. GARDNER (W), Henry GIBBS

(W), Arnold W. GREEN (W), Henry D. GRIMES (W), John GIBBS (B), John GOFF (W), Andrew J. GRESHAM (W), Shadrick GIBBS (W), William A. GARDNER (W), Robert HAWKINS (B), Needam HAMILTON (B), Thomas HILL (B), Samuel HOLMES (B), William M. HICKS (W), Samuel W. HICKS (W), John HURST (W), Enoch W. HURST (W), Frederick HOLLAND (B), Sharod M. HAMILTON (W), Thomas H. HAWKINS (W), Howell S. HAWKINS (W), Izah HOLLAND (B), James HENDRIX (W), Virgil HILL (B), Harrell HOLLAMAN (W), James A. HARRIS (W), William J. HUGGINS (W), Robert A. HUMPHRIES (W), Hartwell S. HARRELL (W), Larkin HARRIS (W), William W. HARRIS (W), William HARRELL (W), Richard S. HOLLAWAY (W), Richard HURT (W), William INGERVILLE (B), Berry JONES (B), John H. JOHNSON (W), Handy JOHNSON (B), Washington JONES (B), John JONES (W), Green JOHNSON (W), John JACKSON (B), Daniel KIKE (B), John W. KENNON (W), Robert A. KENNON (W), David W. LISTON (W), Madison LANE (B), Silas F. LAWSON (W), Benjamin F. LYONS (W), John LLOYD (W), David MILLS (W), James MANDRELL (B), Robert MILLER (B), Stephen MILLER (B), Lewis MORGAN (B), Amos H. MEEKS (W), James P. MORGAN (W), Henry H. MOSELEY (W), William J. MURPHY (W), William J. MICKLER (W), John C. MIZELL (W,7m), Charles McNEIL (W), Ira L. McCOLLUM (W), Bryant NIXON (B), William J. NEWMAN (W), Joseph C. PONCHIER (W), Seek POLITE (B), Hiram ROUSE (B), Isreal ROUSE (B), Adam REED (B), David SIMMONS (B), Jacob SUTTON (B), Simon SUTTON (B), John SMITH (B), James SHANNON (B), Henry STOCKTON (B), John V. SOWELL (W), William SCOTT (B), Henry G. STEWART (W), Willoughby TULLIS (W), Adam THOMAS (B), Samuel WHITE (B), Arnett WILLIAMS (B), George WALLACE (B), Henry M. WOOD (W), Henry WILLIAMS (B), Richard WILLIAMS (B), George YOUNG (B), Jesse BIVIN (W), Daniel M. BLUE (W), Thomas P. DELEGAL (W), William F. GARDNER (W), Felix HURST (W), Samuel JONES (W), David SIMONS (B), George WYNN (W), Sopator HURT (W), Thomas S. EVERS (W), H.T. KENNON (W), Joseph SNEAD (B), Isaac WILLIAMS (B), George E. McCLELLAN (W), Hamilton POLITE (B), James YOUNG (B), Frank BELL (B), Oliver WILDER (B), John CATE (B), Ted GOLPHIN (B), Willis HENRY (B), London MORGAN (B), Abram HUGHES (B), Charles McKEEVER (B), David H. MERCHAND (W), Elkanah GOFF (W), Joseph S. SESSIONS (W), Evan H. TUTEN (W).

LIVE OAK - Coster ALLEN (B), Lancaster AUSTIN (B), Jerry AUSTIN (B), Enoch ALLEN (B), Robert ALLEN (B), George W. ALLISON (W), William P. ALLISON (W), Robert F. ALLISON (W), John W. ALLISON (W), William ALLISON (W), Sampson ALTMAN (W), Elija BUTLER (B), Monday BROWN (B), George BELL (B), Adam BENJAMINE (B), Washington BROOKS (B), John BLACK (W), Alfred BLACK (W), Albert BONDS (W), Sanford B. BONDS (W), Robert BRUINTON (B), Chance BACON (B), Henry BRADFORD (B), Sharrad BIRD (W), John BOATWRIGHT (W), Emanuel BOATRIGHT (W), Andrew J. BASS (W), Junius E.S. BARNES (W), John E. BROSON (W), Joseph BAKER (B), William R. BEVAN (W), George W. BEVAN (W), Thomas A. BALEY (W,8m), Merideth E. BROCK (W), Wright CUNNINGHAM (B), Stephen CASON (B), Edward B. CATES (W), George W. CLARK (B), Elisha CURL (W), Anthony CAROOTH (B), Nelson CONNER (W), Richard COLDING (B), Thomas R. COMPTON (W,8m), Harry COPELY (B), Charles CARLILE (B), George CURRIE (B), William W. COATES (W), William S. CARAWAY (W), Philip G. COATES (W), John O. CARROLL (W), Joseph CARAWAY (W), Peter DELIONS (B), Edinborough DAVIS (B), Monroe DAVIS (B), George DAVIS (B), John B. DAVIS (W), Abraham DAVIS (B,5m), Charles DORSEY (B), Charles

DAVIS (B), Zachariah DEES (W), Philip S. DUVAL (W), Thomas FLOYD (B), Jerry FULJUM (B), Lewis FIELDS (B), Gabriel FORTH (B), Randall FULCHIER (B), Benjamin FIGG (B), Moses FOREST (B), Thomas M. FORSON (W), Nathaniel GOODMAN (B), George GLENN (B,6m), Nathaniel GODWIN (B), John W. GRANTHAN (W), Walter GWYNN (W), Abram GAULDING (B), James GIBBS (W), Benjamin GRIFFIN (W,6m), Jackson GIBBS (W), Jehu GOFF (W), Peter GRAHAM (B), Aleck GAINER (B,4m), Eli HARRIS (B), James HIGDON (B), Clem HALL Sr.(B), Clem HALL, Jr.(B), Richard HURST (W), Thomas T. HURST (W), Lewis HENDERSON (B), Tony HARDGREE (B), John H. HARRELL (W), John HIGDON (B), Caleb W.P. HOWELL (W), John J. HARRELL (W), Elijah F. HENDERSON (W,9m), Jesse HART (W), James S. HALL (W), Thomas HART (W,9m), Cornelius HARDEE (W), Julius HILL (B), Barney HAY (B), William B. HARDEE (W), William H. HOLZENDORF (W), William HOLLAND (W), Ned IVEY (B), Nathaniel IVEY (W), Cuba IRVINE (B), Hays JENKINS (B), Peter JACKSON, Jr.(B), Peter JACKSON, Sr.(B), Aleck JOHNSON (B), Handy JONES (B), Early JACKSON (B), Henry JACKSON (B), William JONES (B), Charley JONES (B), John JOHNSON (B), Benjamin JEFFRIE (B), Berry JEFFUS (B), George H. JOHNSON (W), William H. JONES (W,7m), Frank KING (B), Samuel LONSOME (B), Richeous LANGWOOD (B,9m), Edward R. LUNDAY (W), William E. LIVINGSTON (W), Levin A. LANE (W), David LINSAY (B), Lawrence LONSOME (B), Isaac LAWRENCE (B), Alfred LAMB (B), James R. LEWIS (W), Thomas LLOYD (B,3m), John F. LEGGETT (W), Bryant MOSELEY (B), Carter MOTON (B), London MACK (B), James S. MIKELL (W), James MIMS Sr (W), Obid MARSHALL (B), Jackson MOSLEY (B), James MIMS Jr (W), Downing MATTAIR (W), Green MEEKS (W), Henry MEEKS (W), Oceola MILLANS (B), Tony MITCHEL (B), Thomas MITCHEL (B), Elias B. MILLS (W,8m), Howell MEEKS (W), Jackson MORGAN (B,7m), Thomas J. MITCHELL (W), Hanson K. MILLS (W), George MILLER (W), John McKEEVER (B), Samuel McKEEVER (B), Moses McKINNIS (B), Samuel McCARDELL (W,3m), Joseph McKEEVER (B), Aaron McKINNAN (B), Henry McGEE (B), William F. NOBLES (W), John A. NOBLES (W,7m), Aleck ODUM (B), George E. OVERSTREET (W), Augustus POLITE (B), Jacob PRICE (B), Richard PHILIPS (B), James PERRY (B), John PARSHLEY (W), John PLATT (W), Antney RAWLS (B), Henry ROBERTSON (B), Jackson ROUSE (B), John B. ROBERTSON (W), Charles RADDICK (B), Thomas P. RANDOLPH (W), Samuel STEWART (B), Jake SIONS (B), Joseph SILAS (B), Elijah SMITH (B), Solomon SULLIVAN (W), Lancaster STEWART (B), John G. STINSON (W), Harry SCRANTON (W,9m), James STAPLETON (W), William SAVAGE (B), Edmond SMITH (W), Lofton SHIP (B), William STEWART (B), Ostin STEPHENS (B), Elija SMITH (B), Moses L. STEBBINS (W), Francis M. STEBBINS (W), John SKEEN (W), Joseph TIMMONS (B), Peter TABB (B), Abner THOMAS (B), Shade TAYLOR (B), Charles THORNHILL (B), Dairy TAYLOR (B), David TAYLOR (B), Joseph TYSON (B), William TILLMAN (B), Benjamin B. TAVEL (W,5m), Levi TAYLOR (B), Jackson THOMAS (B), Allen WILLIAMS (W), Titus WOOD (B), Jackson WILSON (B), Willis WILLIAMS (B), Abner WILLIAMS (B), Andrew WILLIAMS (B), Robert WATSON (B), Solomon WILKINS (B), March WEEKS (B), Henry WILLIAMS (B), Wiley WILLIAMS (B), James WRIGHT (B), Brister WRIGHT (B), Nero WEST (B), Thomas WATSON (W), Sherry WADE (B), Peter WIGGINS (B), William C. WHITE (W), John WESLEY (B), Timothy WILLIAMS (B), Benjamin WHITE (B), Kato WALLACE (B), Emry WILLIAMS (B), Alexander WILSON (W), Elisha WINBORN (W), Edward WILSON (B), Crawford WILLIAMS (B), Nathan H. WALKER (W), Council WARD (W), Wellington

YOUNG (B). NOTE - The following names were late registering and are out of alphabetic order. George MANKER (B), Abner R. CREEKMORE (W), Wade H. REDDING (W), John W. ROBERTSON (W), Philip D. WIGHTMAN (W), Edward BUCHANAN (B), Hugh A. BLOUNT (W), John COLSON (B), Ezekiel DENARD (W), Thomas FLOYD (B), Haris HERRING (B), Robert ROBERTSON (B), George T. TURNER (W), Daniel WILLIAMS (B), Isah WILLIAMS (B), Henry A. WYSE (W).

COLUMBUS - James A.M. BROWN (W), Jacob BUCHANAN (B), Francis T. BUCHANAN (W), James L. BOLER (W), William H. BOYETT (W), George CORNWALL (W), Jackson J. CLAYTON (W), Samuel M. DEAS (W), Charles DEAN (W, from Ireland. Naturalized by John Gill Shorter on Oct.10, 1854 in Henry County, Alabama), Adam FORT (B), Soloman FORT (B), William B. FULFORD (W), William R. FULFORD (W), George GALE (B), Nathan L. HALL (W), Thomas LEVY (B), Benjamin F. MEEKS (W), Hamilton McDANIEL (W), William P. NOBLES (W,6m), John C. OVERSTREET (W), William P. PARKER (W), Daniel J. PARKER (W), Thomas P. QUIETT (W), David ROBISON (B), Jacob SMITH (B,9m), Stephen J. TYLER (W), Benjamin WILLIAM (B), John WATSON (W), George WILLIAMS (B), Adam YOUNG (W), Daniel JIMERSON (W).

PLOWDEN - Berry ALLEN (B,8m), John M. BROWN (W), Henry W. BELTON (W), Edmond BANKS (B), Anderson COMER (B,6m), Ostin COLLIER (B), Charley DAVIS (B), Joseph DENSLER (W), Nathaniel T. ELLIOTT (W), Madison EDDINS (B), Peter FLOYD (B,6m), William P. GAMBLE (W,9m), Stephen C. GOENS (W), Alfred J. GLOVER (W), Isam HARVEY (B), John A. IRVINE (W), Henry IVEY (B), Robert A. IVEY (W), Charles T. IRVINE (W), Chance JACOB (B), Reuben B. KELLY (W,7m), Alex MOSELEY (W), Monday y MILLER (B,6m), Felix McINTOSH (B,6m), James McINNIS (W), Calvin PEACOCK (W), Leroy B. PEACOCK (W), Ned PEACOCK (B), Aleck RIVERS (B), Dubbin ROLLINS (B), John L. ROSS (W), John W. RICE (W), York SHAFFER (B), Zaches SHEPARD (W), Samuel W. SHEPHARD (W), Francis J. SANDERS (W), William B. TELFORD Sr (W), William B. TELFORD Jr (W,7m), William WALKER (B), Lewis WALTON (B), Loucious A. YOUNG (W), John O. ROSS (W), George M. WALKER (W), Alfred WILLIAMS (W), Joseph BROWN (W).

NEW BOSTON - William ALLEN (B), Nathaniel Y. BRYAN (W), Lewis CLARK (W), Robert K. ELLIOTT (W), Thomas J. EDWARDS (W), Fortune JACKSON (B), Andrew J. LISLE (W), James D. LEE (W), Waubee MULLER (B), Anthony STEPHENS (B), Thomas SPENCER (B), George WILLIAMS (B), Thomas WALKER (W), Berry WALKER (W), Scott HALL (W), Albert PETERSON (W).

Wills, Probates, & Inventories
(Chapter 5)

These records are nearly 150 years old...old enough to have information for the past 5 generations. The will is one of the most important records for research purposes. These wills were found in an old loft in a Suwannee County government building. The book was in very bad condition...warped with yellowed pages, however, we were able to record it.

BIRD, Reddin - Recorded in the Darlington District of South Carolina on January 19, 1853. The will was certified in the same place on July 25, 1856 and certified again in Suwannee County on May 21, 1860 by Joshua Caraway, County Clerk. It shows his wife's name as Hannah and his children as 1) Harvey L., James E., George W., Andrew J., Sarah E. McElveen, Stephen D.N., Mary L. Mimms, Margaret C., and Francis C. Mr. Bird had grandchildren as follows: Harvey L. had 3 children, James E. had 2 children, Andrew J. had 1 child, and Sarah E. McElveen had 3 children. The executors were James E. Bird (a son) and Levy F. Goodman. The witnesses were Elisha Smith, Thomas M.K. McElveen, and Robert L. McElveen (one of the McElveen men was probably the husband of Sarah E. McElveen). His wife Hannah and each of the children (and the grandchildren) received Negro slaves, sums of money, and various tracts of land. Joshua Caraway was clerk of Suwannee County, Fl.

COATES, Martha Elizabeth - Recorded in Lawrence County, Georgia on May 6, 1850. It was entered into Suwannee County records on August 21, 1860 by Joshua Caraway, County Clerk. She left her entire estate to the children-to-be of her only son John J. Coates and his wife Priscilla H. Coates. She "loaned" the use of her estate to her son John J. Coates and his wife. The will further stipulated that if her son did not have children that her estate should be given to the children of her brother John W. Gray. No mention of a husband. He either died or they had been divorced. The executors were to be her beloved son John J. Coates and a trusted friend named Andrew T. Hampton. Witnesses were D.N. Young, John B. Thomas, A.E. Norris, & Lorange MacConnell. Joshua Caraway was clerk at Suwannee County, Fl.

POWELL, John - Will was made in Suwannee County, Florida on May 23, 1861. His wife's name was Martha (commonly called Patsy) to which he willed 160 acres situated in T3,R15E,S30. Children named were James, Sidney (dau.), Martha, Milly Smith, Mary, John and 2 other sons (these last three were married...making 8 children in all...the earlier five being single at the time of the will). George E. McClellan was appointed executor. Witnesses were Sampson Carver, Mary Powell, John Powell, and V.T.? McClellan. C.L. Carruth was the Judge of Probate.

HACKNEY, Brantley J. - Will was created in Wellborn, FL. on Dec.13, 1862. The will states that he had a wife and 3 children. The executrix was his wife Eliza J. Hackney. Witnesses were John J. Taylor, Jesse T. McLeran, and Hyder D. Rigsbee. Mr.

Hackney died prior to January 12, 1863. Judge of Probate was C.L.Carruth.

SPEIR, John R. - Will was created in Suwannee County, FL. on July 18, 1862. Martha F. Speir was his wife and one of the executors of the will...the other being Brantley J. Hackney. Children are mentioned but not by name. The witnesses were Samuel R. Sessions, Hyder D. Riggsbee, and Jesse T. McLeran. The judge of probate was C.L.Carruth. Mr. Speir died prior to January 12, 1863.

JOHNSON, William E. - Will was created in Suwannee County, FL. on December 2, 1862. His wife's name was Harriot to which he bequeathed 159 acres located as follows: 40a in T4,R13E,S15,SE1/4 of NW1/4; 40a in T4,R13E,S15,NE1/4 of NW1/4; 79a in T4,R13E,S10, S1/2 of W1/4. Harriott, his wife, was the executrix. Witnesses were E.B. Sealman, Owen Parker, and Henry T. Ingerville. Judge of Probate was C.L. Carruth. Mr. Johnson died before April 3, 1863.

STEELE, Augustus - Will was created in the city of Atseena Otie, Levy County, FL. on November 3, 1860. All his properties and goods were left to his wife, Elizabeth Anastatia and his daughter, Augusta Florida. His wife was the executrix and the Judge of Probate was George E. McClellan. Mr. Steele died before December 21, 1864.

LANE, Thomas A. - Will was created in Suwannee County, FL. on October 6, 1863. His wife, Sophia F. Lane was appointed executrix. Mr. Lane had several children but only his younger son James McRee Lane is mentioned. At this time James was without issue. He also speaks of "interest accrued from land sold" left by his father Levin Lane in the state of North Carolina as well as his own stock in the Wilmington & Weldon Railroad in North Carolina. He then speaks of his plantation. Witnesses were John Hart, B.J. Roberts, and W.M. Hicks. Angus McAuley was the Judge of Probate. Mr. Lane died before March 6, 1864.

INGERVILLE, Henry J. - Will was created in Suwannee County, FL. on July 9, 1861. He wills his property to 1) his brother James E. Ingerville, 2) his niece (and daughter of his brother James) Adeline Dora Ingerville. James E. Ingerville was appointed his executor. Witnesses were William B. Ross, John M. Godfrey, & S.R. Mattair. In a codicil dated January 25, 1863, all of Henry's goods go to Adeline Dora Ingerville...and in the event of her death, the goods go to his sisters 3 children. The sister married a "Trimmous". It would appear that his brother, James E. Ingerville had died since a new executor was appointed...an uncle named James Glenn. Witnesses for this codicil were S.H. Bunker, Andrew McClellan, and W.H. McClellan. Mr. Ingerville died before March 24, 1866.

McCLELLAN, George E. - Will was created in Suwannee County, FL. on August 25, 1866. His wife was Celestia R. McClellan who was appointed as executrix of his estate. His children were,

Julia, Ellen, Clifford, Bell(dau), Virginia, and William. He gave his Piney Mount land to his wife. He had a mule named Beck. Witnesses were William P. Bethea, John J. Taylor, and Jesse F. McLeran. In a codicil dated September 3, 1866, a married son named Webb is mentioned. Same witnesses as above. Mr. McClellan died before November 5, 1866. Thomas A. Carruth was the Judge of Probate.

CARAWAY, Adam - Will was created in Suwannee County, FL. on January 15, 1867. The following statement shows the beneficiary..."For the love I bear to Emoline Stewart, I will and bequeath the following property". To wit, 40a (T2,R14E,S14,NE1/4 of the SE1/4), 7 cattle marked Swallow Fork. Executors were Archibald & Joshua Caraway (Joshua died between February 3, 1872 and August 1, 1887). Witnesses were J.H. Thomson, Craven Lassiter, and James A. Hill. Thomas A. Carruth was Judge of Probate.

NEWMAN, James A. - Will was created in Suwannee County, FL. on July 31, 1867. He bequeaths to his two grandchildren...Mary Adeline & Martha Alice McCollum...all his cattle. The remainder of his estate was to be divided between Elizabeth McCollum (wife of Ira McCollum), William James Newman, Jason W. Newman (these last 3 are said to be his youngest children). He further bequeaths to his "beloved" son Andrew A. Newman and to Harriet Triplett. He appointed his "esteemed" son-in-law, Ira McCollum as executor of his estate. Witnesses were John F. White and James A Hill. Thomas A. Carruth was the Judge of Probate. Mr. Newman died before September 3, 1867.

WATSON, John - Will was created in Suwannee County, Fl. on October 14, 1868. He bequests were awarded to John P. Watson's (his son) daughter, Delaina; to his daughter's (Nancy F. Hall) daughter, Bunevista S. Hall, to his 2 daughters...Avy Ann E. and Charlotta O.E. Watson. He appointed William A. Brinson as executor. Witnesses were Charlton Brinson, Levi J. Davis, and George W. Bevan. Judge John W. Rice was judge of the county court. Mr. Watson died before February 1, 1869.

ROUSSEAU, William H. - Will was created in Hillsborough County, FL. on December 10,1869. His wife, Mary Ann, and a son, John L. Rousseau were appointed executors of his estate. He then lists his minor children: Thaddeus, Willie W., Adelaide R., Edward P., Stonewall J., and Ida Viola Rousseau. He directed that his son Stonewall J. be given a good education seeing that he cannot work. He then lists his "other" children, John L., Virginia C., and Mollie. Witnesses were Julius D. Rodgers, A.B. Rodgers, and M.T. Howard. Mr. Rousseau died January 24, 1870 in Hillsborough County, Fl. At the time of his death he had a "mansion" in Suwannee County, Fl.

POWELL, Martha - Will was created in Suwannee County, FL. on February 14, 1870. She states in accordance with the will of her "late" husband John Powell, her assets are to be given to her daughter Sidney, to son James Mack Powell, and to Polly Grimsley. Sidney and James are said to be the youngest children. A further division is to made and given to the remaining children, Joseph Powell, the above mentioned Polly Grimsley, Milly Smith, and Martha Dees. Five dollars is also to be given to the heirs of John Powell Jr. Property is shown as: 80a (T3,R15E,S29,S1/2 of the NW1/4), as property formerly purchased from the P&G RR. Ishom Deas is mentioned as being granted 1/2 of what he makes from a crop then being planted. Thomas A. Carruth of Wellborn was appointed by Mrs. Powell as executor of the estate. Witnesses were Mary A. Carruth and Francis Preston. Mrs. Powell died before November 3, 1870. John W. Rice, County Judge.

IRVINE, John R. - Will was created in Suwannee County, FL. on December 3, 1868. He bequeaths his estate to his wife, Emily G. Irvine, and he appointed his son, Charles T. Irvine as his executor. Lands involved were 80 acres (T4,R11E,S14 & S23, S1/2 of SE1/4 of SE1/4, and NE1/4 of NE1/4, and E1/2 of NW1/4 of NW1/4). Witnesses were D.D.McLeroy, L.M. Balentine, & William P. Gamble. Mr.Irvine died before July 15, 1871. His condition at the time of the will was described as "old, infirm, and palsied".

CONNER, Nelson - Will was created in Live Oak, Suwannee County, FL. on August 1, 1871. His wife is listed as Virginia Connor and his children as, Mary Virginia, Margaret Anna, Jesse Nelson, and Sidney B. Connor. His life insurance policy was for $3000 dollars at the Equitable Life Assurance Company of the United States, based at 130 Broadway, New York, N.Y. All his children were minors at the writing of this will. He name his wife Virginia as executor of his estate. Witnesses were William B. Taylor, S.T. Overstreet, and E.W. Ervine. Mr. Connor died before August 8, 1871. John W. Rice was County Judge. William B. Taylor, E.W. Ervine, and M.M. Blackburn were ordered to appraise Mr. Connor's possessions and submit the list to the court on August 8, 1871.

DEES, Nathaniel M. - Will was created in Suwannee County, Fl. on December 18, 1871. He bequeathed to his wife, Henrietta, land as follows: SW1/4 of SE1/4 of Section 5, NW1/4 of NE1/4 of Section 8, and 27 2/3 acres on West side of NE1/4 of NE1/4 on Section 8, also all rights, title, & interest in my homestead on NE1/4 of NW1/4 of Section 8...all in T3,R14E. He appointed his wife Henrietta as executrix. Witnesses were Angus McCauley, Zachariah Dees, and James W. Harris. Mr.Dees died before January 13, 1872. John W. Rice was County Judge.

HAIR, John A. - Will was created in Suwannee County, FL. on January 28, 1872. He willed his body be buried in the cemetery at Mt. Pleasant Church. He willed the homeplace of 160 acres located at (T4,R15E,S6,W1/2 of NE1/4 & E1/2 of NW1/4) to his son, William W. Hair. He then gave $5 each to daughters Ann, Mary Ann Catherine, Matilda, and to the heirs of his son Rolen. After paying just debts he wills more goods to other children as follows; Sarah A., John A., Bethel, and Permelia. He named his son-in-law, Thomas R. Tedder as executor. Witnesses were James A. Griffin, Velerius W.A. Huchinson, Henry A. Mosely, and W.J. Huggins. In a later affidavitt a Kinsey Chambers is also shown as a witness. Mr. Hair died on October 31, 1872. John W. Rice was County Judge.

CAROWAY, Lucretia - Will was created in Suwannee County, FL. on August 26, 1872. She wills goods to her "adopted daughter, Emily, and her children. She also wills certain goods to her grandmother, Wayne? Johnson, and to a daughter, Biney? Grantham. She named William Gardner, a neighbor, as her executor. Witnesses were Thomas Kenaddy, C.T. McMannan, and W.A. Gardner.

MIXSON, Miller W. - Will was created in Suwannee County on June 17, 1872. His will is directed to the following; this first group are by his first wife: Simon, John, Townson, Sarah Nancy, and Martha Jane. The children of his second wife, Lucretia, born out of wedlock were William, John, Joseph, and James while those born "since our marriage" were Mary and Sariah. Land to be willed was T2,R13E,S22,E1/2 of the NE1/4, and ?1/4 of the NE1/4, and SE1/4 of the NW1/4. John C. Pelot and Lucretia Mixson were named as executors of the estate. Witnesses were John F. White, J.O. Hail, and John S. Pernance. Mr. Mixson died before March 19, 1874. Judge was Michael A. Clonts.

MOFFETT, Sarah E. - Will was created in Suwannee County, Fl. on Sept.7, 1874. Executor was named Harvy Moffett (her brother-in-law). The beneficiaries of her will are her brother, James Harvy Pondergrast, to her sisters Rebecca, Caroline, & Angeline Pondergrast, and to her nephew Harrie A. Moffett. She mentions her mother...but not by name. Land in Shenendoah & Page Counties, Virginia are also mentioned. Witnesses were W.B. Taylor, W.T. Lonis, and Virginia Connor. Mrs. Moffett died on or shortly after Sept.7, 1874. Testimony states that she executed the will on Sept.7, 1874 and died. The Judge was Michael A. Clonts.

BLACKMAN, Kitty - Two wills were created in Live Oak, Suwannee County, FL. on October 20, 1874 and November 28, 1874. The beneficiaries were Joab (a son), and to Calvin (a grandson). Land granted was located in T2,R14E,S21, NW1/4 of the SW1/4. Her executor was ?. Witnesses for earlier will were H.T. Dexter, C.J. Cobb, and M.L. Stebbins. Witnesses for the latter will were John Skeen, Joab Blackman, and M.L. Stebbinss. Mrs. Blackman died before December 15, 1874. Judges were Michael A. Clonts and W.S. Hennly, Justice of the Peace.

PAGE, William - Will was created in Suwannee County, FL. on April 6, 1872. The executrix was his wife, Miley. Beneficiaries were his wife, Miley (or Milly). Children and grandchildren are mentioned but not by name. Witnesses were W.B. Taylor and John C. Blount. Judge was Michael A. Clonts. Mr. Page died on or near April 6, 1876.

MOSLEY, Lewis T. - Will was created in Suwannee County, FL. on January 31, 1875. He stated that 90 days after his death he wanted Charles T. Irwin to apply to the Piedmont & Arlington Life Assurance Co. for $2000 dollars to be disbursed as follows: $1500 dollars to his infant son Louis T. Mosley and $500 to his wife Sallie. He also gave a horse & saddle to his "younger son" Dave. He named his brother Alexander Mosley as executor. Witnesses were Isham Murry, Cordlia A. Irwin, & John W. Rice. Mr. Mosley died before February 2, 1875. The judge was Michael A. Clonts.

KIRK, August - Will was created in Live Oak, Suwannee County, FL. on February 10, 1875. Mr. Kirk states that he has used his present name for 40 years and that his original name was August Keuck (a German form of Kirk?), and that he was from Wittstock Province, Randenburg (or Brandenburg which is the province of Berlin, Germany). His beneficiaries were Matilda Kupman of Kerchheim Balander Paltinto (Germany?). She was also his executrix. She was to distribute monies to Mr. A. Brunswig & to Mrs. Menkin, and to Mr. Kirk's foreman, Henry Chipier. She was to "deliver all my painting tools in remembrance of me". The witness was T.M. Stebbins. The clerk of the circuit court was M.L. Stebbins. Michael A. Clonts received a translation of the will on April 23, 1875.

STOKES, James Monroe - Will was created in Suwannee County, FL. on January 25, 1875. He names himself as a Minister of the Gospel. His beneficiaries were his wife, Caroline Louisa Stokes. He named his wife as executrix. Witnesses were W.H. Reynolds, William Brison, and William Brison Jr.

HARVEY, Alfred R. - Will was created in Live Oak, Suwannee County, Fl. on January 4, 1876. He lists himself as a merchant. His beneficiaries were his daughter Kitty A. Smith, his granddaughter Roberta B. Fisher. He wanted certain of the monies invested in Bonds of the State of Georgia, bearing interest of 6% per annum, to be turned over to his granddaughter, Roberta B. Fisher when she turns 18 years of age. He named M.M. Blackburn as his executor. He also appointed Peter McGlashan of Thomasville, Thomas County, Georgia to be Trustee of Bonds purchased for his granddaughter. Witnesses were H.A. Wyse, R.A. Ivey, and J.S. Hankens. Mr. Harvey died before February 28, 1876. Michael A. Clonts, Judge. Mr. Blackburn was to receive $5000 for duties performed as his executor. Witnesses to this were R.A. Ivey and S. Bird. Codicil dated February 29, 1875. Appraisers of his possessions were W.S. Hamby, Sherwood Bird, and W.S. Bynum. Estate was valued at $3256.29.

GAMBLE, W.P. - Will was created on May 14, 1877 about 1 hour before his death. Court advertised action for 60 days in the Florida Expositor, a paper of Suwannee County. Beneficiaries were stated..."I want George & Lizzie to have the old place with 40 acres where Johnson Brown lives". He wanted his wife and children to have the rest of the land. He assigned the executorship to his two brothers, John .W. and Josiah .N. Gamble. Witnesses were J.N. Gamble, George H. Ballentine, John W. Gamble, J.H. Dazler?. Witnesses (and those co-signing for $4000 to the Governor of Florida) were, John W. and J.N. Gamble as principles, Robert T. & John W. Allison, William H. McClellan, W.T. Bynum Jr., and J.C. Baisden. An inventory was to be taken by S.A. Young, S.J. McIntosh, and G.S. Telford. Judge was Michael A.

Clonts.

HERNDEN, Rhodes N. - Will was created in Granville County, North Carolina on January 3, 1863. Beneficiaries were: Cupid (a negro male slave), his 2 daughters and their children; Jenny (a negro woman), Bit (a negro woman) and her children; Ella R. Davis (possibly Divino)(a niece), Atlas Burnett (a nephew), Zechariah Burnett (a nephew), Robert B. Longmire (a great-nephew), Ianna (a niece and wife of James P. Montague), Emma R. Burnett (a great-niece a daughter of the late Addison R. Burnett), and to the other children of the late Addison R. Burnett, John R., Duncan C., and Bartlet H. Hernden (all brothers), Henry C. & William G? Hernden (1/2 brothers), Sylvania George (1/2 sister), and Elizabeth (1/2 sister and wife of David A. Hunt). Executors were John R. and Duncan C. Hernden, and Henry C. Hernden. Witnesses were R.N. Kingsbury, Robert B. Gilliam, and M.V. Lanier. Clerk of Granville County, N.C. court was Thomas D. Clement and County Judge of Suwannee County, FL. was Matthias M. Blackburn. The will was entered at Suwannee County, FL. on March 15, 1882.

GOFF, Jehu - Will created in Suwannee County, FL. on August 27, 1878. Beneficiaries were, Jane Goff (his wife)...a parcel of land located on T3,R12E,S6,SW1/4 of the SE1/4, sons Dangerfield, Alexander, Jehu, George W., and Winfield, daughters Frances (daughter of first wife...unnamed), Jennie, Adeline, Henrietta, and Feliuos? (children of second wife Jane). He named his son George W. Goff as executor. Witnesses were William F. Bynum Jr., and Matthias M. Blackburn. Jehu died on November 9, 1883. Matthias M. Blackburn was the County Judge. Those in charge of the inventory were, George W. Goff, executor, J.J. & J.R. Robinson, J.T. Clark, T.G. Baxter, and A.J. McLeod. The governor of Florida was William D. Bloxham. Witnesses of the inventory codicil were J.F. Newland and D.L. Mathis.

FAGG, George W. -Will was created in Gadsden County, Fl. on May 19, 1878. Beneficiaries were his wife Sophia C. Fagg. He named his wife Sophia C. Fagg as his executrix. No children were mentioned. Witnesses were G.J. Davis, F.J. Davis, and B. Howe. The judge was J.R. Harris. Entered in Live Oak courthouse on September 27, 1884 by judge Matthias M. Blackburn.

DELEGAL, Thomas P. - Will was created in Suwannee County, FL on October 28, 1868. Beneficiaries were Mary L. Delegal, Henry L., Mary S., James J., Edward T., Louiza? J., Albert S., Louisa M., Philothia E., "and any other children that may yet be born to my wife". His homestead was named The Longwood Place. The executor was named to be Henry E. Delegal. Witnesses were A.B. Hagan, Ishum P. Walters, and George H. Johnson. Mr. Delegal had died on or before August 18, 1884. Matthias M. Blackburn was the judge.

WIGGINS, James A. - Will was created in Suwannee County, FL. on March 12, 1882. Beneficiaries were "my beloved son, Rev. R.L. Wiggins", to daughter Mrs. D. Sherwood, to sons Richard, Thomas R., James A., my grandson Lewis A. Wiggins (son of George Wiggins, deceased), and to daughter Margaret E. Wiggins, and to his wife Elizabeth C. Wiggins. Richard Wiggin, a son, was named to be executor of estate. Young children are mentioned as being, Richard, Thomas R, James A. and Margaret E. Wiggins. Witnesses were called "beloved friends" John F. White, Samuel E. Philips, and James L. Haddock. Mr. Wiggins died before March 7, 1883. The judge was Matthias M. Blackburn.

BYNUM, William Forsyth Jr. - Will was created in Suwannee County, FL. on January 26, 1886. Beneficiaries were his wife (whom he also named as the executrix of his estate) Carrie E. Bynum, and daughter Blanche (under 18 at this time). Witnesses were Henry A. Blackburn, James B. Evans, and Wilson H. Sessions. Mr. Bynum died before February 11, 1886. Judge was R.W. Philips.

HARRELL, William - Will was created in Suwannee County, FL. on February 3, 1872. Beneficiaries were his wife, Altina J. Harrell, and to his children; Sarah R.A., Hartwell S., Mary E., Martha W.?, Roxey L.J., Harriot? L.T., John B., and any children that may yet be born. A married daughter, Eliza E. Fuquay, also is included. He named his wife Altina J. Harrell and his son Hartwell S. Harrell as executors. Witnesses were Joshua Caraway, Shadrick Gibbs, and J.H. Privett. W.L. Stebbins was the Clerk of the court and R.W. Philips was the judge. Mr. Harrell died before August 1, 1887.

HAWKINS, Howell S. - Will was created in Suwannee County, FL. on September 14, 1883. Beneficiaries were Jackson B. Hawkins, a son. He was to receive land located on T4,R14E,S3,SE1/4 containing 160 acres. Another son, Bartow J. Hawkins received the following land: T4,R14E,S10,N1/2 of NE1/4 containing 80 acres. Howell Hawkins, another son is mentioned as are the following children: Thomas H., Julia Williams, John W., George E., Mary Holtzclair, and Susan? Goff. Thomas H. and John W. were named as executors. Witnesses were T.J. Hackney, J.W. Gassett, and H.W. Mosely. Judge was R.W. Philips.

DEXTER, Mary Ann -Will was created in Suwannee County, Fl. on October 8, 1874. Beneficiaries were Rebecca S. (daughter), George E. Dexter, and Horace F. Dexter (sons). Horace F. Dexter was named as executor. Witnesses were W.B. Taylor, John S. Purviance, and Charles J. Cobb. R.W. Philips was the judge. Mrs. Dexter died before February 7, 1888.

DORMAN, Orloff M. - Will was created in Norfolk, Virginia on June 2, 1876. Benificiaries included, Margaret E. Dorman (his wife), Mrs. Charity Dorman (his mother), the American Bible Society, the Presbyterian Church, Rushton W. Dorman of Chicago, Illinois (nephew), Rodney Dorman of Jacksonville, FL. (brother), Miss Rachel Gould (sister of his wife)...and at Miss Gould's demise...this money is to be given to the Biddle Memorial Institute in Charlotte, N.C. to help educate and fit "colored youths" to preach the gospel, Miss Sarah Gould (another sister of his wife), Mrs. M.B. McClure (sister of his wife), Mrs. M.L.G. Patton (sister of his wife), Miss Gurgine V. Gould (niece of his wife),

Miss Mary Ann Hoey, Mrs. Laititia Louisa Kinney (his niece), Mrs. Agnes M.C. Alden (niece of his wife), Hannah Tole of Morgan Ashtabola County, Ohio, Clinton C. Clark (nephew), Celia C. Hammond (niece), Mary Dean Louisa ? , Mrs. Crawford, Mary G. Gardiner, Board of Foreign Missions of the Presbyterian Church, Scotia Seminary in N.C. He appointed his wife, Margaret E. Dorman to be his sole executor. If she were to die, Rushton M. Dorman (the nephew) of Chicago, Illinois would be the executor. If for some reason his nephew could not do this, then Rodney Dorman (his brother) would take the responsibility. If none of these are able to be executor, he appointed his friend, Charles B. Duffield of Norfolk, Va. to be executor. Witnesses were George M. Bain Jr., Holt Wilson, and J.H. Towner?, all of Portsmouth, Va.

BRIDGES, John M. - Will was created in Suwannee County, FL. on August 24, 1889. His wife, Mary Ann, named the executor, was to dispose of the following land: T2,R13E,S14,N1/2 of the NW1/4, NW1/4 of the NE1/4 containing 120 acres. Benificiaries included children of his first wife, to wit, Mary Jane Letsoun (wife of J.C. Letsoun), Adnanna Scott (wife of J. Scott), and Emma Tyner (wife of John Tyner), my son Frank R. Bridges, and to my 2 grandchildren (heirs of the estate of the late Minnie Letroun (wife of J. Letroun). He also bequeaths to "his beloved wife (the present wife), Martha Ann Bridges, and to his beloved children, to wit, John A., Jesse F., Mary C., Virginia D., Paul L., and George F.P. Bridges (all minors). Witnesses were, S.T. Overstreet, C.H. Brinson, and A.A. Barnette. Judge was W.P. Mosely.

LEWIS, James R. - Will was created in Suwannee County, FL. on July 11, 1887. He notes an indebtedness to H.F. Dexter for "making his crop"in 1886-1887. He also states he had been an invalid for 21 years under the care of his daughter Amanda. He wills the following land to Amanda: T2,R14E,S6,S1/2 of SE1/4 and T2,R14E,S5,SW1/4 of SW1/4 and T2,R14E,S8,NW1/4 of NW1/4. Beneficiaries included: Amanda Lewis and her two children Eula & Florence. Witnesses were J.C. Skeen & T.T. McDaniel. Judge was W.P. Mosely.

HURST, Richard M. - Will was created in Suwannee County, FL. on December 26, 1889. Property to held in trust "for my children now living with me", to wit: Martin B., Mary Anna, Ellie Etta Black, and Caroline Lucretia Jervis. Witnesses were J.B. Hobbs, A.J. Bass, and W.C. Robinson. Judge was W.P. Mosely.

LINDSEY, Nathan - Will was created in Suwannee County, FL. on February 19, 1881. Beneficiaries were Mary J. (his wife), Ada L. (daughter), and Benjamin H. (son)...children under 21 at this time...,his 3 youngest children; Lura J. Clayton, Ada & Benjamin Lindsey. He appointed his wife, Mary J. Lindsey, as his executrix. Witnesses were M.G. Clayton, J.J. Albritton, and W.W. O'Hara. Judge was W.P. Mosely.

FRASER, John - Will was created in Live Oak, Suwannee County, FL. on April 9, 1890. Beneficiaries were Sophia (his wife),

Ella Sessions (daughter...now married to Wilson H. Sessions), Irene Sessions (his granddaughter...daughter of Ella). He appointed his daughter Ella to be his executrix. Witnesses were W.M. Wood, L.H. Kennerlin, and Matthias M. Blackburn. Judge was W.P. Mosely. Mr. Fraser died before July 8, 1890.

OMANS, Rebecca F. - (late Rebecca F. Hall). Will was created in Suwannee County, FL. on August 22, 1883. Owned a note by Charles Engalls for $138.00 to be divided between James J. & Morgan B. Holly (2 orphaned children raised by her and her late husband). She appointed Robert F. Allison as her executor. Witnesses were W.J. Carroll, C.L. Dickens, and H.P. Breen. She died before November 21, 1890. Judge was W.P. Mosely.

HODGES, J.L. - Will was created in Wellborn, Suwannee County, FL. on December 22, 1890. Beneficiaries were Caroline F. (his wife), to his youngest son Thomas F., to his 4 children...naming at least 2 more: J. Wesley & Albert H. Hodges. He named J.Wesley and Albert H. Hodges, and Charles B. Olliff to be his executors. Witnesses were J.W. Bell, R.B. Mordsen?, and S.W. Gary. Judge was W.P. Mosely. Mr. Hodges died before January 21, 1891.

BLACKBURN, Andrew A. - Will was created in Live Oak, Suwannee County, FL. on August 22, 1882. Beneficiaries were his wife, Ellen E. Blackburn, a daughter, Charlotte Allen (wife of J.A.Allen), a son, Henry A. Blackburn. He appointed his son Henry A. Blackburn as his executor. He spoke of his home situated in Live Oak on the east side of Ohio Avenue bordered on the north by the property of Mrs. N.M. Parshley and on the south by H.A. Blackburn (his son). Witnesses were W.S. Hamby, J.A. Collins, and Walter I. Cole. Judge was W.P. Mosely. Mr. Blackburn died before August 10, 1891.

WILLIAMS, Simon L. - Will was created in the town of Wellborn, Suwannee County, FL. on August 5, 1872. Beneficiaries were his wife, Eliza Williams, and his children (unnamed). He named his wife as executrix. Witnesses were Philip E. Lowe, John W. Campbell, and John J. Taylor. Judge W.P. Mosely presiding. It is also stated that both Mr. Williams and two of the witnesses, namely Philip E. Lowe and John J. Taylor had died before December 12, 1892.

BLACKBURN, Mathias M. - Will was created in Suwannee County, FL. on August 22, 1893. Beneficiaries were his sister, Mrs. Eliza Clark (of Jefferson County, Tennessee), the Presbyterian Sunday School library in Live Oak, the Presbyterian Church in Live Oak, Claude I. Allen (son of Charlotte I. Allen of Live Oak) 280 acres described as follows: the E1/2 (except the NW1 4 of the NE1/4 of Section 21, Township 9, Range 9E, lying in Taylor County, FL., the remainder of his possessions to his niece, Charlotte I. Allen (wife of Julius A. Allen) of Live Oak. He also appointed Charlotte I. Allen as his executrix. Witnesses were H.M. Wood, E.G. Allen, and W.P. Mosely. J.N. Connor was the County Judge.

RIXFORD, George C. - Will was created in Rixford, Suwannee County, FL. on October 4, 1892. He lists himself as a "manufacturer and merchant" and lists his beneficiaries as his beloved wife, Lydia J. Rixford. He appoints his wife and his stepson, George E. Robbins, as executors. Witnesses were A.R. and W.P. Creekmore (farmers) and Frank White (dealer in real estate). Mr. Rixford died before July 14, 1894. J.N. Connors was county judge.

RIGGSBIE, Eliza J. - Will was created in Suwannee County, FL. on July 16, 1894. She requested that tombstones be provided for herself, B.J. Hackney, and H.D. Riggsbie (this latter may have been her husband). Beneficiaries were her daughter Callie Baker (among other things she inherited a note of debt owed to Mrs. Riggsbie by an A.D. Hemming), to her granddaughter, Scylla Griffin, to Minnie Hackney (wife of her son Thomas J. Hackney), her son Thomas J. Hackney (who also received a note payable to her from George F. Griffin), and to grand children, George F. Griffin, Callie Hemming, Scylla Griffin, Brantley Griffin and Maude Griffin. Her grandchildren were given the following lands in the town of Wellborn...Lots #3&4 in block 17, lots #1&2 in block 24...all total about 4 acres. She also appointed her son, Thomas J. Hackney, as executor. Witnesses were A.W. McLeran, W.R. Moore, and S.W. Gary. J.N. Connor was county judge.

TAYLOR, William Burwell - Will was created in Suwannee County, FL. on June 19, 1886. Beneficiaries were his wife, Mary Linton Taylor who he willed certain lands as follows... T2,R13E,S24,SE1/4 of SW1/4...and "all of my interest in the estate of Henry Lucas of the town of Mount Meggs, Montgomery County, Alabama, deceased, who was an uncle of Mary Ann Taylor, daughter of William Lucas and wife of my father Henry L. Taylor, now deceased". He appointed his wife Mary Linton Taylor as executrix of his estate. Witnesses were W.S. Hamby, S.H. Howard, and G.E. Dexter. J.N. Connor was the county judge. Mr. Taylor died before October 6, 1886.

JOHNSON, Edith - Will was created in Suwannee County, FL. on May 8, 1891. Beneficiaries were Martha Homer, Henrietta Daniels, and Rebecca Jackson (all nieces). All three nieces were appointed as executrixes of the estate. Witnesses were, M.E. Broome, W.E. Gainey, and Eustas Long (all from Live Oak). An affidavit by Hattie Jefferson states that Mrs. Johnson died on June 9, 1896 in Suwannee County, FL. Judge was Jesse N. Connor.

PARSHLEY, Nancy M. - Will was created in Live Oak, Suwannee County, FL. on May 21, 1890. She is shown to be a widow. Beneficiaries include...daughters Maria A. Brock, Arrabella E. Ives, and Emma L. Parshley. Sons were John Howard & William Brown Parshley. Her late husband, John Parshley, is mentioned in relation to "reserve from sale 80 square feet in the home lot in Live Oak, Florida as the grave of their father John Parshley". Executors appointed were Emma L. Parshley, John Howard Parshley, and a son-in-law, Wash M. Ives. Witnesses were Wm. P. Mosely, George Wolfe, and Daniel M. McAlpin. On February 10, 1897 it was declared by the lone surviving witness, George Wolfe, that by this time the other two witnesses had died, and that Nancy M. Parshley died on January 21, 1897. Judge was Jesse N. Connor.

DUTTON, Charles K. - Will was created in the city, county, and state of New York on January 30, 1895. Beneficiaries were his wife, Alice B. Dutton, James Otis Dutton (a son), Bessie K. Stephens (a daughter). The monies to the children are to be given to them when they become 30 years of age. He appointed his wife to be the executrix. Witnesses were Hugh D. Auchincloss of 17 W. 49th St., New York, P.O.Box 2, John W. Auchincloss of 12 W. 34th St., New York, P.O. Box 2, and S.S. Auchincloss of 24 East 48th St., New York. J. Fairfax McLaughlin was Clerk of the Surrogate Court of New York. Other witnesses were John H.V. Arnold and Jacob Washburn, both of New York. Mr.Dutton had died before May 18, 1897. Will was filed and recorded in Suwannee County by Judge Jesse N. Connor on December 22, 1897.

HOWARD, John L. - Will was created in Suwannee County, FL. on July 18, 1896. Beneficiaries were his wife Mary S. Howard, Jamie Victoria Johnson (daughter), Ada W.S. Grant Mitchell (daughter). The following land was willed to the above as follows: T2,R14E,S19,E1/2 of the SE1/4 to his wife, after her death T2,R14E,S19,NE1/4 of the SE1/4 to daughter Jamie...except for 1/2 acre for a graveyard, and T2,R14E,S19,SE1/4 of SE1/4 to daughter Ada. Witnesses were J.H.T. Bynum, J.W. Hawkins, and J.N. Connor. Judge was Jesse N. Connor.

LEWIS, H.K. - Will created in Live Oak, Suwannee County, FL on August 28, 1893. He is shown as a merchant of Live Oak. Beneficiaries were his wife, Flora Lewis, and his children (unnamed). His wife was his executrix. Witnesses were M.E. Browne, J.S. Hawkins, M.D., and W.P. Mosely...all from Live Oak. County judge was Jesse N. Connor.

MALLORY, William C. - Will was created in Wellborn, Suwannee County, FL. on November 20, 1899. Beneficiaries were Frost (son), Ralph (son), Maud (daughter), Grace (daughter), and his wife (unnamed). Frost, his son, was named executor. Witnesses were A.H. Hodges, C.B. Olliff, and J.W. Bell. Jesse N. Connor was the judge. Mr. Mallory died on May 24, 1900.

WILKINSON, Maurice - Will was created in Richmond County, Georgia on April 10, 1894. He owned real estate in New York City, in Newark, New Jersey, and Branford, Florida. Beneficiaries were Hattie W. Burwell of Charlotte, North Carolina, Fanny M. Wilkinson of Augusta, Georgia, Arthur Wilkinson of the city of New York, Lily W. Wright (all sons and daughters). He appointed his son Arthur of the city of New York, and John M. & William A. Walton of Augusta, Georgia as executors. Witnesses were J.E. Tarves?, John Moore, and Maurice Walton. J.Fairfax McLaughlin was Clerk of the N.Y. Surrogate Court. In a later statement dated February 27, 1900 Arthur Wilkinson is living in Hackensack, New Jersey. Mr. Maurice Wilkinson died before Feb.27, 1900.

AIRTH, W.S. - Will was created in Live Oak, Suwannee County, FL. on June 29, 1900. Mr. Airth was a medical doctor. Beneficiaries were his wife, Nellie, and Willie (his son). He appointed his wife Nellie as his executrix. Witnesses were L.T. Boatwright, A.J. Robertson, and Cary A. Hardee (all of Live Oak). Mr. Airth died before July of 1900. Judge was J.N. Connor.

WHITE, Joseph S. - Will was created at a temporary residence of Mr. White on Lookout Mountain, Tennessee on July 25, 1900. Beneficiaries were his wife, Jessie S. White. He states that he and wife have three small children. He appoints his wife as executrix. Witnesses were George T. White, O.W. Whetsel, and William C. White. Jesse N. Connor was judge. He was a resident of Suwannee County, Fl. at the time of his death which was before August 3, 1900.

FLETCHER, George N. - Will created in Detroit, Wayne County, Michigan on December 6, 1884. Beneficiaries were his sister, Mary Ann L. Fletcher, Addison T. Fletcher (a son?), to his nieces (daughters of his deceased sister, Maria Adams), Sarah Stone, Maria Adams, and Mary Adams...now of Boston, his wife Sarah A.G. Fletcher and his children. Executors of his estate were his wife and two sons, Frank W. and Allan M. Fletcher. Witnesses were Samuel McCoskey Stanton and Edward Payson Shelden. Judge of probate was Edgar D. Dunfee. Mr. Fletcher died on November 6, 1899 in Wayne County, Michigan. His wife, Sarah, had died before November 6, 1899. Filed in Suwannee County, FL. on August 28, 1900. Judge Jesse N. Connor presiding.

WHITE, Frank - Will was created in Suwannee County, FL. on September 6, 1900. Beneficiaries were all kinfolk...each received $1.00, the rest of his estate was to go to John Douglas of Dade County, FL. "for all his kindnesses". John Douglas was also appointed executor. Witnesses were Franklin L. Rees, Melvin Porter, and Dr. J.S. Hawkins. Judge was Jesse N. Connor.

WHITE, John Fletcher - Will was created in Live Oak, Suwannee County, FL. on January ?, 1901. Beneficiaries were his second wife, Sally A. White, his youngest child, Midget. He willed 575 acres of land to his wife as follows: T2,R13E,S23, T2,R13E,S26,E1/2 of NE1/4, also 10 acres in T2,R13E,S24,in SW1/4 (known as Brown's University lands), T2,R14E,S19,NW1/4 of SW1/4 & SW1/4 of SW1/4 & NE1/4 of SW1/4, T3,R13E,S3,NW1/4 & E1/2 of SW1/4, and SW1/4 of SW1/4. Midget is said to be "deaf & dumb". Other beneficiaries include a son, William C. White, and Rachel Cate (colored), the SE1/4 of SE1/4 of T2,R14E,S33. His appointed executor was his son William C. White. If William C. died before estate is handled, then he appoints another son, John Fletcher White Jr. to take over the executorship. A daughter Annie H. is also named. Witnesses were Z. Graham, H.F. Dexter, and J.N. Connor. Mr. Jesse N. Connor was the judge.

WILLIAMS, Jeptha V. - Will was created in Suwannee County, FL. on June 12, 1901. Beneficiaries were his wife Harriet who received land as follows: T3,R12E,S4,SW1/4 of NE1/4...40

acres..., to sons William, & John D., to daughters Mary Chancey, Laura Sapp, and Martha Robinson. Martha Robinson was appointed his executrix. Witnesses were James Tillman, John Crawford Watson, A.Sanford Bends, and Berry I. Brown. Judge was Jesse N. Connor.

MORGAN, James P. - Will was created in Suwannee County, FL. on October 7, 1901. Beneficiaries are as follows: "Julia H. Clark of Villa Rica, Georgia, sister to my last wife". Julia H. Clark was also appointed executrix. Witnesses were Cary A. Hardee, Robert T. O'Neal, and J.D. Parnell (all of Live Oak). Jesse N. Connor was judge.

PEACOCK, Helen B. - Will was created in Suwannee County, FL. on March 23, 1899. Beneficiaries were children, to wit, Pearl, Fletcher, Heber, Avon, Eunice, and Edith Peacock, and to his unnamed wife. No executor is named. Witnesses were W.F. Hodges, J.F. Dorman, and J.W. Bryson...all of Live Oak. Mr. Peacock died before January 9, 1902. The judge was Jesse N. Connor.

MILTON, Henry R. - Will was created in Suwannee County, FL. on June 28, 1894. Beneficiaries were two daughters, Hattie S. and Mary L, and his unnamed wife. Witnesses were S.M Martin, N.H. Green, and H.J. Green (all of Branford, FL). Mr. Milton died before December 30, 1901.

WALLS, Andrew J. - Will was created in Suwannee County, FL. on August 23, 1903. Beneficiaries were his wife, Martha Walls. She was also his executrix. Witnesses were J.C. Gallaher, J.C. Baisden, and E.P. Groover. Judge was Jesse N. Connor. Mr. Walls died before January 11, 1902.

WALLS, Martha A. - Will was created in Suwannee County, FL. on August 22, 1902. She was Andrew J. Walls wife. Beneficiaries were her sister Mary Lundy...she received "all my land and residence in block bounded by 1st Street on South and Scriven Street on West in the Northwest Division of Live Oak". A condition was that Mary Lundy serve as executrix and live with Mrs. Walls as her companion and nurse as long as she lives. Witnesses were Ira J. Carter, W.R. Dorman and H.E. Carter...all of Live Oak. If Mary Lundy died before her then her estate would go to Mary's son and Mrs. Walls' nephew, Hugh Carter. Witnesses to this 2nd codicil were Ira J. Carter, Mary A. Carter, and H.E. Carter...all of Live Oak. Judge was Jesse N. Connor. Mrs. Walls died before July 16, 1903.

KIMMONS, J.A. - Will was created in Palatka, Putnam County, FL. on May 20, 1890. He was a minister of the gospel. Beneficiaries were Antoinette Clark (wife of John Clark of Tupelo, Mississippi), to son-in-law John Clark of Tupelo, Mississippi, to his wife, Anna Maria Kimmons. The executor was John Clark. Witnesses were Gustave A. Schneider, W. & W.A. Hocker. A codicil was witnessed by Calvin Gillis andd C. Gillis Jr. An additional witness was B.W. Helvenston. The judge was Jesse N. Connor.

KIMMERLIN, L.K. - Will was created in Suwannee County, FL. on March 16, 1907. Beneficiaries were his 3 brothers and his 3 sisters (all unnamed). His executor was Winder J. Hillman. Witnesses were Cary H. Hardee, J.W. & H.C. Skeen. Judge was Jesse N. Connor.

ATWELL, John - Will was created in Suwannee County, FL. on May 8, 1875. Beneficiaries were his wife Caroline Atwell. He appointed a good friend, Joseph M. Talbert as executor. Witnesses were C.H. Brinson, J.D. Ivy, and William Bryson. Judge was J.N. Connor.

WOOD, Henry M. - Will was created in Live Oak, Suwannee County, FL. on July 8, 1907. Beneficiaries were his son Harry J., his wife Jessie, and his daughter, Jessie Wood White. He appointed his wife Jessie and his son Harry J. as his executors. Witnesses were Thomas Dowling and J.B. Johnson.

DEXTER, Horace F. - Will was created in Suwannee Couty, FL. on March 11, 1907. Beneficiaries were his 4 younger children (his stock in the Live Oak Bank for their education), to his daughter Lizzie, to his son Kenneth B., Thomas D., George, his wife Lizzie, daughters Ruby and Clair, and a son Worth. He appointed his wife and daughter Ruby as executrixes. Witnesses were W. Bird, B.W. Helvenston, and Franklin L. Rees. Judge was Jesse N. Connor.

STEWART, Sam - Will was created in Suwannee County, FL. on December 3, 1907. His beneficiary and executrix was his daughter Laura Winson, and several unnamed children. Witnesses were Henry Smith and Nathaniel Garrett. Judge was J.N. Connor.

SESSIONS, Ella - Will was created in Live Oak, Suwannee County, FL. on October 6, 1898. Beneficiaries were his uncles...to wit, William Frazer of South Vale, Upper Seiracki, Nova Scotia, and David Fraser of Hopkins, Hennepin County, Minnesota, to cousin James N. Coombs of Apalachicola, Franklin County, FL., and to Henry L. Parker of Live Oak. Mr. Parker was also made the executor of the estate. Witnesses were W.B. Mickler, Mahone Rees and F.L. Rees. Mrs. Sessions died before March 15, 1909. Judge was J.N. Connor

HOYL, Albert A. - Will was created in Suwannee County, FL. on July 30, 1906. Beneficiaries were his wife Eliza, his 2 grandsons Bleman & Albert Williams, his 2 step-children Mary Jane Lane and Tobe Brown. He appointed J.B. Johnson, attorney at law to be his executor. Witnesses were J.B. Lamb and Webster Ross. Judge was J.N. Connor.

ALLPORT, William - Will was created in Suwannee County, FL. on August 10, 1909. Beneficiary was a nephew John Haughton. Witnesses were C.E. Humphreys, Arch Blount, and Alex H. Key. Judge was Jesse N. Connor.

JOHNSON, Henry M. - Will was created in Suwannee County, FL.

on December 2, 1899. Beneficiaries were a daughter, Louisianna M. Johnson, a son, Thomas W. Johnson, to his wife Kitty Phillips Johnson, another daughter, Alice H. Johnson. He named his wife, Kitty Phillips Johnson as his executrix. Witnesses were A. Lee Humphreys, S.C. Humphreys, and Ira J. Carter. Judge was Jesse N. Connor.

TOMPKINS, Annette L. - Will was created in Suwannee County, FL. on June 18, 1910. Beneficiaries were a niece, Lula A. Everett, her sister-in-law, Florida Nelson and Mrs. Nelson daughter, Vanisia Bush. Her executor was a good friend, John B. Smithson. Witnesses were T.J. Mallory, E.H. Pickard, and W.H. McClellan. Judge was Jesse N. Connor.

WILLIAMS, John Henry - Will was created in Suwannee County, FL. on June 25, 1910. His wife had already died. His beneficiaries were Addie Holmes (daughter), Marietta Washington (daughter)...40 acres located at T3,R13E,S22,SW1/4 of NE1/4..., Essie Washington...20 acres located at T3,R13E,S22,N1/2 of NW1/4 of NE1/4..., Bessie Williams ("the little girl whom I have raised from infancy")...20 acres located at T3,R13E,S22,S1/2 of NW1/4 of SE1/4. A statement is made "Marietta Washington's daughter Essie Washington" showing a relationship. He named Sherman Washington and Robert Lee as executors. Witnesses were Ida Platte and L.E. Robinson. He died before February 24, 1911. Judge was Jesse N. Connor.

BLACKMON, Joab - Will was created in Suwannee County, FL. on February 22, 1902. Beneficiaries were his first wife Rebecca, his present wife Mary Elizabeth, and his unnamed children. He appointed his 2nd wife, Mary Elizabeth, to be his sole executrix. Witnesses were J.B. Johnson, S.T. Overstreet, and N.T. Elliott. He died before March 31, 1911. Judge was Jesse N. Connor.

LAMB, W.H. - Will was created in Newburn, Suwannee Cty, FL. in 1913. Beneficiaries were his wife, Ella F. Lamb, and Millie M. Robinson (daughter and wife of John J. Robinson). Witnesses were A.M. Mosely, and H. Brown. Judge was Jesse N. Connor. Later witnesses were sheriff G. Potsdamer and W.W. Hawkins. Mr. Lamb died before August 23, 1913.

LANIER, Porch M. - Will was created in Suwannee County, FL. on December 22, 1916. Beneficiaries were his wife, Eliza Lanier, to receive the following land: 400 acres, T3,R12S,S27,W1/2 of SW1/4 and E1/2 of S28, to sons Barney & Arthur, to daughters Eva Grant, Burtis Brannan, Dora Mills, Mary Lanier, and Rosa Gill. He appointed J.W. Grant as his executor. Witnesses were A.S. York, and J.B. Johnson. Jesse N. Connor was judge. Mr. Lanier died before March 10, 1917.

WOLFE, George - Will was created in Live Oak, Suwannee County, FL. on Feb.24, 1893. His sole beneficiary and executrix was his wife, Mary S. Wolfe. Witnesses were B.B. Blackwell, J.H.T. Bynum, and J.N. Connor. Mr.Wolfe died on May 12, 1911. This was attested to by M.E. Broome and Cary A. Hardee, friends.

Judge was Jesse N. Connor.

DOWLING, Thomas - Will was created in Live Oak, Suwannee County, FL. on June 9, 1911. He speaks of a $15,000 loan he had made to C.H. Tedder and to C.H. Brown in relation to the Gulf Pine Company at Odessa, FL. of which he is president. His beneficiaries were his wife, Laura Dowling, and his children, Fannie Williams, Georgia Butler, Lillie Radford, Waterman, William H., and James H. Dowling. He mentions debts owed to him by his son-in-laws O.O. Williams and George Butler. His executors were his wife and his two sons...William H. and James H. Witnesses were Burr A.L. Bixler and Ira J. Carter, both of Live Oak. Judge was J.N. Connor.

GREEN, Narcissy E. - Will was created in Suwannee County, FL. on July 20, 1910. Beneficiaries were her daughter Haddie V. Banks to whom she willed the following land...T2,R13E,S11&12,E1/2 of NE1/4, & NE1/4 of SE1/4 of Section 11, and W1/2 of SW1/4 of Section 12, to her husband R.R. Green, to her son Dr. O.F. Green, son Benjamin F. Green, daughter Sadie Atwater, daughter Opal Smith, son Worth C. Green, son Gordon R. Green, son Porter Ord? Green. Executor was son-in-law George P. Banks. Witnesses were Blanche Gometo? and L.E. Robinson. Judge was J.N. Connor.

BROWN, David W. - Will was created in Suwanne County, FL on March 18, 1914. His sole beneficiary was his wife Sarah Elizabeth Brown. She was also his executrix. Witnesses were Guy Gillen, A.P. Rivers, and R.T. Boozer. Mr. Brown died before June 1, 1914. Sworn before Notary, Gussie Miller and Columbia County judge W.M. Ives. Suwannee County judge was Jesse N. Connor.

HORNE, Simeon A.J. - Will was created in Live Oak, Suwannee County, FL on March 26, 1913. Beneficiaries were his wife Hattie R. Horne, children: James A., Mrs. Mary Fryer, Mrs. Annie Long, Robert M., Mrs. Nancy McCuller, Mrs. Francis Dees, and Mrs. Effie Ivey. Land left was 80 acres located at T2,R13E,S27,SE1/4 of SW1/4 and T2,R13E,S34,NE1/4 of SW1/4. He appointed his son-in-law, Galien M. Dees of Jennings, Hamilton County, Florida as his executor. Witnesses were J.B. Johnson, J.W. Bryson, and H.E. Carter. Notary was J.L. Lee, judge was J.N. Connor. Mr. Horne died before November 9, 1915.

BROCK, Smithy - Will was created in Wellborn, Suwannee County, FL. on Feb.22, 1908. Beneficiaries were Dr. Galen B. Smithson of Wellborn. She had no children and she did not mention a husband. She also appointed Dr. Smithson to be her executor. Witnesses were C.W. Hemming and F.J. Mallory...both of Wellborn. E.H. Pickard was the Notary.

PINKHAM, James Jackson - Will was created in Suwannee County, FL. on January 5, 1907. Beneficiaries were his (2nd?) wife, Amanda Pinkham (a clause in the will demands a tombstone be put on his 1st wife's grave and his grave). He appointed his son, Samuel Pinkham, as his executor. Witnesses were W.F. Tummand? and W.A. Miller. Notary was G.G. Register.

SEARS, Richard W. - Will was created in Chicago, Illinois on November 18, 1911. Beneficiaries were his wife, Anna L. Sears of Chicago, Illinois. She was also his executrix. Witnesses were Arnold J. Lethan, and E.T. Boland. Clerk of record was Lew A. Hendee and the judge was Perry L. Persons. A codicil was made in Lake County, Illinois stating that Mr. Sears died on or about September 28, 1914 in Lake County, Illinois. Will was recorded in Suwannee County, FL. by judge Jesse N. Connor on June 1, 1915.

CARVER, Raymond M. - Will was created in Suwannee County, FL. on July 5, 1913. Beneficiaries were his wife, Annie M. Carver. Property willed to her is described as, "An undivided one fourth interest in and to lots 1 and 2 in block 14 in the town of Wellborn, Florida. Also an undivided 1/2 interest in and to the south 1/2 of the north 1/2, the north 1/2 of the SE1/4, the SW1/4 of the SE1/4, and the NE1/4 of the SW, all in Section 10, Township 3, and Range 13 east". He appointed his wife as his executrix. Witnesses were J.B. Johnson, W.P. Moore, and T.J. Hackney. Mr. Carver died before December 31, 1915. Judge was J.N. Connor.

HAMLIN, E.D. - Will was created in Suwannee County, FL. on July 26, 1915. Beneficiary was his stepdaughter, Mrs. Mollie Parker. She was also his executrix. Witnesses were J.W. Griffin and Mrs. S.A. Griffin. The judge was J.N. Connor.

BONNELL, Robert O. - Will was created in Suwannee County, FL. on July 5, 1913. Beneficiaries were his wife, Eva A. Bonnell. She was also his executrix. Witnesses were M.E. Broome, J.M. Barclay and E.J. Blume, all of Live Oak. Mr. Bonnell died before August 25, 1915. Judge was J.N. Connor.

BEVAN, Amanda C. - Will was created in Live Oak, Suwannee County, FL. on November 6, 1914. Her sole beneficiary was her niece, Julia Della McLeod. She was also her executrix. Witnesses were F.J. Green and J.B. Johnson. J.N. Connor was the judge.

WEST, Eugene Edgar - Will was created in Jacksonville, Duval County, FL. on June 21, 1916. Beneficiaries were his wife, Lula Frances West, to his daughter Lois Evelyn, to his son Joe Hunter, to his sister Mary J. Lane of Valdosta, Ga., sister Laura F. Peacock of Valdosta, Ga., son-in-law John O. Coffee of Valdosta, Ga., to brother Abraham H. West of Duval County, Fl., to nieces Mamie Sue Dasher and Lizzie Lee Coffee, to the children of his deceased brother John W. West, to the children of my deceased brother William S. West, to my wife's brother Joseph A. Brady of Madison, FL., to my wife's sister Elizabeth E. Wadsworth of Madison, FL., to my wife's sister Marion I. Henderson of Williston, FL., to my wife's sister Catherine V. McClelland of Madison, FL., to my wife's half sister Mary Bridges of Madison, FL., to my wife's nieces (children of William G. Jones), and Miss Jennie Murray. The executor of the estate was the American Trust Company of Jacksonville, FL. He appointed friends Charles Darby and James J. Sullivan to be the appraisers of his properties. Witnesses were Charles H. Wyche, Charles E. Pepperday, and Frank F.

Maxwell, all residing at Jacksonville, FL. Mr. West died on December 3, 1918. H.B. Philips was the Duval County judge. Jesse N. Connor, judge, filed the will in Suwannee County, FL. on December 19, 1918. A special deputy, Calvin Rahn Hankins is mentioned.

PARIS, Moses - Will was created in Suwannee County, FL. on September 7, 1917. Beneficiaries were Isaac Lovett, Rosa Lovett, and Isaac Lovett Jr. The inheritance consisted of 1 house and lot in Gainesville, Alachua County, FL. Witnesses were P.L. Hemming, I.W. Chandler, L.R. Blanton, and E.W. Wordlaw?. According to an affidavit submitted by Isaac Lovett, Mr. Paris died on September 24, 1917. He was Mr. Lovett's step-father, having married his mother many years ago. However there were no children by this marriage. At his death, Mr. Paris was an aged man. Jesse N. Connor was the judge.

DEVALL, S.R. - Will was created in Suwannee County, FL. on December 9, 1908. Beneficiaries were his sister, Mrs. W.F. Benet, sister Mrs. A.M. Kimmons, sister Mrs. H.D. Wilson, sister Mrs. E.W. Gillis, to Weddell and Donald Gillis. He appointed as executors, Mrs. Gillis, Mrs. Kimmons, Mrs. Wilson, Weddell and Donald Gillis. Witnesses were Oscar O. McCollum and J.F. Harrell. Jesse N. Connor was the judge.

PETERS, Sarah Jane - Will was created in Suwannee County, FL. on September 27, 1907. Her sole beneficiary was her niece, Jamie Williams. Witnesses were J.B. Johnson and L.T. McQueen. Jesse N. Connor was the judge.

ROBERTSON, John - Will was created in Suwannee County, FL. on October 9, 1916. Mr. Robertson was a resident of O'Brien, FL. His sole beneficiary and his executrix was his wife Mamie C. Robertson. Witnesses were John L. Wells and L.M. Wilson, both residents of O'Brien, FL. The judge was J.N. Connor. Notary was W.F. Register. Mr. Robertson died before January 10, 1917.

RILEY, Martha - Will was created in Suwannee County, FL. on December 5, 1904. She requested her body to be buried in the Mount Pleasant Church cemetery where her husband and children are buried. Beneficiaries were granddaughters Pearl Ray, Nova Scotia Johns, and Leola Moore, daughter Mrs. Sylvania Clemmons and her children, Viola Summer, Either, Arthur, and Johnnie Riley, Lena Naley, Luther Stansel, Alice Boston and Clarence Parker. She appointed a friend, William H. McClellan "whom I have known from his boyhood days" her executor. Witnesses were N.A. Gaylord, R.J. Long, and L.C. Gaylord. Judge was J.N. Connor. She died on April 25, 1909.

SPERRING, John W. - Will was created in Live Oak, Suwannee County, FL. on November 21, 1913. Beneficiaries were as follows: Eugene Encine (son), born July 6, 1859, Melvin Wallace (son) born November 21, 1860, Emma Elizabeth (dau.) born November 17, 1863, and Eddie Lewis (son) born January 30, 1869, his wife Sarah A. Sperring, children as follows: William Leonard Sperring, Mrs.

Abbie Elizabeth Griffin, Mrs. Ella Dixon, Mrs. Hattie Newman, James Wesley Sperring, Mrs. Annie Helvenston, Mrs. Mattie Fletcher, Grover Cleveland Sperring, Mrs. Cora May Davis, and Frank Sperring. He appointed his wife, Sarah, as his executrix. In the event of her death, his son William Leonard Sperring will be his executor. Witnesses were F.L. and Mahone Rees. Judge J.N. Connor presided. Mr. Sperring died March 16, 1914.

MURRAY, Orissa J. - Will was created in Suwannee County, FL. on November 28, 1913. Beneficiaries were a son, Harry E. Murray of Lowell, Massachusetts, and to grandsons, Harry F., Roy Nelson and Edgar Lambert Murray of Missoula, Montana, and to son Frank E. Murray of Branford, Suwannee County, FL. Frank E. Murray was also appointed executor. Witnesses were William S. Elsbree, Loie A. Wilcox, and Roy B. Swasey. Jesse N. Connor was judge.

COMER, Eldredge - Will was created in Suwannee County, FL. on February 8, 1918. Beneficiaries were his sister, Mrs. M.A. Idlett, sister Mrs. Susan Wilburn, brother John Comer, nephew Eldredge Gray (all of Suwannee County), and Mrs. Frances M. Smith of West Palm Beach, FL. ("a step-daughter by marriage to her mother, now deceased"). He appointed his sister, Mrs. M.A. Idlett, as his executrix. Witnesses were M.E. Broome, Lewis Washington, and William Morant, all of Live Oak, FL. Mr. Comer died before February 13, 1918. Judge was J.N. Connor.

HALL, Harriet - Will was created in Suwannee County, FL. on January 2, 1916. Beneficiaries were her children Mamie, Drew, Lillie, and Bessie Hall. She names the father as Alex Hall (apparently her husband). She named John W. Bryan as executor and in the event of his death, James J. Hall and James Jenkins are to succeed him. The children's inheritance was to be placed in the First National Bank of Live Oak until they reached the age of 21. Witnesses were J.J. Hall, J.W. Jenkins, and J.W. Bryan. Notary was W.F. Register. Judge was J.N. Connor.

BARRETT, Eliza Ellen - Will was created in Leonardsburg, Ohio on May 23, 1914. The will shows she was from Brown, Delaware County, Ohio. Beneficiaries were her husband, G.W. Barrett, her 3 sisters, Mrs. Elizabeth Fleming of Oberton, Ohio, Mrs. Mary Jane Main of Leonardsburg, Ohio, and Mrs. Edith Main of Geneva, Ohio, her niece Mrs. May Right of Aldridge, Missouri, and the heirs of my sister Sarah Sherwood, deceased, to wit: Mrs. Carrie Trapp of Geneva, Ohio, Jennie May and Frank Sherwood of Marysville, Ohio. Her executor was named as her husband, G.W. Barrett. Witnesses were Henry R. Smith, and Celia L. Smith, both residents of Leonardsburg, Ohio. Commissioner of Suwannee County was J.M. Schaffner. The county judge was A.E. Leslie.

WILKINSON, John M. - Will was created in the Borough of Phoenixville, Chester County, Pennsylvania on July 17, 1884. His sole beneficiary and executrix was his wife Ada B. Wilkinson. He was described as a merchant. Witnesses were A.J. Hughes and John H. Harden. E.N. Pennypacker and H.H. Gilkyson verified the signature of witness A.J. Hughes. Granville Prizer was Register of Phoenixville, Pennsylvania. Register of Wills for Chester County was Lewis H. Miller. J.William Butler, President Judge of the 15th Judicial District of Chester County, Pennsylvania also attested to the correctness of the will. Mr. Wilkinson died before August 22, 1918. Suwannee County judge was A.E. Leslie.

LANIER, Porch M. - Will was created in Suwannee Co County, FL. on December 22, 1916. Beneficiaries were his wife, Eliza Lanier, two sons, Barney and Arthur who are to each receive 160 acres as follows: T3,R12E,S27,28, W1/2 of SW1/4 of Sec.27, and E1/2 of Sec.28, to daughter Eva Grant he gave, T3,R12E,S27,W1/2 of SW1/4, to daughter Dora Mills he gave, T3,R12E,S28, N1/2 of NE1/4, to daughter Burtis Brannan he gave, T3,R12E,S28, S1/2 of NE1/4, to daughter Mary Lanier he gave T3,R12E,S28, N1/2 of SE1/4, to daughter Rosa Gill he gave T3,R12E,S28, S1/2 of SE1/4. He appointed J.W. Grant as his executor. Witnesses were A.S. York, and J.B. Johnson. Judge was Jesse N. Connor. Mr. Lanier died before March 10, 1917.

Inventories

Wills are usually looked for because most folks feel they reveal the most information about a family...but we need to remember another record that reveals much more in personal areas.. and that is the "Inventory Book". Early history has a certain degree of interest in that it takes us back to the "good old days"...which quite frankly, weren't always that good. Early records also tell us a lot about how folks lived...but none is so revealing as the "Inventory". This is a record that is taken after someone had died. The following inventories show the kinds of information one might find in "inventories" taken in the 1860's.

INVENTORY BOOK: 1859-1870

CRAWFORD, Mrs. Eliza E. - Suwannee Cty, FL. dtd Jan.27, 1860. William A. Dunn, Thomas H. Lane, W.E.N. Cousins, and E.J. Lutterloh, were the appraisers. Mr. S?. Crawford was her husband. They had 1 sorrel horse, 1 cow, and 6 Negro slaves. (p.17-18). An affidavit dated Jan.16, 1861 re sale of slaves is as follows: Sale was conducted at the Houston Court House door. Highest bidder was given 4 months with 8% interest. Sales were 1)Sooky alias Susan, aged 65 yrs. to A.M. Crawford; 2) Essy, aged 34 yrs. and child named Helo?, 13 yrs. and Tom, infant, to A.M. Crawford; 3) Ross, aged 11 yrs. to John P. Rogers; 4) Bell Isabella, aged 8 yrs. to Amelia L. Crawford; 5) Edward, aged 6 yrs. to A.L. Crawford. L. Crawford was Administrator. (p.32).

BOATRIGHT, Chisley J.D.- Feb.7, 1860. Rachel Boatright, wife?. Witnesses to her X were J.A. Hill and T.D. Dexter. Appraisers were George E. McClellan, Green Johnson, and Fleming Deese. (p.18-19).

TILLIS, T.A.- Apr.14, 1860. 1 note on Henry Herrod, T.A.Tillis, and J.M. Whitfield; 1 note on Aldrich Wiley; 1 note on Joseph Caraway. Appraisers were Green Johnson, J.W. Green, William S. Parker. (p.20).

McCLELLAN, Sidney S.- 1860. Had 17 slaves. Appraisers were Joseph M. Hull, Wm. A. Dunn, and T.D. Dexter. George E. McClellan was administrator. Estate amounted to 14,935 dollars to be equally divided between John Webb McClellan, George E. McClellan, to wife Ellen McClellan, to wife Julia McClellan, and 4 minor heirs. Joshua Caraway was the judge. (p.21-23). A second document dated Dec.27, 1861, shows the name of the following slaves: Frank, Clarissa, Bob, Monimia, Mary Ann, Old Mary Ann, Aara?, Frederick, Robert. A family member, Melinda C. McClellan is said to be "the only heir at present". Appraisers were T.D. Dexter, Sampson Carver, and John J. Taylor. (p.53-54). On Oct.15, 1863 a listing of slaves was shown to be Jane & infant, Mary Ann, Old Mary Ann, Maria & infant, Fred, Robert, Bob, Manimia. Isabella S. McClellan is said to be his wife. Appraisers were John J. Taylor, Robert M. Mosely, and Jesse T. McLeran. (p.119).

RAINEY, Samuel - Dec.1, 1860. Notes on David Silas, Leander Green, Gary M. Daniel, Lewis Ivey, and John Parker. Appraisers were A. Niles, W.H. Watson, L.L. Hardee, and Wm. G. Carver. Sold goods to James Hardee, Howell Meeks, Cornelius Hardee, A. Mills, S.S. Hardee. Wm. G. Parker was sheriff.(p.23 & 28).

McLERAN, W.T. - Nov.3, 1860. His possessions and perishables were sold to the following: S.R. McClellan, M.A. McLeran, R.R. Moore, H.H. Mosely, J.C. McLeran, James Mims, James Hutchenson, A. McCaskill, Jon Evers, V. Carver, T.H. Lane, W.A. Collins, D.M. Blue, N.R. Gailard, J.S. Goodson, J.M. Hull, H.F. Ingerville, H. Hawkins, and B.J. Hackney. Appraisers were M.A. McLeran and J.T. McLeran. (p.24-25). In a later statement J.J. Taylor, J.M. Hull, M.A. McLeran, Dr. Dunn, R.R. Moore, Dr. Hill, J.T. McLeran, W.A. Collins, B.J. Hackney, Mrs. M.A. McLeran, Dr. Hackney, H.D. Rigsbee, J.B. Turner?, Walden Groyner, and J.W. Green are spoken of. This document was dated April 13, 1861 and was signed at Houston. Joshua Caraway was judge of probate. (p.29).

MOORE, Wm. L. - Nov.29, 1860. Thomas D. Dexter, Admin. Appraisers were J.R. Lewis, Wm. Harrell, Harris Hollyman. His wife, Mahilda and their children: Eliza, Thaddeus, and Andrew are mentioned. (p.26).

BLOOME, Wm. - Nov.10, 1861. Appraisers were M.W. Postell, John R. Evers, Thomas S. Evers, and H.M. Bloome. (p.27)

COATS, John .J. - May 29, 1861. Administrators were Mrs. P.H. Coats and Edward .R. Coats. M.W. Mixon, Auctioneer, N.L. Creekmore for making coffin, W.T. Townsend for printing. (p.28)

LEE, Moses - Feb.26, 1861. Sales to N.A. Hull, W. Bryan, G.

Walker, Mrs. Lee, T.W. Fielding, N. Bryan, David Wiley, M.L. Moore, George W. Lyons, L.B.? Fielding, Thomas Graham, Ira McCollum, James W. Rawls, Annie Lee. A widow and 2 unnamed children are mentioned. Appraisers were D.W. Tedder, Thomas Graham, and Albert Peterson. (p.30-32).

DEESE, Fleming - May 4, 1861. Administrator was Mrs. Sarah Deese. 2 male slaves, Augustus and Caesar were part of the property. Notes on Wm.G. Parker & Isaac J. Wiley, D.C. Landers. Appraisers were T.D. Dexter, P.W. Cato, and R.M.D. Peacock. Wife Sarah Deese, and 6 children: George W., Ann Elizabeth, Wm. Bartley, Malinda, Julia V?, and Nathaniel Deese are mentioned. (p.33-34). A second document listing sales of property dated May 25, 1861 shows the following individual buyers: P.W. Cato, Sarah Deese, L. Deese, James Ellis, Z. Deese, George Allison, James A. Hill?, W.E. Johnson, E.B. Lealman. (p.36-37). A third document shows additional purchasers of his property...Joseph U. Wise, Leonard Dees, E.B. Lallemand. (p.50-51).

ROWLAND, Mary A. - July 25, 1861. Executor was N.A. Hull. An unnamed negro man, woman, and two children are mentioned. Appraisers were James A. Newman, Dan? W. Tedder, and Dan J?. Lee. (p.35). Document dated 1863 shows, cash collected from George W. Lyons and Dr. Bynum. Section dated 1861 shows M.L. Moors, Hugh McPherson, W.B. Ross, minors Lewis, Adaline, Leroy, Elijah, and shoes for George. (p.138).

RILEY, Jesse - Nov.23, 1861. Mentioned were "Receipt on M.L. Odom for note on J. Green", and 1 note on Robert B. Chambliss, and 1 account on William Blum, dec'd. Martha Riley was the administrater. Appraisers were N.R. Gaylard, John R. Spier, and John Powell. Also mentions he had 1 wife and 7 children aged 14 down to 1 year. (p.37-38).

GOODBREAD, J.M.B. - Jan.2, 1862. Appraisers were James S. Hall, James C.A. Polk, and John H. Parker. John S. Goodbread was administrator. A Mrs. J.M.B. Goodbread is mentioned. (p.51).

POWELL, John - Jan.3, 1862. Executor was George E. McClellan. Appraisers were T.D. Dexter, John J. Taylor, Thomas S. Evers. Notes were on James E. Ingerville and Gillum Watson. Slaves were Lean, Jesse, Richard, Rachel, Alford, Clarissa, January, Turner, and Rachel. (p.51-53). A second document dated Jan.18, 1862 lists further sales of his property as follows: M.M. Hutchingson, John Powell, Sampson Carver, Joseph Powell, and Martha Powell. (p.54). A second document dated Sept.25, 1863 lists additional possessions. Appraisers were A.D. Wilder, John R. Evers, and Sampson Carver. S.V. Powell was administrator. (p.117). Document dated April 1, 1864, shows Mrs. Martha Powell in charge of "Guardian account" for minors of John Powell's estate. Lists, "balance due James", "Sale James Colt", "Bill of expense Martha, Sidney, Isham's Negroes, and James". (p.133).

MATTAIR, Lewis - Jan. 10, 1862. Slaves were: Isaiah, Peggy,

Henry, Heronena & child, Delorias, Hannah, Joe Shade, Kate, Caroline, Douglas, Charles, Thaddeus, Charlotte, and Jeremiah. Administrators were Louisa and Lewis H. Mattair. Appraisers were T.D. Dexter, George E. McClellan, and Arch Caraway. Witness for Mr. Caraway's mark was G. W. Bell. His family is shown to be, Louisa, Downing, Philothea, Maxey, and William. (p.54-56). An appendage listing purchasers shows, John H. Johnson, Thomas Urquhart, L.H. Mattair, John Harrell, A.J. Byrd, P.W. Cato, Joseph M. Hull, Louisa Mattair, Cyprian Brinson, William Oates, & James Foster. (p.114-115). A second document lists amounts paid to Workman, Mrs. Taylor, Herman & Emetsina, Benton & Graves, T. Brown, Mrs. Barnes, G.S. Wilson, W.B. Fairchild, Bisbee & Canova, Hyman Rothschild, H.H. Bengheine, P. & George R. Road, W.H. Hart, J.H. Bengheine, Leharn E. Brycke, Henry Lathrope & Co., E. Remington & Son, Jefferson? Manufacturing Co., Adams & Zipperer, W.H. Hunt, Cline & Cathy, Denham & Palmer, Mrs. P.H. Coates, J.T. Baisden, ?. B. Spencer, Mahala Caraway, A.W. Knight, D.J. & J.W. Sheffield, Z.U. Paschal, & Mrs. Frink. Administrators were L.H. Mattair & Louisa Mattair. (p.116-117). Notes paid: D.T.Trezvant, J.V. Brown, Mrs. Frink, J.G.W. Gillespie, A.J. Smiley, B.M. Bryan. Dated May 16,1864. (p.132-133).

ZIPPERER, Elizabeth - Aug.16, 1862. Appraisers were John H. Parker, Wesley Philips, and Wiley Meeks. W.J.J. Duncan was the administrator. 5 children were mentioned. (p.57-58).

ZIPPERER, Solomon - Aug.16, 1862. Appraisers were John H. Parker, Wesley Philips, and Wiley Meeks. W.J.J. Duncan was the administrator. (p.58).

BRYAN, Nathaniel - June 16, 1862. 1 negro boy, Amos, is mentioned. 1 due bill against W.H. Edwards, 2 notes against Hardy Daughtry and J.J. Langford, and 1 account against G.W. Lyons. Appraisers were William Lyons, Thomas Graham, and D.W. Tedder. Administrator was Timothy? Bryan. (p.58).

WATSON, W.H. - June 25, 1862. Accounts: J.J. Todd, Amon Barnes, L.H. Mattair, William Barnes, Augustus Moore?, Mrs. Rogers, David McDonald, Jonathan Jarvers (to Columbus Ferry), W.H. Watson (for building courthouse), D.P. Jones, J.P. Harrison, C.F. McCall, D. Green, I.H. Caraway. Appraisers were E.J. Boyet, James Mims, and A.I. Glover. (p.59).

SAUNDERS, Daniel C. - May 1, 1862. Owned 1 Negro boy & 1 Negro girl plus child. Notes against A.J. Lisle?, J.A. Newman, M.L. Moore, accounts against W.F. Bynum, H.R. Hull, Josiah Douglas, W.A. Grant, George N. Durrell, C. Peacock, N.T. Elliott, A. Munson. Appraisers were Daniel W. Tedder, James A. Newman, and David Mills. (p.60).

DEXTER, Thomas D. - Nov.6, 1862. Appraisers were John J. Taylor, Joseph M. Hull, and John Hart. Administrators were George E. McClellan and Mary A. Dexter. The following notes date from 1854. Willett W. Snell, Moore & Smiley, A.J. Smiley, William Frink, John Frink, J.R. Haddock, John H. Thompson, Cyprian Brinson, J?. Linton, A.M. Crawford, William H. Rousseau, D.P. Snell, Adam Caraway, Isaac N. Moat, G. Hall, Edward F. Wrede (or Reed?), John Skeen, Joseph M. Hull, Joab Blackman, C.W.P. Howell, R.S. Foster, Angus McAulay, Arch Caraway, R. Hurt, Fleming Dees, J.H. Parker, Lewis H. Lawson, Benjamin C. Jackson, W. Lee, A.S. Cutts, William S. Moore, James Moore, Banks & McCloud, U.A. Shelton, Thomas Urquhart, William P? Allison, James C.A. Polk, Judge R. Hodges, Smith & Ives, Thomas Amerson, Richard Tillis, William Barnes, W.L. Yarborough, B.F. Owens, J.B. Carter, Silas L. Lawson, John Caraway, J.S. Jordan, C.T. Burroughs, Arthur Carraway, William Hines, Joseph Dial, William Brinson, E.J. Boyt, Craven Lassiter, William Harrell, L.B. McNeill, Eliza Oliff, J.R. Lewis. Book accounts: Mrs. R.S. Scott, Mrs. Pipkins, J. Haddock, Naomi? Blackman, E. Hines, J.B. Quince, Hiram Roberts, Mrs. Mims, B.R. Walker, Mrs. Demery, James Foster, Amon Barnes, L.A. Moree?, A.J. Smiley, J.E. Fletcher, Hateley?, Allen McLean & Bulkley, James Owens, Valentine Mims, J.N. Green, Mrs. Mary Trezvant, M.E. Brock, J.S. Ponchier, James Mims, W.W. Oates, James S. Hackney, Richard Hurt, W.W. Snell, James Moore, Mrs. P.H. Coates, Miss Maria Bass, Joab Blackman, F?. M. Bryde, Harris Brock, John H. Johnson, Thomas Urquhart, W. Harrell, W. I?. Huggins, James Newsome, George E. McClellan, Angus McLoud, J.P. Owens, John J. Harrell, John W. Ivey, John Caraway, E.B. Lealman, Richard Tillis, Daniel Snell, A.L. Wilder, William Collins, Rev. J.J. Taylor, McAuley, Mrs. Jane Gerry, D. McQueen Blue, Howell Meeks, Wm. L. Moore, James Cheshire, Benjamin Holland, Estate Dr. Cousins, Sarah Dees, Dr. N.P. Marion, Mrs. Blackman, T. McLoud, P.W. Cato, Mrs. Eliza Wood, C. ?. Carruth, Wm. A. Gardner, F?. P. Brannan, Boston & Villalonga, Thomas Houghens, John Hart, J.A. Warrock, Dr. Hicks, Carter, Daniel Keith, King (Negro) McClellan, Tom (Negro) McClellan. Slaves were: Cally (50 yrs) and his wife Agnes (25 yrs), Joe & his wife Lizzie & son Primics?, Maryland & Jenny & dau. Emily, Wilson (a boy), Claude (a boy), Rick & Kizza (old woman), Bill & wife Flora, Elijah (a boy), Rosanna (a girl), & Thomas (infant), Stephen & Susan (wife) & Hicks (6 mon), Sandy & Pheby (wife) & Alexander (son), Sarah, Margaret, Isaac, Edward, and Dianna, Addison & Margaret (wife) & Gintrilla, Allene, & David, George & Julia (wife) & Jerome and Stephen, Granville & Delphi (wife) & Elizabeth (infant), Bryant (50 yrs) & Eve (wife) & Sarah Ann, Moses & Anna, Sevenia & child Eliza, Richard (28 yrs), Solomon (25 yrs), and Needham (25 yrs). His wife was Mary A. and his children were, Jacob S., Horace F., Florence, George E., and Rebecca S. Dexter. Also listed is his mother Abby Dexter. The following listing consists of purchasers of his property.... Dr. Cato, Mrs. John Frink, Samuel McNeil, J.M. Hull, G.E. McClellan, Andrew Mills, John Hart, James Hendrix, Robert Lang, Green Johnson, Dr. Dickson, F.S. Wesson, Lewis Mattair, Judge Carruth, T.J. Williams, J.C.A. Polk, Robert Thomas, Sherrod Bird, Daniel Keith, A. McLeod, G.W. Allen, C.H. Treadwell, John Allison, Mrs. Jacob Goodbread, J.B. Brown, N.M. Creekmore, Mrs. Jane Thompson, Benjamin King, Jasper Evers, C.Y. Savage, T.P. Branning, David Clemons, A.B. Brown, John Johnson, C. Brinson, I?. B. Cole, Wiley Lee, Thomas Stewart, Matthew Mickler, L.T. Hodges, J.B. Ellis, Daniel Mims, David Clements, Dr. Collier, Judge Hines, J.O.A.

Gerry, E.B. Lealman, Joseph Thomas, Rev. J. Sealy, Rebecca Blackman, Henry M. Bloom, Simeon Poncheir, Wm. A. Gardner, N.A. Hull, Thomas Urguhart, J.L. Hodges, C. Dean, Silas Lawson, J.D. Godbold, B.E. Grantham, Meredith Brock, F.S. Hastings, Wilson Carver, Thomas Pleasant?, Richard Tillis, I.? M. Curl, D. McQueen Blue, Vincent Carver, Judge Dyall, Wm. H. Rosseau, Harris Hollomon, Sampson Carver, R.M.D. Peacock, C.H. Steadwell, Gibbs, Adam Caraway, James Lewis, Major? Delegal, T.P. Brannen. (p.61-94).
A document of "annual settlement" dated Jan.17, 1863 by Commissioners George E. McClellan, Angus McAuley, R.M.D. Peacock, Henry T. Ingerville, and Joseph Ponchier listed J.W. Green, Dr. Davis, Joshua Carraway, A.H. Meeks, Henry Woods, J.A. Johnson, B.A. Tedder, John Hart. (p.96-97). Another document dated April 13, 1863, was an accounting by Dr. George E. McClellan & Mary A. Dexter. Paid Mr. Gardner & Col. Hart (for cotton), T.P. Brannan, Adam Caraway, Mrs. Brock, Dr. Cato, W.W. Snell, and George E. McClellan. (p.105). A document dated 1863 shows the following, Mary P. Trezvant, William Harrell, Dr. James S. Hackney, Dr. O?. P. Luther, Dr. Hicks, B.J. Hackney, George D. Miller, J.A. Warrick, Green Johnson, Howell Meeks, T.P. Brannen. (p.131-132).

INGERVILLE, James E. - Jan.10, 1863. Administrator was Henry J. Ingerville. Appraisers were John J. Taylor, George W. Allen, and James P. Godbold. Sales of property to the following; Henry J. Ingerville, S.R. Sessions, D. Mickler, Peter Mickler, Mr. Harris, J.D. Godbold, F?. W. Allen, T.R. Tedder, Mr. Amerson, A. McAulay. (p.95). Document dated May 17, 1864 shows, "Sale of boy Toney in Savannah", S.R. Sessions, W. Bryant, L. Mattair, Isaac Wiley, J. Ponchier, S.B. Mickler, D. Mickler, D.M. Mickler, M. Mickler, E.M. Mickler, R.J. Mickler, P.T. Mickler, L.R. Mickler, J.T. McLeran, H.? D. Rigsbee, Dr. Hutchingson, Dr. Hicks, J. Caraway, J.O.A. Gerry, N.A. Hull. (p.133-134).

McLERAN, W.T. - 1861-1863 (Various dates). J.T. & M.A. McLeran, Administrators. Others mentioned were P.J. Caraway and C.L. Carruth...the latter being the judge of probate. (.97)

SPEIR, John R. - Jan.26, 1863. Executor was M.F. Speir. Appraisers were J.T. McLeran, Hyder D. Riggsby, and Joseph Powell. (p.98).

HARDEE, Thomas E. - 1863?. Notes by David Jowers, Robert Barrow, E.J. Boyet, James Holland, John Dinor?, Charles Hardee, Silas Overstreet, J.F. McCall, J.A.M. Brown, John S. Parker, Alexander Bell, Barrow & Rouse, J.C.A. Polk, and the following slaves: Virginia & her child; William & Lindy, & their 2 children. Administrator was W.B. Hardee. Appraisers were Wiley Meeks, B.R. Williams, and J.C.A. Polk. (p.99).

WATSON, Lucy - May 10, 1862. 1 Negro girl Julia (aged 15 yrs), and 1 Negro boy Henry (aged 13 yrs). Appraisers were John A. Irvine, Charles Dean, and Zacheus Sheppard. (The following appears to belong to Lucy Watson's inventory although dated Jan.1, 1863. It is an account of sales under administrator Julia A. Goodbread on behalf of the Clark family (minors) under the guardianship of Noble A. Hull. It is as follows: One negro woman slave belonging to Adaline Clark, minor; One sorrel filly belonging to Levy Clark, minor; and one sorrel filly belonging to Elijah Clark, minor. (p.100).

HACKNEY, B. J. - Feb.16, 1863. Notes dating from 1858 on T.C.Griffin, J.R. Speir, Simeon Sheffield, John Thompson, James P. Gibbs, Henry Gibbs, W.A. Brinson, James H. Caraway, C.T. Boroughs, John T. Coates, Isaac H. Mote, W.W. Thompson, Wiley Meeks, Thomas W. Brinson, John Watson, J.H. Keith, John Loyd, J.R. Smith, Howell Meeks, T.L. Overstreet, C.W. Howell, Archibald Caraway, James S. Hackney, J.B. Roundtree, John A. Hunter, A. Tedder, Joab Blackman, J.B. Ellis, Henry E. Harrod, J.V. Chewing, Theopilus Tompkins, A.C. Rawles?, S.E. Rawles, J.T. McLeran, James A. Griffin, F. McLeod, N.A. Murdock, S. E. Baisden, D. McQueen Blue. Accounts: Mrs. Margaret Pipkin, James Owens, L.K. Mickler, Fielding Stephens, ? Mathis, Isreal U?. Stewart, P.Roebuck, Capt. William Frink, William Eady, S.Harris, H.J. Stewart, Theopilus Caraway, Sheffield & Bro., A. Perviance, J.S. Davis, W. Demfro?, W.J. Meeks, John Hately, James C. Hately, James Bailey, Dan Matthis, Lewis P. Dunn, Wiley Meeks, A.B. Funderburk, Nathaniel Hall, Benjamin Boatright. Slaves: 1 woman named Lucy & child Jenny, 1 girl named Margaret. Administrator was Eliza J. Hackney (wife), and appraisers were John J. Taylor, J.T. McLeran, and George E. McClellan. (p.100-102). An additional document dated April 14, 1863 was an accounting by Mrs. E. J. Hackney (p.108). Document concerning vouchers dated May 13, 1864. Administrator was E.J. Hackney. (p.132).

FORD, Elya J. - March 14, 1863. Notes on N.A. Alford, James English, Benjamin Williams, Alefair Chastain. The deceased had 3 unnamed children. Luke U. Jenkins was administrator. Appraisers were W.C. Langston, S.L. Sparkman, and James A. Newman. Purchasers of property were, S.L.Sparkman, Moses Simmons, James A. Newman, C.E.W. Collins, Elias Osteen, Winfield Jenkins, J. Trubuck, Sampson Gunter, Benjamin Williams, John Goodman, William C. Langston, Jesse Clements, Luke Jenkins, James Chastain, Hugh McPherson, and Alfred Moore. W.C. Langston & S.L. Sparkman are designated as "Clk" (clerks). (p.102-104).

INGERVILLE, J.E. & WATSON, Gillum - Dr. George E. McClellan, Executor, collected the following for J.E. Ingerville & Gillam Watson - from Niblack & Young, John Powell. He paid Drs. Paschal, Hill, Hutchingson, and Davis, and J.T. McLeran for services. Took place at Little River, FL. on April 1, 1863. C.L. Carruth was Judge of Probate. (p.104).

WILEY, Aldridge - April 1, 1863. List of property as shown by Administrator Elza B. Lealman, appraisers were Albert Peterson, James A. Newman, and Daniel Hall. Property to Susan A. Wiley, William Williams, and R.M.D. Peacock. (p.105-106).

KEITH, Daniel - June 2, 1863. Slaves are shown as Moses (age 55), Mira (age 60), Maria (age 45), Charles (age 21), Sophia (age 35), Mary (age 40), Dolly (age 21), Charlotte (age 12), Michael? (age 14), Alexander (age 10), Maria Jane (age 8), Francis (age 6), Lewis (age 4), Eloey? (age 7), Hannah (age 6), Fanny (age 3), Farabey (age 1), Philip (age 8), Sam (age 6). Administrators were James R. Lewis and Lydia W. Keith. Appraisers were W.H. Rosseau, A.J. Byrd, and William J. Bevan. (p.106-107). On June 20, 1863 two additional slaves were included: John (age 46) and Ben (age 55). Same appraisers minus William J. Bevan. (p.120)

PONCHIER, John S. - 1863. Notes on T.P. Brannan, Lewis Berry, James A. Hill, Absolam W. Smith, James Moore, Simeon B. Driggors, John W. Ivey, James M. Clarely, M. Ponchier, William Bevins, Amon Barnes, John M. Smith, Joseph B. Keen, J.C. Callwell, Paul Hatch?, Andrew McClellan, P.W. Cato, Dennis M. Drigors, J.W. Clemons, John Ponchier, J.A. Hill, Isaac Hatch, H. Keith, Isaac W. ?, Joel Adams, William Bivens, James, Oglesby, John L. Ponchier, A.J. Smiley, J.M. Byrd. E.B. Lealman, Administrator, appraisers, Philip W. Cato, Angus McAulay, J.A. Harris. His wife was Martha A.E. Ponchier, and her 10 month old child named John Simeon Ponchier. (p.108-109). In October 1862 & January 1863 a separate listing of purchasers was given. They were J.J. Wiley, John Glisson, E.B. Lealman, John Edwards, T.P. Brannen, Martha A.E. Ponchier, J.C. Buff, J.J. Cherry, L. Snodgrass, and Adam Caraway.

DEES, Fleming - June 23, 1860. Sarah Dees, Administrator. Notes on J.D. Tillis, J.W. Allen, Green Johnson, J.A. Harris, J.W. Green, A.L. Johnson, Joshua Caraway, Dr. P.W. Cato, James M. Hull, William M. Truitt, Malcolm Hurst, J.R. Hodges, E.B. Lealman, Leonard Dees, Mrs. John Frink, J.B. Wood, J.B. Ellis, S.R. Sessions, Col. Hart, J.B. Spencer, H.R. Hull, Dr. W.M. Boyd, Mrs. V. Johnson, W.H. Foster. (p.110).

EVERS, Jasper - 1863? Thomas S. Evers, Administrator. Notes on W.H. Ivey, James E. Ingerville, J.P. Johnson, Wm.L. Evers, Francis M. Ingram, R. Hurt, John Caraway, J.H. Tedder, W.L. Powell. Sales to T. Stewart, J. Hull, Mrs. Sarah. M. Evers, J.T. McLeran, R.W. Peacock, Ben Bryan, Wm. Gardner, J.C. Bugg, A. Caraway, Mrs. Dowless, Brannen, Mrs. Lane, R. McKenzie, Gillam Walston, J. Williams, J.B. Adams, G.W. Allen, A. Caraway, John Johnson, James Latimer, James Hendrix, L. Bryan, W. Oates, Dr. McMillen. Appraisers were Randal McKenzie, G.W. Allen, and L.K. Mickler. (p.110-112). Document dated 1864 shows, James O. Gerry, W.L.F. Evers, J.H. Tedder, F.W. Ingram, William A. Powell, J. Caraway, James E. Ingerville, S.R. Sessions, William Hunt, L.K. Mickler, Joseph F. Rogers, A.J. Davis, Benjamin Bryan, James Jamison. (p.135-136).

LANG, Robert - 1862? Notes on Julia A.H. Carter, M. Whit Smith, Dr. M.M. Carter, S. Atkinson?, James M. Baker. Appraisers were John J. Taylor, Robert Thomas, Robert M.D. Peacock. W. Fricks?, W. Crawford. Slaves were Jim, Jim Crow, Patience, Hortense, Augustus, August, America & child Grover, Mariah Jane, Jane, Billy Wilson, Sealy, Victor Immanuel, John, Big Peter, Mariah Sen? & child Preston, Callie, Henrietta, Thomas, George, Henry, Florida, Alabama, Joe, Joe Wright, Theresa, Malinda,

Liney, Little Peter, Martha, Abraham, Hannah, and Garibaldi. (p.112-113). Document dated May 31, 1864 shows Margaret Lang & W. A?. Hicks as Administrators. Others mentioned were Mrs. McNeill, Col. Hull, Mrs, Howell (for tuition of Lillian), McLeran (for board), Lealman, Mrs. Wood, Dr. Roberts (for Jim's shoes), Miss Stewart, Mrs. Lane (for Susan's dress), it's stated that Ann, Adeline, Susan, and Lillian were paid in gold, Mrs. Dexter, Mr. Hurt, Mr. Stewart, Mr. Allen, Lillians expenses to Gainesville. (p. 137-138).

COUSINS, William E.M. - May 2, 1861. Lists Negro slave boys: William, Henry, & Moses; Negro slave women: Amy & 2 children Frank & infant Ellen, Julia & child Milly, and Judy. He is addressed as "Dr.". Administrator was John H.J. Dunston. Appraisers were S. Crawford, T.H. Lane, and R.M.D. Peacock. Notes & Accounts for M.A. Murdock, Wm.A. Dunns (note dtd Nov.1860), Hiblack & Young (note dtd Dec.1860), T.A. Tillis, E.J. Lutterloh, Joseph McClellan, Jesse Curl, Palmer, Amos Thompson, Daniel Mickler, Thomas H. Lane (note dtd Aug.1860), Andrew McClellan (note dtd Jan.1858), T.A. Tillis (note dtd Jan.1858), James A. McQueen (note dtd Jan.1858), R.H. Wrede (note dtd Jan.1852), Samuel Wadsworth (note dtd Jan.1856), record of John Hadeley, attorney at law, for various notes, M. Whit Smith, A.J. Smith, Joseph McDaniels, David? Gurganus (note dtd Oct.1860), Rev. J.J. Taylor, Rev. K. Chambliss, A. McAuley (note dtd May 1859), L.K. Mickler (note dtd Jan.1858), Andrew Caraway, Rev. Mr. Caldwell, S. Crawford, A.M. Crawford, Richard Hurt, Wishard, T.H. Lane, C. Boatright, Brooks, Banks & McLeod's note on V.T. Hart, Mary M. Murdock, Samuel McClellan, H. (or K.) Graham, R.G. Washington, Jesse Boatright, Riley Wright, Henry T. & Jame E. Ingerville, J.W. Wilkins, Lovit Smith, Moses Lee, S.A. Keller. Joshua Caraway was the administrator...but had died. New administrator was John H.J. Dunston. (p.117-119). Another document dated Nov.7, 1863 lists the sales of his property as follows, Dr. P.W. Cato, Dr. J.R. Dickson, Dr. W.M. Hicks, John N.J. Dunston, George E. McClellan, A.J. Gresham, Dr. Paschal, A.J. Bryan, Andrew McClellan, Dr. Roberts, N.A. Hull, S.R. Sessions, D.W. Tedder, Mrs. Curl, Capt. Newman, James Hadduck, John Davis, Wilson Carver, J. Stone?, Mr. Snodgrass, Mr. L.H. Creekmore, C.Y. Savage, A.J. Byrd, J.W. Cannon, H.T. Elliott, T.J. Stewart, James Mims, A.D. Wilder, M.W. Mixon, Angus McAulay, G.W. Dupree, Rev. J.J. Taylor, D. Mickler (note), Dr. Dunn (note), Mrs. Murdock, J.Caraway. George is listed as an "agent" for the inventory. One other is David Lang (for surveying). (p.121-125).

IVEY, William H. - 1862? Ann W. Ivey, Administrator. Appraisers were John W. Rice, Jasper H. Ivey, and A.J. Glover. List of property included the following slaves, Luke (68), Silva (40), Alex (30), Isham (24), Tempe (27), Daniel (19), Sally (18), Dolly (15), Sue (10), Aurelia (7), George (6), Amanda (4), Ellen (1), Andrew (1), Alonzo (4 mon.). (p.120). Document dated May 18, 1864 shows, Z. Sheppard, William Telford, A.J. Glover, S.T. Overstreet, John W. Rice, W.L. Irvine, C.L. Carruth, L.M. Moseley, Dr. Peacock, Henrietta Glover, Mitchell Hunter, James Davenport. (p.134-135).

BURROUGHS, Cornelius T. - Oct.10, 1863. Appraisers were Cyprian Brinson, Archibald Caraway, and John Lloyd. Cordelia A. Boroughs, his wife, was administrator. Notes are as follows, S.S. Hardee, C.W.P. Howell, John Lloyd, Benjamin Tompkins, D. Mattair, W.A. Brinson, A.S. Smith, John Armisted, Charlton Brinson, C.W. Howell, William Hines, James A. Hill, John C. Hateley, H. Brock, G.H. Brock, H.B. Blount, J.A. Keith, Simeon Ponchier, H.H. Henry, J.H. Bozeman, E. West, Ann D. Johnson, D. Higdon, B.G. Davenport, P.G. Coates, W.B. Davenport, A. McLeod, Urban Hayne, Dr. Allison, Wiley, W. Allison, B.C. Jackson, Thomas G. Footman, Rev. R. Wilson, J.J. Smith, William Caraway, Israel Stewart, Joseph Day, H.J. Stewart, Mr. Turner, Dr. Thompson. Purchases were, A.J. Byrd, John Lloyd, A. Moseley, Mrs. Jones, Adam Caraway, William Frink, L.M. Moseley, Mrs. McClellan, Henry Walker, C.A. Boroughs, Joe Tuters. (p.126-128).

CLARK, Levy - Dec.23, 1863. 1 16 year old slave named Arch, 1 negro slave named Sarah & child. N.A. Hull was administrator. Appraisers were James A. Newman, Green Johnson, Joseph M. Hull. (128).

PARKER, W.G. - Dec.19, 1863. Notes on Henry Grigs, Henry Walker, John Skeen, Thomas Hardee, E.M. Graham, J.R. Wimberly, William Lyon, H.R. Hull, Dan Tedder, William F. Bynum, J.A. Hull, A.J. Lisle, J.B. Miller, R.R. Elliott, B.F. Harrison, Leander Green, H.F. Simmons, T.R. Sanders, James A. Newman, H.P. Jones, George W. Carter, D.R. Townsend. E.B. Lealman, Administrator. Appraisers were W.L. Irvine, Andrew Caraway, and C. Peacock. Sales were, W.L. Irvine, W.M. Hicks, J.A. Irvine, T.P. Brannen, N.A. Hull, T.H. Lane and E.R. Lealman. 2 negro slaves were mentioned as follows, Clarrisa & child, and Jordan. (p.128-129).

DELEGAL, Henry H. - May 4, 1864. Thomas Urguhart, Justice of the Peace, E.W. Delegal, Executor, and John Bailey, Archibald Caraway, Thomas Urguhart, Apppraisers. Slaves: Titus (36 yrs), Oseola (29), Sam (23), Nero (19), Buck (45), Ned (23), Fanny (21), Adam (16). (p.130)

EVANS, Rees - May 17, 1864. Shows George E. McClellan as in charge of guardian account for heirs of Rees Evans. Document executed at Little River, Fl. (p.133).

CLARK, Lewis - 1861. N.A. Hull, guardian of minor, Adaline Clark, G.W. Lyons, Levy & Lewis for instruction. "hire of Syndia". Document dated May 31, 1864 shows, "Tuition to Mosingale", John Goff, Warrick, M.L. Moore, Col. Hart, Dr. A.J. Davis, Mrs. Hull, Mr. Bugg, Mrs. M.O. Bugg. Document for 1861-62 shows N.A. Hull, guardian of minor Elijah Clark, "hire of Elizabeth", Masingale, John Goff, Mr. Warrack, M.B. Ross, R.M.D. Peacock, Andrew McClellan, J.C. Bugg, E.R. Powers, George W. Lyons. Document dated May 31, 1864 shows N.A. Hull, guardian of minor Levy Clark. Shows "hire of Sarah", and "hire of Arch, 1861-1862". Names same as above except, Silvey Hernden, and Kitty Newman...attention to

Sarah, "for cloth for Sarah & child". (p.139-140).

MOORE, William J., dec'd had an inventory taken which revealed the following information. His wife's name was Mahilda (or Matilda), and he had three children named Eliza, Thaddeus, and Andrew. His total estate consisted of 50 bushels of corn valued at $62.00, 15 head of hogs with 1 spinning wheel at $40.50, 1 bed and clothing at $5.00, 6 hide bottom chairs and 3 pine tables at $6.00, 1 lot of kitchen furniture at $8.00, and 1 pine bedstead at $3.00....total value $124.50. This brief inventory was dated 1860.

RILEY, Jesse dated November 23, 1861 not only reveals the nature and value of his personal possessions... but quite importantly reveals individuals he had business relations with...for example, "Received on M.L. ODOM for note on J. GREEN, $43.50", "1 note on Robert B. CHAMBLISS for $466.25", and "1 account on William BLUM, deceased for $8.15". It also lists the appraisers by name...N.R. GAYLARD, John R. SPIER, and John POWELL, along with his wife who was the executrix, namely, Martha RILEY. This is quite a bit of information.

WOOD, J.B. . On an inventory dated November 24, 1861 made in Houston, Florida, several pages are dedicated to people who he owed money to and people that owed him money..163 in all. It may prove to be a "census" of every family in the area for 1859-1861. I am going to list the names found in the accounts of J.B. Wood, a storekeeper. These should prove invaluable in establishing the identity of some of our early settlers. On November 24, 1861, shortly after Mr. J.B. Wood died, George E. McClellan, Green Johnson, and Robert M.D. Peacock made an appraisal of Mr. Wood's property. Notes on the following adults were listed as follows: Daniel McQueen BLUE, Thomas H. LANE, J.M. NELSON, T.M. MICKLER, Craven LASSITOR, Alvin BRANNEN, Angus McAULAY, Mary A. HARDEE, A.J.T. WRIGHT, W.G. PARKER, N.A. HULL, George W. HARRIS, Job MANNING, Howell Sharp HAWKINS, C. PEACOCK, T. HOUGHINGTON, Zachariah DEES, H.R. HULL, George LANGFORD, Dr. P.W. CATO, C. BRINSON, James MIMS Sr., Sarah DEES, J.E. FLETCHER, J.E. INGERVILLE, Jack ROBERTS, W.N. FOSTER, James McNEILL, Berry McCALL, W.H. WATSON, John McINNIS, E.G. HEWITT, and G.H. BROCK. Orders and due bills were against, James F. HENDRICKS, James A. HILL, H. HOLLYMAN, H.M. BLOOM, Jasper B. EVERS, Daniel KEITH, and A.H. MEEKS. Accounts were against, (the year in brackets shows when the bill was made), J.M. BAKER, Garrett VINZANT, and S. SCARBOROUGH (all 1859); Craven LASSITOR, J.W. GREENE, T.J. STEWART, A.S. JOHNSON, John BAILEY, John H. JOHNSON, W.A. DYALL, J.R. SPIER, T. OVERSTREET, Downing MATTAIR, B.R. WALKER, J.H. CARAWAY and O.W. PARKER (all 1860). The following alphabetized accounts were all for 1861. William, John, and George W. ALLISON, Joab, Cullin, and Arthur BLACKMAN, Mrs. N. BLACKBURN, Daniel McQueen BLUE, W.S.J. BLOUNT, John BAILEY, Terrell P. BRANNEN, Andrew Jackson and Sherwood BIRD (or BYRD), Harris, G.H. and M.E. BROCK, Cyprian, B.F., and A. BRINSON, Amon BARNES, J.H. BOZEMAN, J.C. BUGG, George W. and W.J. BEVAN, Mrs. C. BRYANT, Archibald, Adam, Joshua, and John CARAWAY, S. CRAWFORD, R.W. CAIN, Mrs. P.H. and P.G.

COATES, W.A. and William COLLINS, P.W., Homer, and Lassiter CATO, J.M. COKER, W.E.M. COUSINS, Jesse CURL Jr., W.L. and C.L. CARRUTH, George W. DUPREE, Joseph DYALL, Fleming, Mrs, Sarah, Zachariah, Leonard, and Nathaniel M. DEES, Thomas D. DEXTER, J.A. ELLIS, W.N. and J.M. FOSTER, John FIELDS, J.R. FRANCIS, Henry GIBBS, J.W. GREENE, N.R. GAYLARD (or GAYLORD), James A. and John GOFF, John W. GUFFEY, H.H. HERRING, Joseph M., H.R., and N.A. HULL, Henry HARWOOD, James A. and Mrs. Sarah HILL, James A. HARRIS, Howell Sharp HAWKINS, C.W.P. HOWELL, Mrs. M.A. and James HARDEE, Cornelius HOLLYMAN, T.T. HURST, John A. HUNTER, John HART, H.T. and James E. INGERVILLE, W.L. IRVINE, A.L., John H., Green, W.M.T., and H?. JOHNSON, James H. and Daniel KEITH, A.W. KNIGHT, John LOYD, Thomas H. LANE, George LANGFORD, James R. LEWIS, Augustus MOREE (or MORSE), James P. MORGAN, Andrew MILLS, Louis and Downing MATTAIR, James Sr., and Valentine MIMS, A.H. MEEKS, George E. McCLELLAN, Amos and Thomas McCASKILL, Berry McCALL, L.B. McNEILL, Angus McAULAY, Miss Ann NEWMAN, W.J., Y.P., Wesley OATES, Mrs. D. ODUM, John C. OVERSTREET, J.P. OWENS, Mrs. E. OLLIFF, Dr. C. PEACOCK, Joseph PONCHIER, J.C.A. POLK, Miss Martha PIPKIN, Owen W. PARKER, W.G. PARKER, Henry L. PARKER, W.H. REDDING, Berry ROBERTS, William H. ROSSEAU, T.J. STEWART, John SKEEN, J.R. SPEIR, D.P. SNELL, W.W. SNELL, D.C. SANDERS, Richard TILLIS, Benjamin TOMPKINS, B.A. TEDDER, J.F. UNION, H.N. WALKER, W.H. WATSON, W.C. WATSON, Another document dated February 1, 1862 lists Amon BARNES, Adam CARAWAY, Dr. Philip CATO, Jesse CURL Jr., Nathaniel M. DEES, James A. FOSTER, Mrs. Sarah DEESE, J.W. GREENE (blacksmith), Howell HAWKINS, John HART, John H. and Green JOHNSON, Dr. C. LASSITOR, Lafayette SNODGRASS, Thomas DEXTER, James HENDRIX, W.J. BEVAN, and Coatsworth L. CARRUTH (Judge of Probate). It also lists his 6 children, not by name, but by age (18, 15, 12, 8, 7, and 2). That can be useful in verifying ages. Another document dated January 12, 1863 lists Mrs. Eliza WOOD, George E. McCLELLAN, Mary A. & Thomas D. DEXTER.

LANE, Thomas H., dec'd, over and above the regular household/farm equipment, there was listed another kind of property...slaves. He had no less than 25 slaves valued from a high of $4,000 each to a low of $500. All in all, his slaves were worth over $50,000 dollars.

PROBATE RECORDS: 1877-1884

The records in this book deal with a number of legal transactions including WILLS, HOMESTEAD, GUARDIANSHIPS, APPRENTICES, SALES of PERSONAL PROPERTY, DOWRIES, REAL ESTATE SALES, MINER HEIRS, & SETTLEMENTS. This is the first book. It has over 400 pages. In the next section, we will include the names in Book 2 (1884-189?). Some of the accounts have been "abstracted" and will be included with the name. Where "db" is found in parenthesis after the name, it means they "died before" the date of the entry.

These books are too extensive to share, but I will list the index of those who are listed in the book. For additional information on any of these names, write to the Suwannee County Genealogical Society, % Live Oak Historical Society, 208 North Ohio Avenue, Live Oak, Fl. 32060. The following names are listed in alphabetical order.

Henry ATWELL, William ALLISON, R.F. ALLISON, W.P. ALLISON, George W. ALLEN, Edmond & E. James BRANNEN, T.E. BRANNEN, Sherrod BIRD, G.S. BRADLEY, Lafayette BALEY, Kitty BLACKMAN, George BROOKINS, R.C. BERRITT, John BALEY, Francis M. BAREFIELD, M.J. BULLARD, William BRYSON Sr, W.H. BRINSON, Washington BROOKS, L.M. BALLENTINE, L.N. CREEKMORE, Archibald CARAWAY, H.W. CARVER, J.J. COLLINS, William CASON, N. CONNER, P.J. COATS, T.J. CROWSON, Walter R. CSORAN?, R.L. COLSON, G.B. CASONS, V. CONNER, W.A. DEMPSEY, S.A.? DEAS, John T. DENT, J.?P. DELEGAL, Mary S. DELEGAL, Anbie DEXTER, D.H. ELLIOTT, Ruth FIELDING, W.P. GAMBLE, George T. GAMBLE, Carie E. GAMBLE, Indinna GAMBLE, W.H. GOODBREAD, P.A. GREEN, W.H. GAMBLE, M.F. GAMBLE, R.B. GOSHONO, Jehu GOFF, E.T. HENDERSON, J.F. HUNT, Homestell? HAGENS, W.T. HALL, J.M. HALL, J.C. HOLLAND, Richard HURST Sr. Sallie L. HALLMAN, Annie E. HALL, William HAWKINS, R.N.? HERNDON, H. INGERVILLE, W.L. IRVINE, Martha A. IRVINE, Lura V. IRVINE, Julia H. IVEY, Robert JOHNSON, William JORDAN, Chancy JACOBS, James V. JOHNSON, John F. KINSEY, N.A. LONG, Robert LANG, L.S.? MOSLEY, Thomas MADDEN, J.O. McCORMICK, M. MIKLER, John MORE, M.C. McCARDLE, L.B. MIKLER, G.M. MARSHALL, P.J. MESSER, Alex McDONALD, Isam MURPHY, Charlie L. MILLS, H.K. MILLS, J.D. McCORMICK, Thomas MEEKS, S.S. MOODY, Temperance MICKLER, George F. NUTTER, Alfred OLIVER, J.C. OVERSTREET, W.F. O'NEAL, John POWELL, M.M. POWELL, Ann W. PEACOCK, W.J. PARISH, William PAGE, W.H. READING, E.J. RIGGSBEE, G.E. ROBBINS, John W. ROBERTSON, Sarah A. ROBERTSON (guardian of Susan L. Boler), E. SMITH, J.B. SPEAR, A.C. STEPHENS, Marietta & Robert O. SELLARS, John B. SPERRING, Eliza J. SELLERS, Florence, Willie & Elizabeth SWAILS, Sarah B. SPENCER, A.L. SPENCER, J.D. & Sarah F. SPENCER, Joseph TAYLOR, A.E. TAYLER, Richard TILLIS, James N. TAYLOR, S.E. WILLIAMS, Robert WRIGHT, H.A. WYSE, Augustine WARD, Isaac WESLEY, Isaac F. WILLIAMS, James N. WRIGHT, and Adam YOUNG.

PROBATE RECORDS: 1884-1902

William P. ALLISON, George W. ALLEN, Dr.W.J. AIRTH, William H. BIRD, Calvin BLACKMON, Susan BOWLEN (minor), Sherrod BIRD, F.E. BRANNEN, William Forsyth BYNUM Jr.(db 1886) His wife was Carrie E. He was a store owner. His inventory list list 146 names of those who had accounts with him; Jack BERTHA or BETHEA (db 1885) He was a store owner; Annie D. BRINSON (db 1887) J.W. Brinson was the administrator; William BRYSON (db 1890) He left a wife, Margaret Ann and 4 children. He was a lawyer.; M.A. BRYSON (guardian for Evelyn RIGDON?), A.A. BLACKBURN, Amanda BIRD, J.H. BENNETT Sr., Calhoun Yancy BYRD, David C.T. COLLINS (db 1885) His wife was Pensy E.; Nelson CALHOUN (db 1886); Elizabeth CORBETT (db 1889) Names associated with the inventory were James J., E.L., and Jacob Corbett; S.M. CARSON, A.R. CREEKMORE, Thomas P. DELEGAL (db 1885)0; Joseph V. DRISLAN?, A.H.(or N) DAVIS, Lilly E. DEES (minor), Ruth FIELDING (minor), Dr. J.L.FISH, Sophia FRASER, John FRASER, T.A.J. FORT, B.T. FISHER, Jehu GOFF (db 1884) His wife's name was Jane and his children were Jehu, George, Winfield, Dangerfield, Mary, Frances, Jennie, Alexander, Adelline, Henrietta, Sallie, Filmore, and Louvinia. He was a cattleman by trade; R.B. GOSHORN (db 1885); W.P. GAMBLE, F.M. & P.A. GREEN (both db 1880, minors) their children were Lenora, Joshephine, and Francis M.; J.A. GRESHAM, CALLAHAN, E.F. HENDERSON db 1885); Annie E. HALL db 1884); Elias HARRELL db 1885) His administrater was Mrs. E.J.Fry; William HAWKINS (db 1885); Ellis H. HULL (db 1890), James L. HODGES, Presley HUGHES, Rebecca F. HALL, Washington L. IRWIN (db 1883) His wife was Martha A.; Sura V. IRVINE, W.S. IRVINE (db 1884) P.A. McInstosh was guardian over Lura V.; L.V. IRVIN, Jasper N. IVEY (db 1889) His wife was Mary J. and a minor daughter named Mary L.; J.D. IVEY, Mary L. IVEY, Jesse A. IVEY, Thomas H. JONES (db 1885); Caroline B. JONES, H.K. LEWIS, J.W. LONG, M.W. MIXON, James MIMS (db 1886) His administrator was Thaddeus Mims; Homer S. MIMS (db 1886) James Smith was appointed guardian over his children...Margaret, James Edward, and Thomas; A.W. McCASKILL (db 1881); S.A. McCASKILL, M.A. MARABLE (db 1888) His wife was Sallie J.; Bird MATTAIR (db 1888) He left a wife and several children. His administrater was Harry Mattair; Florence R. MOSELEY, Henry Harley MOSELEY, J.F. Page MOSELEY, William C. MALLORY, James P. MORGAN, Mary A. McLERAN, Wm. H. NOBLES (db 1885); William NIXON (db 1886) He was a cattlemen; Martha E. OSTEEN, William PAGE (db 1885); H.J. PARRISH (minor), N.M. PARSHLEY, W.J. PETERSON, Margaret ROBERTSON, Mrs. Sarah A. ROBERTSON, Elisabeth ROBERTS, J.E. ROBERTS, John B. SPENCER (db 1884) Sarah B.(Spencer) GARY was guardian over John's minor children...Arrana S., E. Dean, and Eliza G.; J.J. SWAIL db 1884) R.J.Swails was the appointed guardian for J.J.'s minor children...Elizabeth and Florence E.; J.B. SPENCER, James SMITH (guardian), John R. SESSIONS, Tempey SLATE db 1890) The administrator was Tempey Key (probably a married daughter; Dr. William SIMPSON, Walter L. SESSIONS, Mamie C. and Margaret SHAW, W.H. SESSIONS, Rebecca SCOTT, Frank L. SMITH, S. TIMMERMON (db 1889) Labo WRIGHT, R.U. WILLIAMS, W.W. WILLIAMS, Simon L. WILLIAMS, John Fletcher WHITE.

Military & Pensions
Chapter 6

INDIAN WAR - 1835-1842

The following list is a listing of early Suwannee County men who served in the Indian wars and were buried in Suwannee county. The list shows the name of the individual with his date of birth in parenthesis. They are, William ALLISON (b.1820), Thomas CROSSGROVE (b.1811), A.E. DANIELS (b.1823), Howell Sharp HAWKINS (b.1818), W. LEAK (b.1806), John A. MARABLE (b.1818), Thomas R. MERCER (b.1809), M. MICKLER (b.1812), George E. McCLELLAN (b.1807), John W. ROBERTSON (b.1815), Thomas Jefferson STEWART (b.1804), and T.J. WILLIAMS (b.1822)

Over 4000 soldiers died as a result of the Seminole War of 1835-1842 throughout Florida. This listing involves soldiers largely from other states that fought in Florida. Most died from tropical diseases during these years but a large number also died as a result of battle. The following are those who died in battle. If you believe your ancestor is among those in this listing please write to me for additional information...Reverend Harold Bennett, 9584 116th Place, Live Oak, FL. 32060.

They are, Charles F. BUSHMAN, Isaac CHILDS, George CLARIDGE, John HYDE, John A. HODGE, Patrick HACKETT, William HOLMES, John JACOBUS, John JEFFS, William H. JOHNSON, Job LUTHER, Edward MEE, Horace NICHOLAS, William P. NORTON, George NEWELL, Edward PROCTOR, Job SIMMONS, Robert THOMPSON, Richard WHITE, Aug. R. WANDELL, David YORK, A.W. FULLERTON, Benjamin GRIFFETH, Augusthia JOHNSON, Jacob KEPLER, James W. MOODY, Thomas SHARPE, John SYKES, W.E. BASINGER, G.W. GARDINER, R. HENDERSON, Charles MELLON, Constantine SMYTH, John ALLENDER, Edward BELTON, William BLACK, Richard BOURKE, Rufus BARTON, Owen BOYEN, Richard R. BOWEN, Henry BONDON, Daniel BRADY, Phillip COOPER, Nicholas CLARK, William CURNEY, John CRAIG, Edward DeCOURCEY, James DUNLAP Thomas DAVIS, Francis DUNN, Peter DeGRAFF, William P. DAVIS, Robert GREEN, Isaac C. GRANT, Alpheus GILLETT, John HOOD, Charles T. HECK, George HOWARD, John HALTER, John HURLEY, William HOLMES, Cornelius HILL, John HOLLAND, Aaron JEWELL, Michael KENNEY, Thomas KNARR, John KEIRNS, Anthony LAUGHLIN, John LOVIS, John McCARTNEY, John McWIGGIN, James McDONALD, Robert MULVAHAL, Hugh McMEE, William McGRAU, William NEELEY, Hugh PERRY, John A. PATTEN, Reuben PHILIPS, Patrick ROONEY, Michael RYAN, William ROBERTSON, Patrick RAFFERTY, John REILLY, Thomas SAVIN, Caspar SCHNEIDER, John STAFFORD, Andrew SHEARECKER, William TAYLOR, Isaac TAYLOR, Hiram TAYLOR, Thomas THORNTON, Joseph WILSON, Orville WORCESTER, William WRIGHT, U.S. FRASER, I.L. KEAIS, W.S. MAITLAND, R.R. MUDGE, Jacob BANGS, Parker BROWER, Edward BURKE, Frederick BALZ, Thomas BOYCE, George BERTRAM, Benjamin CHAPMAN, John COULTER, B.C. CARPENTER, Patrick CUMASKY, Henry CHILDS, John CAIN, George W. COOK, Kinsley H. DALTON, Samuel E. DODGE, A.C.W. FARLEY, H.C. FIELDS, William FLANAGAN, John

C. FOLK, Abel FULLER, Frederick K. FORD, C.R. GORDON, George HURLYHIGH, Jordan HALL, Edward HOPKINS, John HORN, Alexander JONES, Henry JACKSON, John JACKSON, Samuel KINKERLY, Jacob KNEELAND, Michael KENNEY, Samuel LEMON, David LANE, C.D. MONTGOMERY, William MINTON, Donald MONROE, John MULCAHY, Joseph MUSTELL, John NOBLE, John QUINN, William B. RANDALL, Christie RUNER, Willard SARLES, John SCHAFFER, Henry SENNAN, Washington TUCK, Charles TREAT, James THATCHELL, John VAILING, Richard VREELAND, Philander WELLS, Henry WAGNER, Samuel S. WRIGHT, John WILLIAMS, Sylvester, WELCH, Daniel WESHING, George C. YOUNG, George YORK, John HARDING, Harvey P. MATTISON, John PARDON, Joseph SHARPE, William SPENCER, William THEIS, Hiram WOODRUFF, Michael CLARK, Morris CALL, Theodore DEVOR, Samuel GLENN, John HEIMER, John LAME, Henry S. PHILLIPS, Gabriel YEARICK, Samuel L. RUSSELL, Robert ARCHER, Daniel CLIFFORD, Edward CARNES, Philo C. GRIGGS, Calvin HOTCHKISS, Patrick JEFFERS, Robert LANG, John McKEAVY, Edward MURPHY, Lewis MERRICK, Daniel SWEATMAN, John SHAW, Henry STUHLMAN, Walter THOMPSON, William ZEIGLER, Edward BROWN, William GRAHAM, Samuel G. KNOWLTON, John TOOLE, Frances L. DADE, John BARNES, Enoch CATES, Donald CAMPBELL, Martin CUNNINGHAM, Levi CLENDENING, John DOUGHTY, Cornelius DONOVAN, William DOWNES, William FOSTER, Samuel HALL, David HILL, Wiley JONES, Wm. MARKHAM, David McLAUGHLIN, Felix McCANN, John STEWART, Barthol SHUMARD, William WALKER.

The following list is a listing of Suwannee County soldiers who served in the wars listed in the headings. They were all buried in Suwannee County. The list includes the name of the soldier and the date of his birth.

UNION ARMY

Luther ANGUS (b.1835), Joseph A. BOYD (b.1843), Ned CAMAL (b.1831), George W. GROOMS (b.1820), George C. RIXFORD (b.No date), R.H.M. STARLING (b.1838), Frank M. THOMAS (b.1832), and Allen F. WRIGHT (b.1818).

CONFEDERATE ARMY

James M. ADAMS (b.1837), Andrew J. AGEE (b.1836), Julius A. ALLEN (b.1839), George W. ALLISON (b.1822), John W. ALLISON (b.1825), Robert ALLISON (b.1819), Samuel AMERSON (b.1835), T.M. ARRINGTON (b.1846), Jeremiah S. BADEN (b.1840), Jesse Y. BAILEY (b.1838), Madison BAILEY (b.1850), J.N. BARNETT (b.1835), Joseph F. BARROW (b.1839), John H. BASS (b.1836), Thomas G. BAXTER (b.1830), W.I. BEACH (b.1836), W.R. BELL (b.1842), Thomas N. BEMBRY (b.1828), Charlie BERRY (b.1845), George Washington BEVAN (b.1838), William Ramsey BEVAN (b.1832), Thomas BIGGARSTAFF (b.1843), Sherrod BIRD (b.1823), J.W. BOATRIGHT (b.1833), Joab BLACKMAN (b.1835), Elbert W. BLAND (b.1847), David T. BLANTON (b.1825), Henry M. BLUME (b.1830), Albert BOND (b.1845), Sanford BONDS (b.1847), Joseph J. BONNELL (b.1846), Millard F. BOYETT (b.1852), Henry E. BRADDOCK (b.1840), Benjamin V. BRANNAN (b.No date), Frank W. BRANNAN (b.1842), David Jacob BRIDGES (b.1843), John BRIM (b.1832), David Alex BRINSON (b.1845), Charlton H. BRINSON (b.1841), Martin BROCK (b.1846), Ben BRYAN (b.1822), James Madison BRYAN (b.1813), Nathan L. BRYAN (b.1839), James H. BURNETT (b.1814), James H. BURNETT (b.1845), Marcus D. BUSH (b.1842), William Forsyth BYNUM (b.1832), Jackson CANNON (b.1823), Birton CARROLL (b.1808), Patrick CARROLL (1836), William J. CARROLL (b.1831), John Waine CARVER (b.1848), Ridgon CARVER (b.1835), William CARVER (b.No date), John W. CHALKER (b.1843), Irwin Westlly CHAMBERS (b.1839), William C. CHAMBLISS (b.1837), Dan CLARIDAY (b.1849), George CLARK (b.1834), J.H. CLARK (b.1839), John T. CLARK (b.1844), John Wesley CLARK (b.1830), Milledge CLAYTON (b.1836), M.V. CLAYTON (b.1839), Edward B. COATES (b.No date), Philip G. COATES (b.1841), William W. COATES (b.1842), Thomas J. COBB (b.1830), James J. CONNELL (b.1846), James T. CRAWFORD (b.1833), A.R. CREEKMORE (b.1846), Leroy CROFT (b.No date), William R. DAUGHERTY (b.1845), Arthur N. DAVIS (b.1839), Charles E. DEAN (b.1814), Jeremiah B. DEAS (b.1822), Samuel M. DEAS (b.1832), Henry E. DELEGAL (b.1847), Perry L. DELEGAL (b.1853), William Stevens DELEGAL (b.1849), George H. DORMAN (b.1841), Formy S.J. DUVAL (b.1843), Dred E. ELLIOTT (b.1837), Flemon Pope ELLIS (b.1845), Thomas W. FERGUSON (b.1836), James J. FIELDING (b.1829), James B. FLETCHER (b.1846), George W. FLETCHER (b.1842), Washington FLETCHER (b.1836), James M. FOSTER (b.1837), Watkins W. FOSTER (b.1837), Andrew Jackson FUTCH (b.1844), James C. GALLAGHER (b.No date), Josiah N. GAMBLE (b.1842), G.or C. F. GARDNER (b.1845), W.T. GARDNER (b.1824), R. Nathan GAYLORD (b.1820), Henry GIBBS (b.1815), James GIBBS (b.1835), Shadrack GIBBS (b.1837), Elkanah K. GOFF (b.1847), Jehu GOFF (b.1818), John L. GRAMLIN(G) (b.1839), John H. GRANT (b.1841), Thomas J. GREEN (b.1843), Andrew J. GRESHAM (b.1819), James A. GRIFFIN (b.1836), L.L. GRIFFIN (b.1829), John W. GUFFERE (b.1816), Elisha HALL (b.1831), John M. HALL (b.1849), Henry HOLTZCLAW (b.1844), Isaac R. HARDEE (b.1841), Benjamin D. HARRELL (b.1836), Thomas W. HART (b.1840), Azerah HATCHER (b.1820), John HATCHER (b.1832), Franklin Leroy HELTON (b.No date), Washington HELTON (b.1808), H.C. William HENDRICKS (b.1843), George W. HERRING (b.1849), William W. HERRING (b.1843), Doc William HICKS (b.1843), A.D. HIGDON (b.1822), William Henry HILLHOUSE (b.1844), John R. HINGSON (b.1842), Joseph S. HOGAN (b.1841), C.W.P. HOWELL (b.1837), John P. HOWLAND (b.1847), Enoch W. HURST (b.1810), T.T. HURST (b.1831), Sofater HURT (b.1847), V.W. HUTCHINSON (b.1840), A.W. JACKSON (b.1836), James H. JENKINS (b.1832), Henry JOHNS (b.1847), William JOHNSON (b.1846), Edward John JONES (b.1849), Gideon JONES (b.1838), John H. JOWERS (b.1837), Jacob E. KEITH (b.1842), Thomas T.(J) KENADY (b.1833), Gilford R. KIRKLAND (b.1835), Henry C. KITE (b.1845), Wade H. LAMB (b.1836), Arnett LANDING (b.1847), Thomas P. LANDING (b.1846), R.J. LANIER (b.1819), S.B. LAW (b.1830), Edgar James LAWSON (b.1848), Alexander LEE (b.1848), Gilford LEE (b.1842), James R. LEWIS (b.1821), John LLOYD (b.1815), John W. LLOYD (b.1834), Nathaniel LONG (b.1831), Philip Edward LOWE (b.1835), James H. LYLE (b.No date), Samuel M. MARTIN (b.1847), David L. MATHIS (b.1833), Green A. MEEK (b.1846), James S. MIKELL (b.1834), William A. MILLER (b.1842), Elias B. MILLS (b.1835), H.K. MILLS (b.1838), Henry L.

MILLS (b.1842), J.J. MITCHELL (b.1845), William MIXON (b.1837), A.W. MIZELL (b.1845), Alex B. MORGAN (b.1845), Henry H. MOSLEY (b.1835), Robert McCreary MOSLEY (b.1827), William McCreary MOSLEY (b.1849), James E. MURDOCK (b.1836) and F.C. MURPHY (b.1839), Thomas J. McCALL (1835), W.H. McCALL (1847), George E. McCLELLAN (1807), William Henry McCLELLAN (1845), Benjamin Franklin McCOLISTER (1848), Ozias Wesley McCORMICK (1833), Harrison A. McCOY (1892), David M. McCULLERS (1874), Hugh B. McDANIEL (1898), T.T. McDANIEL (1821), J.E. McDONALD (1841), Robert Fulton McDONALD (1895), Andrew J. McLEOD (1822), C.T. McMANNEN (1834), James T. NEALEY (1843), George Francis NEWLAN (1880), James Ralph NEWLAN (1848), William P. NOBLES (1830), Charles Francis O'HARA (1814), William W. O'HARA (1847), Robert T. O'NEIL (1848), G.R. OGDON (1839), John C. OVERSTREET (1841), Ben OWENS (1834), Solomon M. PARKER (1847), William PARKER (1815), Sewell W. PARNELL (1815), James PARRISH (1840), Robert E.L. PARSONS (1875), Thomas F. PLATT (1898), James H. PRIVETT (1830), Joseph D. RAGAN (1838), Asa G. RANKIN (1839), Jackson J. RAWLINS (1847), Robert A. REID (1843), Owen J. REVELS (1838), Daniel B. RICHARDSON (1846), Alexander G. RIDEOUT (1844), George C. RIXFORD (Union Army), John W. ROBERTSON (1815), W.W. ROGERS (1822), John O. ROSS (1846), Anthony SAPP (1834), W.M.J. SAUCER (1838), John R. SCOTT (1843), John R. SESSIONS (1841), W.H. SHELFER (1827), William Franklin SHEPHERD (1842), W.M. SIMPSON (1837), Hezekiah SMITH (1838), Hobson SMITH (1897), J.G. SMITH (1833), Willis H. SMITH (1829), Alexander SNIDER (??? WW1), John E. STANSEL (1894), Sampson F. STANSEL (1891), Truby STANSEL (1910), David STAPLETON (1847), Levi STARLING (1838), R.H.M. STARLING (1838), J.N. STEPHENS (1833), Asa STEVENS (1822), H.M. STEVENS (1844), Daniel STEWART (1844), Thomas Jefferson STEWART (1804), Arthur STOCKTON (1894), Solomon SULLIVAN (1838), Alfred H. SURRENCY (1840), Joseph K. TAYLOR (1836), Daniel W. TEDDER (1833), Thomas R. TEDDER (1831) Frank THOMAS (??? Civil War), Frank M. THOMAS (1832), Horace Augustus THOMPSON (1887), Henry TISON (1813), William A. TISON (1845), Cecil TOMLINSON (1898), John W. TOMPKINS (1837), Sidney TOMPKINS (1896), J.H. TURNER (1894), Thomas W. ULM (1892), George W. UMSTEAD (1827), John A. URSY (1872), Perry VAYLES (1824), Andrew J. WALLS (1822), F. William WALSTON (1846), William M. WARREN (1841), William C. WATSON (1830), Leam B. WHALEY (1832), George C. WHITE (1818), James L. WHITE (1846), John Fletcher WHITE (1824), Alfred WILLIAMS (1836), Allen WILLIAMS (1826), James WILLIAMS (1895), Joseph A. WILLIAMS (1847), Shelton Eddie WILLIAMS (1893), T.J. WILLIAMS (1822), Thomas C. WILLIAMS (1847), William Paul Hill WILLIAMS (1844), Edward F. WREDE (1825), Rev. Allen F. WRIGHT (1818), David YOUNG (1897), Ephraim J. YOUNG (1831), L.A. YOUNG (1825).

The preceding list provides not only the name and the war, but rank, organization, birth and death dates, and place buried. Write to me if you have an ancestor among these that have been listed IF you need the rest of the information, write to Rev. Harold B. Bennet, 9584 116th Place, Live Oak, Fl. 32060.

PENSIONS

I have just received a "pensioner's list" issued in 1903. It includes, for the most part, men who served in the civil war AND the names of their next of kin, mostly wives, who made claims for pensions. It also includes the company and/or captain with the regiment they served in. Because of space limitations I will list the names of the servicemen. Where a widow is mentioned I will include her name in parenthesis. These are all Suwannee County people.

Samuel DEES (Zilpha), John C. OVERSTREET, Robert REID (Hattie), T.P. QUIETTE (Harriet), Riley TURNER (Elizabeth), J. LEE (Sarah), Thomas P. LANDING (Jane), T. FERGUSON (Eliza), E.W. VANN (Mary), W.O. JACKSON, James M. FOSTER, M.C. BURNS, Matthew McCORMICK, J.M. DUCKER, Levi STARLING, Joseph D. RAGAN, V.W.A. HUTCHINGSON, Samuel AMERSON, John A. BONNELL (Zilpha A.), Robert S. WILLIAMS, James H. CLARKE, R.C. MURDOCK (Eliza R.), Dred E. ELLIOTT, James T. NEELEY, James M. STOKES (Caroline L.), Benjamin M. BRANNAN (Mahala), John S. PONCHIER (Martha A.), William P. NOBLES, Thomas ADAMS, George W. CLARK, Sanford BONDS, Watkins FOSTER (Elizabeth), George W. CARTER, Thomas J. MITCHELL (Sarah E.), David T. BLANTON, Lemuel B. WHALEY, M.G. CLAYTON (Sarah A.), D.L. MATHIS, John H. JOWERS, James S. MIKELL, G.C. NEWMAN, William McDANIEL, Thomas KENADY, James H. JENKINS, R.W. PHILLIPS, J.N. BARNETT, John R. SCOTT, Patrick CARROLL, Matthew JOHNS, W.T. BEACH, Shadrack GIBBS, Alford WILLIAMS, G.W. MARTIN, John W. CAMPBELL, James T. CRAWFORD, Robert F. ALLISON, Thomas J. McCALL, John BRIM, Thomas R. TEDDER, A.J. FUTCH, R.J. LEGGETT, Eli STANFORD, J.W. CLARK, B.F. MEEKS, William J. HOLSTEN, Martin BROCK, J.J. HOGANS (Patience), Elisha HALL, Mandon V. CLAYTON, W.J. CROSIER, John W. BOATWRIGHT, A.W. MIZELL, James A. GRIFFIN, E.B. MILLS, William R. WHEELER, Daniel CARROLL, Sterling W. GARY, John SWEAT, J.J. STAFFORD (Nancy J.), Reuben ROBERTS (Harriet), James J. FIELDING (Elizabeth), A.G. RANKIN, J.F. BARROW, R.J. STEWART, Joshua MATHIS, Joseph H. EPSEY, Albert BOND, John F. TATUM, Hezekiah SMITH, W.J. TURNER, B.D. HARRELL, A.M.R. SESSIONS, John E. ALLEN, James PARRISH, George C. WHITE, Joab BLACKMAN, W.H. SHELFER, James J. DIXON, John J. PAINTER, and L.M. SKELTON.

The remaining names are all preceded by Mrs.! R.J. BLACK, Jane E. CARROLL, Esther E. ELLISON, Mary HARPER, Polly HOLLIMON, M.A. MILLS, M.E. WALTON, Bettie G. MALLORY, Mary J. McDANIEL, Martha A.E. CRAWLEY, Caroline C. STANSEL, L.Z. SEALEY, M.A. PRIVETT, Emiline E. BAILEY, Mary LEE, Virginia T. LOWE, B.L. MURDOK, Martha OWENS, Maggie J. MICKLER, Emily GREEN and Mary L. CREEKMORE. When a widow's first name is NOT shown, we can presume that this is the name of the veteran.

Tax Lists
Chapter 7

The following is an 1847 tax list for Madison County. I am going to list only the names that are prevelant among Suwannee County settlers. ADAMS (Charles & Joshua), AVANT (A.), BAILEY (Madison, William S.), BELL (David), BENNETT (Simeon), BEVIN (William), BRANNAN (Thomas, William, Bryant, James, Rachael, Robert), BRYANT, (Edward, Hardy), BYRD (James, Jeremiah M., Sylvanus), CARTER, (James), CARVER (Elisha), CASON (Silas), CHARLES (Andrew), CHURCH (Lucius), CONE (Fountain, Spencer), CARUTH (C.L.), DEAN (Henry), DUTTON (Joseph), FUQUAY (Neil), GAMBLE (John), GARDNER (G.W., W.G.), GOFF (Cle???), GORNTO (David), GREENE (Robert), HALL (Daniel), HAWKINS (B., Dennis, W.W.), HERRING (John, Rufus), HINGSON (Armstead), HOLLAND (James), HOWLAND (Anna, Ed C.), JENKENS (John), KIRKLAND (Aaron, Joshua), LAW (James R.), LAMB (Cravy, Evan, Isaac, James, Luke G.), LEE (Elann, James), LANIER (Benjamin, Roan), LLOYD (J.P., Joseph), McDONALD (Alex), McGEHEE (John C.), McINTOSH (Daniel, John M., M.M., William), MIMMS (John), MOSELY (Lewis M., Wm.A., Will P.), OSTEEN (James, John), OVERSTREET (George D., S.S.), PARISH (Hiram), PARKER (Isaac, Lewis), PARRAMORE (R.A.), POPPELL (Boyett, John A.), ROBERTS (Hiram, James, Lucy, Wiley, William), SAPP (Charnick, Darling, Henry, John, Riley, William), SCOTT (Charles A., Red, Mary), SESSIONS (L.R., Hampton), SISTRUNK (David, William O.), SLOAN (Samuel), STARLING (Allen), STEPHENS (Allen, James), STEVENS (John), STEWART (Daniel), STORY (James), STRICKLAND (Savage), SUMMERLIN (Elisha), TAYLOR (Isham, Jesse, John G.), TILLIS (Richard), VANN (Adamson, James, Washington), TUCKER (E.R., John R.A.), WALKER (A.O., Charles W., David, George, Henry, Isham R., James, Minor, Whitestead), WHIDDON (Jeremiah, William, Willy), WHITE (Anson), WILKINSON (Robert), WILLIAMS (Alfred, Glisson, Lovett, Manning, Rollin, John), WINN (Isaiah, James), WOOD (John, Thomas), WYCHE (George, John T.).

The following is an 1859 "tax list" from Suwannee County directly after it was founded. This would indicate that these people owned land in this area BEFORE it was a county. After some of the names you will find a number in parentheses...this will indicate the number of slaves owned by that individual. If there is no number that individual did not own any slaves.

W.T. ALLISON, T.J. ALDERMAN, T.L. ADAMS, William ALLISON (4), Robert F. ALLISON (8), J.B. ADAMS, J.B. ANSLEY, James ADAMS (1), Thomas AMISON (or AMERSON), Christopher ANDERSON, Thomas ANDERSON, B.N. BRYAN, Mrs. S.BRYAN, William BIVENS, John BAILEY (4), Cyprian BRINSON (5), Mrs. Naomi BLACKBURN, T.P. BRANNAN, R. BYNUM, L.F. BOWLIN, Sherard BYRD, John BIVENS, Benjamin BELL (2), James M. BAKER, E.T. BOYER, Harris BROCK, Joseph BROWN, Samuel BARBER, W.F. BYNUM, T.C. BRADLEY, Harriot BRINKLEY, Wiley BRINKLEY (3), D. McQueen BLUE (16), A.J. BYRD (17), B.F. BRINSON, C.T. BOROUGHS, Synthia BRYAN (1), George W. BELL, Joab BLACKBURN, Kitty BLACKBURN, Cullin BLACKBURN, B.F. BRINSON, W.A. BRINSON, R.C. CARRUTH (10), W.L. CARRUTH, W.E.M. COUSINS (8), Kinsey CHAMBERS, A.M. CRAWFORD (24), S.W. CRAWFORD, Mrs. E. CRAWFORD

(6), J.J. COATES (2), T.W. CARAWAY, Adam CARAWAY, Archibald CARAWAY (2), W.L. CARAWAY, Joseph CARAWAY, Arthur CARAWAY, Joshua CARAWAY (13), John B. CARTER, Vinson CARVER, Wilson CARVER, M.W. CAIN, Jessee CURL, David CLEMMONS, J.N. CHASTAIN, Sampson CARVER, R.M. CAIN, C.L. CARRUTH, Joseph DYALL (23), T.P. DELEGAL (13), T.P. DELEGAL, Sr. (2), H.H. DELEGAL (8), W.A. DUNN (10), Zachariah DEES, Leonard DEES (1), Nathaniel DEES, T.D. DEXTER (49), O.M. DORMAN, John DEMERE (13), H.L.J. DAVIS, T.C. DAVIS, Mrs. Nancy DEAKLE, Fleming DEES (5), G.W. DUPREE, John DICKSON, J.D. DALRYMPLE, T.R. DEAN, L.W. DUBOIS, N.M. DEES, W.H. EDWARDS, S. EDWARDS, J.R. EVERS, W.T.L. EVERS, Jasper EVERS, Daniel L. EVERS, A.E. FOSTER, M.G. FOSTER, E. FOSTER (1), James M. FOSTER, J.E. FLETCHER, R.S. FOSTER, W.M. FOSTER, Pilate FRY, T.M.B. GOODBREAD, Mrs. T.A. GOODBREAD (2), T. GRAHAM (1), T.D. GODBOLD, Willis GURGAMES, William GARDENER, Henry GIBBS, H.P. GIBBS, John GOFF, N.R. GAYLORD, J.A. GOFF, A.J. GLOVER, J.S. GOODBREAD, William GOFF, J.W. GREENE, B.R. GREENE, John A. HUNTER, Harris HOLLOMAN, Joseph M. HULL (20), T. HURST, T.S. HALL, John A. HAIR, Roland HAIR, H.S. HAISTEN, J.S. HACKNEY (6), J.W. HANCOCK (8), William HARRELL, Thomas HURST, John HURST, Richard HURST, W.B. HARDEE (2), Mary HARDEE (4), Howell HAWKINS (5), T.R. HODGE (2), Washington HELTON (6), James HOLLAND, Terry HUNTER, James HENDRICKS, B.J. HACKNEY (5), Daniel HALL, N.A. HULL, Calob HOWELL, N.L. HALL, William HINES (24), Charlton HINES, A.J. HILL, John T. HARRELL, J.S. HALL, D.D. HENY, M.M.T. HUTCHINGSON, J. HART, John W. IVY, J.A. IVY (7), W.L. IRVIN (7), W.H. IVY (14), J.A. IRVIN (11), H.T. INGERVILLE (2), J.E. INGERVILLE (2), John H. JOHNSON, Matthews Z. JOHNS, J.B. JOHNS, W.E. JOHNSON (1), Levi JOHNS, Green JOHNSON (8), G.P. JOHNSON, A.L. JOHNSON, James H. KEITH, Daniel KEITH (12), T.F. KINSEY, B.C. LEWIS, Morris LEE, David LEE, Robert LONG (26), T.R. LEWIS (8), John LLOYD, E.P. LEE, J.H. LANE (29), E.J. LUTTERLOK (7), E.B. LEALMON, J.D. LINDSEY, John LEWIS, J.R. LEWIS, T.E. LOWE, Julius A. MIMS (5), Wiley MEAKES, James M. MIMS, H. McPHERSON, W.L. MOORE (2), M.W. MIXSON (2), Andrew McCLELLAN, W.H. MANCEL, Randall McKINSEY, William McCOMACK, J.T. McLERAN, Eliza Mip McLERAN, Isabella Mip McLERAN, William McLERAN (5), Angus McAULEY (2), Samuel McNEIL, Ferdinand McBRIDE, Sarah McCALL (1), Lewis MATTAIR (7), Valentine MIMS, James MIMS, Sr., Mary MURDOCK (16), D.C. MURDOCK (5), Howell MEAKES, M. MOSELY, Mrs. N. MOSELY, J.C. McGAHEE, A.H. MARTAIN (or MARTIN)(33), John McCOLLUM, Ira McCOLLUM, George McCLELLAN (38), J.W. McCLELLAN, A. MILLS, H.H. MOSELY, Thomas McCASKIN, A.W. McCASKIN (or McGASKIN), William L. MOORE, Jackson MEAKES (or MEEKS), Thomas McCASKILL, M. MICKLER, L.K. MICKLER, M.A. MURDOCK, H.M. McKINSEY, J.A. NEWMAN (9), T.L. OVERSTREET, J.P. OWENS, William T. OATES, Silous OVERSTREET, James OWENS, S.W. OATES, Joseph PONCHER, John PLATT (1), H.E. PURVIANCE, Mrs. Peggy PIPKIN, G.W. PARKER, Albert PETERSON (5), J.F. PEED (1), M.W. POSTELL, J.S. PONCHER, R.M.D. PEACOCK (5), James C. POLK (1), E.D. PLOWDEN (5), N.H. PLOWDEN (30), J.S. PARKER, Daniel POLK, John POWELL (7), C. PEACOCK (17), William PLATT, John POWELL, Joseph POWELL, M.A. ROLAND (1), G.J. ROBERTS, W.H. ROUSSEAU (14), J.W. ROBERTSON, W.T. RAWLS, Thomas ROBBERDS, John W. RICE, H.D. RIGSBEE, Robert SMITH, T.J. STEWART (2), J.W. SMITH, Hirum SEARS, J.L. SMITH, R.C. SMITH, Milly SMITH, Jacob SMITH, J.B. SMITH, V.H. SHELTON (1), D.P. SNELL, W.W. SNELL (10),

John SKEIN, Jessee STANCEL, Mrs. C.C. STANCEL, Robert SPEARS, A. SPEARS (6), Simeon SHEFFIELD, Louisa SUMMERLAND (1), D.C. SANDERS (2), Hirny STEPHENS, Demsey SAWYER, Laf SNODGRASS, R.S. SESSIONS, Moses SIMMONS, T.H. TRIPLETT (20), D.W. TEDDER, Riley TURNER, J.W. TYNER, T.R. TEDDER, Toplet TILLIS, Oseat TILLIS, J.H. TEDDER, W.L. THOMPSON, W.B. THOMKINS, William THOMPSON, J.F. TATUM, J.J. TAYLOR, T.H. THOMPSON, Thomas URGUHART (1), A.A. WYLEY, H.N. WALKER (15), W.H. WATSON (2), Jonathan WALKER, Gilbert WALKER, T.J. WILLIAMS, John WILLIAMS, Sr., Thomas WALKER, John WATSON, Isaac WILLIAMS, Carthy WRIGHT, R.T. WASHINGTON, Ben WILLIAMS, J.B. WOOD, ? YARBOROUGH, and Elizabeth ZIPPERER.

MORE SUANNEE COUNTY SLAVE OWNERS

Before the Civil War, the owning of slaves was a normal circumstance throughout this country. Like it or not, it is an integral part of this country's history...and Suwannee County was a part of that history, therefore I am going to list our county's 10 largest slave owners during the years of 1859-1861. It helps in identifying some of Suwannee County's citizenry. 1) T.D. DEXTER (53 slaves), 2) George McClellan (38 slaves), 3) A.H. MARTAIN (33 slaves), 4) N.H. PLOWDEN (30 slaves), 5) J.H. LANE (29 slaves), 6) Robert LONG (26 slaves), 7) William HINES (24 slaves), 8) A.M. CRAWFORD (24 slaves), 9) James DYALL (23 slaves), 10) T.H. TRIPLETT (20 slaves). There were many other land owners AND slave owners, but these were the more prominent.

COURT CASES
Chapter 8

1860 LOCAL COURT CASES

The following individuals were involved in court cases in Suwannee County in 1860. CLAIMANTS - Isham BAILEY, James M. BAKER, Matthews Whit SMITH, Sarah BIVIN, Hiram SAUNDERS, dec'd, Isaac P. BLAIR, Henry M. BLOOM, William F. BOLEN, Terrell P. BRANNON, James R. CALLAHAN, James CASON, William S. CASON, James W. CATHEY, George W. CLINE, Leonard DEES, Thomas D. DEXTER, Frederick DOUGLAS, Edward J. FORD, William F. GILL, James S. HACKNEY, Rhodes N. HERNDEN, James HOLLAND, Henrietta KEEN, Daniel LADD, Lewis H. MATTAIR, Walter R. MOORE, Melville A. CARRUTH, dec'd, John F. O'NEIL, George E. PACE, Robert M.D. PEACOCK, Abraham J. PREVATT, John S. PURVANCE, Catherine JOHNSON, Pleasant C. ROEBUCK, Philip & Eugene SCHEEFFELIN, William W. SCOTT, Richard TILLIS, Daniel T. TREZVANT, John J. UNDERWOOD, John U. WISE, and Joseph B. WOOD. DEFENDANTS - David J. ALDERMAN, William P. ALLISON, Margaret BARNES, Sherrod BIRD, Daniel BOATWRIGHT, Cornelius T. BOROUGHS, Edward J. BOYT, Meredith E. BROCK, John & Nathaniel BRYAN, William J.J. DUNCAN, William Y. & William Forsyth BYNUM, William CALLAHAN, dec'd, Henry CARAWAY, Sampson & William CARVER, Noah CASON, Elfain CHASTEEN, Edward B. & John J. COATES, Fleming & Leonard DEES, John ECCLES, John R. EVERS, William GARDNER, James McNEIL, Joseph GIBBS, John GOFF, Leander GREEN, Thomas E. HARDEE, Robert HAYS, Henry H. HERRIN, William HOLMES, John A. HUNTER, James E. INGERVILLE, David B. JOHNSON, George LANGFORD, Edward J. LUTTERLOH, Alexander H. MARTIN, Howell MEEKS, Marley, Leton, & Solomon MORGAN, John PALMORE, John S. & William G. PARKER, John PLATT, James C.L. POLK, William T. & Salina E. RAWLS, Elsey SEALMAN, Samuel R. SESSIONS, Simeon SHEFFIELD, James W. SMITH, Joseph STAFFORD, Daniel W. TEDDER, William S. THOMPSON, Thomas URGUHART, John & William H. WATSON, Andrew G. WISHARD, and Willet S. YARBOROUGH.

The following were listed in the 1861 court records. CLAIMANTS - Robert F. ALLISON, William BIVIN, Louis F. BOLIN, Andrew J. BRINKLEY, Lucius A. CHURCH, Hill B. COFFEE, William DOUGLAS, Philip DZIALENSKI, William H. EDWARDS, Charles W. ELLIS, Benjamin F. MITCHELL, Benjamin W. FORCE, Mitchell A. MITCHELL, Elias N. FORT, James J. HACKNEY, William A. HANKEL, William M. TUNNO, Augustus NORRILL, William HARRELL, John HART, Thomas HOWINGTON, William JAMES, Riley JOHNS, Tarleton JOHNS, Dec'd, Thomas F. JONES, George A. KNIGHT, Henley LAWSON, William M. LIVINGSTON, Donald F. LIVINGSTON, William A. SIMS, Benjamin F. WARDLAW, Richard L. MAYS, Pierce B. WILLIAMS, John F.B. McKINNEY, Julius A. MIMS, Milbe W. MIXSON, James M. MONK, Eliza OLLIFF, Sarah Jane PALMORE, James T. PETTIWAY, George E. MITCHELL, Joseph PONCHIER, John B. QUINCE, ??? RAMSOUR, Robert H. SHAFFER, Chandler H. SMITH, James W. SMITH, William S. SMITH, Holmes STEELE, Daniel J. THOMAS, Samuel B. THOMAS, John THOMAS, John BEGGS, William H. WATSON, James WILLIAMS. DEFENDANTS - Thomas AMERSON, Daniel McQueen BLUE, Jacob C. BUGG, Allen S. CUTTS, Samuel W. DEES,

Louis W. DUBOIS, Milton FOSTER, James GOFF, James W. GREEN, Benjamin J. HACKNEY, John J. HARRELL, Noble A. HULL, William F. BYNUM, Leonard B. JOHNSON, James H. KEITH, Benjamin LANE, Thomas H. LANE, Lewis LAWSON, Elzy LEALMAN, Philip W. LOWE, Solomon ZIPPERER, William J. LUTTERLOH, Louis MATTAIR, James McNEIL, Martha A. MIXSON, Wilson Haywood PALMORE, Henry L. PARKER, John H. PARKER, W.H. REDDING, J.C. BRINSON, Hiram ROBERTS, Samuel M., Francis G., James H., Elizabeth, & Thomas SAUNDERS, Hampton SESSIONS, J.J. SMITH, Daniel T. & William J. SNELL, Hiram N. WALKER.

I have also been researching and abstracting a Court Order Book starting at 1884. This is an interesting book in that it lists details on "inventories", "guardianships", and other items. Here are some of the highlights but much of the information sheds insights into the personal lives of these people. The dates shown show a date shortly after the individual's death. 1) E.F. HENDERSON dec'd by June 10, 1884, 2) George W. ALLEN dec'd by Aug.11, 1884, 3) William H. BIRD dec'd by July 17, 1884. He owned a liquor store among other wares. He apparently had a pool hall as well. His worth was $21,721.63 at his death...a lot of money for those days. 4) Calvin BLACKMAN, a minor, was under the care of Shade GIBBS. This was dated July 17, 1884. 5) W.P. ALLISON dec'd by Sept.23, 1884. Administrator was R.F. ALLISON. He was also the guardian of W.P.R., H.D., S.E., & Amelia D. ALLISON all minors. 6) W.L. IRVINE dec'd by Oct.22, 1884, 7) M.W. MIXON dec'd by June 10, 1884. Wife was Lucretia. Children were William, Joseph, John, James, Mary, and Sarah. 8) John W. ROBERTSON dec'd by June 13, 1884. Heirs were Margaret ROBERTSON and Susan A. BOWLES, both minors under the guardianship of Sarah A. ROBINSON. 9) John B. SPENCER dec'd by July 5, 1884, 10) Sherrod BIRD dec'd by Nov.21, 1884. Wife was Amanda.

The people listed in this court order book will have died sometime before the year shown. Julia V. GOODBREAD (formerly Mrs. Joseph V. JOHNS).She began her guardianship of Joseph V. DENSLER in 1869. John R. SESSIONS (1888) was married to Mattie A. J.A. GRESHAM (1888) was a storeowner. Over 80 accounts are named. S.L. WILLIAMS, discharged from guardianship of H.J. PARRISH in 1889. James SMITH, guardian of Edward & Thomas MIMS for 1887-1890. J.L.A.FISH (1890), and Labo WRIGHT (1890). The following are "estate probate records" unless indicated otherwise...the deceased having died sometime before the year shown. The following are all dated 1891. Sophia FRASER, J.L.IVEY, James L. HODGES, John FRASER, John R. SESSIONS, S.M. CARSON, A.A. BLACKBURN, Dr.William SIMPSON, and R.N.(or H.) WILLIAMS.

EARLY COUNTY OFFICES
Chapter 9

The following Suwannee County officers held office during the 1800's (those before 1858 were considered part of Columbia County since Suwannee was not declared a legal county until December 21, 1858). Only the names and years in office (where available) will be listed.

STATE SENATORS - They were, William P. MOSELEY (1847-1854), William A. BRINSON (1854-1858), W.W. McCALL (1858-1861), J.L. KING (1861-1864?), W.H. ROUSSEAU (1864-1866), J.M. UNDERWOOD (1868-1871), Robert W. ADAMS (1871-1873), Angus McCAULEY (1873-1875), William BRYSON Jr. (1877-1887), Bishop B. BLACKWELL (1887-1889), Robert F. ROGERS (1889-1893), A.W. McLERAN (1893-1897), J.H.T. BYNUM (1897-1901).

COUNTY TREASURER COMMISSIONER: - George C. WHITE (1868), M.M. BLACKBURN (1872), N.Y. BRYAN (1875), John M. BRIDGES (1877), T.T. McDANIEL (1881), J.J. ROBINSON (1891), W.A. PARKER (1893), A.J. McLEOD Jr (1897), D.S. GOSS (1899). (Office was abolished in 1917).

TAX COLLECTOR: - Julius A. MIMS (1859), Daniel P. SNELL (1859-64), Elza B. LEALMAN (1864-66), James A. HARRIS (1866-68), George W. ALLEN (1868-76), A. YOUNG (1876), Robert T. ALLISON (1877-83), W.H. SESSIONS (1883-87), J.J. ROBINSON (1887-91), S.W. GARY (1891-93), Joseph A. CAIN (1893-95), J.R. NEWLAND (1895-97), Henry J. DORMAN (died) (1897), 1897-1901 - John T. DORMAN (1897-1901).

COUNTY CLERK: - Angus McAULEY (1859-68), N. CONNOR (1868-70), Moses L. STEBBINS (1871-77), Robert A. REID (1877-85), J.W. NEWMAN (1885-89), J.H.T. BYNUM (1889-97), Zack GRAHAM (1897-1905).

SHERIFF: - Noble A. HULL (1859...resigned in October), Robert G. PARKER (1859-61), Elza B. LEALMAN (1862-64), William D. GREEN (1865-68...removed from office by Gen. Meade who appointed him), Richard HURT (1868), John H. BAKER (1869-72), Samuel W. HICKS (1872-73), George W. ALLEN (1874-76), 1876 - W.H. SLATE (1876), John R. SESSIONS (1877-87), W.H. MOBLEY (1887-89), Gus POTSDAMER (1889-93), J.W. HAWKINS (1893-1905).

STATE REPRESENTATIVES FOR SUWANNEE COUNTY

Note: Before 1858, Suwannee County was part of Columbia County.

1839 - James NIBLICK
1841-42 - William CONE
1844-45 - George E. McCLELLAN
1844 - Florida became a state.
1840 - Alexander MARTIN
1843 - Jacob SUMMERLIN
1845 - Giles U. ELLIS & Wm.B. ROSS

1846 - Robert BROWN, Elisha CARTER.
1847 - James L. KING, George H. SMITH.
1848 - Giles U. ELLIS, George E. McCLELLAN.
1850 - James S. JONES, John W. JONES.
1853 - H. RAULERSON, W.H. ROSSEAU
1854 - Garrett Van ZANT, Josiah T. BAISDEN.
1856 - Hansford R. ALFORD, W.E.M. COUSINS, George B.
1858 - Cyprian BRINSON, R.M.D. PEACOCK.
1858 - Suwannee became a county.
1860 - Noble A. HULL.
1862 - S.R. SESSIONS, W.B. ROSS.
1864 - Arthur ROBERTS, W.B. ROSS
1865 - Craven B. LASSITER, Wm.B ROSS.
1867-71 - Thomas URGUHART.
1872 - J.M. BRIDGES
1873 - Cyprian BRINSON.
1875 - Daniel McALPIN.
1877 - Samuel M. MARTIN.
1879 - B.M. GARDNER, R.A. IVEY.
1881 - G.W. UMSTEAD, Jasper IVEY
1883 - R.T. ALLISON, A.J. McLEOD.
1885 - S.T. OVERSTREET, A.J. McLEOD
1887 - B.T. UMSTEAD, J.R. NEWLAND.
1889 - Samuel M.M. MARTIN, M.M. KNIGHT.
1891 - J.R. NEWLAND, W.B. HIGH.
1893 - Robert A. REED, John O. ROSS.
1895 - J.M.N. PEACOCK, F.L. REES
1897 - J.F. FIELDING, W.H. MOBLEY
1899 - J.J. CORBETT, S.T. OVERSTREET.
1901 - B.F. UMSTEAD, John H. GRANT.

SUWANNEE COUNTY JUDGES

1859-60 - Joshua CARRAWAY
1861-63 - Catesworth L. CARRUTH
1864-65 - George E. McCLELLAN
1866-67 - Thomas H. CARRUTH
1868-72 - John W. RICE
1872-74 - G.R. THRALLS
1874-81 - M.A. CLOUNTS
1881-84 - M.M. BLACKBURN
1885-88 - R.W. PHILLIPS
1889-92 - W.A. MOSELEY
1893-1919 - J.N. CONNER

EARLY SUWANNEE COUNTY MARRIAGES
Chapter 10

The following are all Suwannee County marriages from 1859 through 1869. Records from 1870 to the present may be gotten by writing to County Seat of Suwannee County, Live Oak, Fl. 32060. I will list the groom, the bride, and the date of the marriage.

1859

Benjamin F. BRINSON to Elizabeth A. COATS on Dec.6, John PLATT to Susan ROBERTS on Dec.19, Thomas J. MOAH (or MOORE) to Missouri MEEKS on Aug.20.

1860

William W. WATSON to Caroline DURDEN on Jan.6, Amos BARNES to Virginia E. POUCHER on March 15, Ira McCOLLUM to Betty B. NEWMAN on Feb.27, Hiram N. WALKER to Martha BLAKELY on Apr.18, Jesse CURL to Mary A.C. QUINN on July 2, John R. ROEBUCK to Louisa PURVIS on Aug.25, Duncan BELL Jr. to Sarah Jane BOYET on Aug.11, William W. QUINN to Mary A. CAIN on Sept.15, William S. FRINK to Matilda V. JOHNSON on Nov.8, Sarah MITCHELL to Jane C. URGUHART on Dec.31, James A. GOFF to Winnifred DUPREE on Dec.26.

1861

Arthur BLACKMAN to Jane T. GIBBS on Jan.30, James A. GRIFFIN to Sarah E. HACKNEY on Oct.17, Isaiah L. TILLIS to Nancy HUNTER on Feb. 6, John BLACK to Martha Ann MIMS on Mar.30, Henry CARVER to Mary DUPREE on Apr.6, Jeremiah M. HUNTER to Margaret A. TRUITT on Apr.10, Thomas P. SMITH to A.M. ZIPPERER on Nov.28, Henry T. SIMMONS to Martha JENKINS on Apr.3.

1862

Andrew J. BASS to Nancy CLIFTON on Jan.25, David DALRYMPLE to Frances BASS on Mar.3, Thomas HARRINGTON to Margaret BARNES on Mar.4, Solomon F. HEDGECOCK to Mary STAFFORD on Apr.14, Dr.William M. HICKS to Miss Ann LANG on Apr.29, Daniel HILL to Ann GREEN on July 24, R.K. ELLIOTT to Lizzie Bell LANE on Sept.10, Louis CLARK to Ann LYONS on Sept.26, Thomas P. QUICK to Milly A.L. BOATWRIGHT on Sept.26, John L. HUNTER to Martha Jane QUICK on Aug.18, Green FORESON to Sarah DEES on Oct.20, David M. WILEY to Parmealia Jane FOARD on Dec.29.

1863

Joseph LIVINGSTON to Mary Ann SELF on Jan.7, W.C. LAWRENCE to Martha WALKER on Jan.10, William P. WILLIAMS to Margaret B. WILEY on Jan.16, Aaron DANIELS to Adaline E. ROBERTSON on July 1, Thomas P. QUICK to Francis A.M.J. BOATRIGHT on Aug.12, Dennis C. HAWKINS to Bella McLAURIN on Aug.18, Luke WALKER to Mary STAFFORD on Oct.14, Robert F. ROGERS, to Sarah J. ROBERTSON on Nov.8,

William H. FIELDS to Caroline CARRAWAY on Oct.20.

1864

John F. STEWART to Eliza C. BURNETT on Feb.4, T.T. McDANIEL to Mary Jane BEVANS on Apr.14, Elisha CURL to Rachel BRANNON on Apr.29, Dr. Silas T. OVERSTREET to Lizzie H. GOODBREAD on Apr.5, Alexander WILSON to Eliza A.R. BAILEY on May 6, John GOFF to Elza Jane REID on Dec.25.

1865

Harrell HALLOMON to Polly Ann BLACKMAN on Feb.8, Albert BONDS to Mary BRANNON on Mar.3, William DOWNING to Eliza A. BONDS on May 18, William A. DRIVER to Martha B. ALLISON on May 23, Charles H. KEITH to Virginia C. ROUSSEAU on Dec.6, Zachariah DEES to Eliza JONES on Dec.15, John L. ROUSSEAU to Dora A. McCARDLE on Dec.6, Oscar B. LANE to Martha W. IVEY on Dec.21, Philip G. COATS to Sarah P.J. GUFFY on Dec.28, William W.C. COATS to Mary A.E. GUFFY on Dec.28, William R. DRIVER to Eliza WILLIAMS on Dec.24.

1866

Willoughby TILLIS to Martha L. AMERSON on Jan.3, Robert F. ALLISON to Laura J. DENARD on Jan.9, James R. NEWLAND to Mary J. MITCHELL on Jan.21, Thomas H. HAWKINS to Sophrony A. GOFF on Jan.18, Henry G. STEWART to Emeline CARAWAY on Jan.17, Cornelius HARDEE to Laura D. BROCK on Feb.8, James EVERS to Francis SPIER on Jan.2, Samuel AMERSON to Sarah J. PELUM on Jan.31, John WILLIAMS to Amelia G. ALLISON on Mar.4, Caba IRWIN to Lucy BRINSON on Feb.15, Henry LASHLEY to Elizabeth FUGUA on Mar.5, Sandy HIGDEN to Silva WILLIAMS on Mar. 11, Thomas J. MITCHELL to Sarah E. HALL on Mar.29, Edward R. LUNDY to Mrs. Mary CARTER on Apr.5, John H. HARRELL to Elizabeth WALKER on Mar.6, Elijah SMITH to Maria HIERS on Apr.21, Dary TAYLOR to Rhoda STAFFORD on May 16, Nat GOODMAN to Nancy DUNN on May 13, Shade TAYLOR to Jane POULITTLE on May 13, Harry COKELY to Sibbee COKELY on May 26, Louis JOHNSON to Adaline ???? on May 26, Charles DORSEY to Eliza DORSEY on May 20, Henry RAWLS to Mariah RAWLS on May 20, Jack ROUSE to Dorcas ROUSE on May 20, Cato WALLACE to Jane WALLACE on May 20, Chance DEUSLER to Margaret A. QUARTERMAN on May 20, Anthony CARRUTH to Pebia MIMS on June 3, William STEWART to Salomia DREW on June 3, George CLARK to Jane CLARK on May 24, William SCOTT to Emmas LAUER on July 4, Thomas HILL to Amanda HALL/HULL on July 4, Needham HAMILTON to Salena HALL/HULL on July 23, John HOWELL to Elizabeth HANNOCK on July 24, James HIGDEN to Mary SMILEY on June 3, Samuel McKEEFER to Mary Ann MILTON on July 1, Robert ALLEN to Rebecca CHARLES on May 6, David LINZA to Mirah KEITH on May 6, Lancaster STEWART to Mary MILES on May 6, Titus WORUFF to Elsey MECKENS on June 3, Lancaster AUSTIN to Hannah HAMS on June 3, Jackson WILSON to Mary AUSTIN on June 3, William Joseph DYALL to Mrs. Martha NEWSOME on Aug.14, Elijah SMITH to Caroline SMILEY on June 9, Henry ROBERSON to Catherine STRINGFELLOW on July 29, Joshua NELSON to Jane THOMPSON on June 10, Simon CHAIRES to Phylis McIVER on Aug.26, Tony HARGROVE to Dinah HARGROVE on

Aug.26, London MORGAN to Katey MORGAN on Aug.26, Pierce DELEGAL to Bama DELEGAL on Aug.26, William DUNN to Celia DUNN on Aug.27, William SAVAGE to Flora SAVAGE on Aug.25, T.M. JENKINS to Rebecca A. WILLIAMS on Aug.21, Thomas URGUHART to Saloma E. BAISDEN on Sept.30, Julious HILL to Mary BALDWIN on Sept.27, York DASHER to Sarah QUARTERMAN on Sept.29, Carter MOTON? to Mary BRAZELL on Aug.5, William PARKER to Sarah FRANKLIN on Aug.5, Oceola MELLON to Mary Ann BENJAMIN on Aug.5, Benjamin FIGG to Harriet BIRK on Sept.3, Elijah BUTLER to Jane ROUSE on Sept.3, Abraham GRAHAM to Sallie GRAHAM on Aug.9, John HALL to Pelason BRADLEY on Apr.2, David W. LISTER to Ann E. DEES on Oct. 10, Fred HOLLAND to Jane HOLLAND on July 22, Limas HOLLAND to Dorcas TILLMAN on Oct.7, William T. GARDNER to Elizabeth GREEN on Nov.8, Warren L. KENNON to Fannie GRAHAM on Oct.9, Handy MARTIN to Affa JONES on Oct.9, Wallis BOWDIN to Eliza ANDERSON on Oct.9, Sabe MARTIN to Abby SCOTT on Oct.9, Charles MARTIN to Rebecca PETERSON on Oct.9, William F. NOBLES to Asian F. SMITH on Nov.15, Henry O. GRIMES to Charity DEES on Nov.29, Henry McGEE to Jane SMILEY on May 13, John HIGDEN to Rachel RAMSEY on Oct.7, Berry JEFFERS to Easter ALLISON on Oct.11, Austin STEPHENS Martha S. THOMAS on Oct.8, Henry JOHNS to Falby TAYLOR on Nov.1, 1866, Richard BAILEY to Amanda L. HARRISON on Nov.9, Pealer ADAMS to Mary Agnes ADAMS on Aug. 21, Stephen TREDWELL to Martha HOWELL on Aug.31, J.E.S. BARNES to M.J. KEITH on Nov. 20, Peter GRAHAM to Julia MARTIN on Aug.26, Samuel MAUCEL to Kiziah MAUCEL on Aug.26, Anthony RAWLS to Miley KEITH on Nov.1, Noah GRAHAM to Peggy GRAHAM on Sept.3, George WASHINGTON to Rebecca WASHINGTON on July 20, Auston ??? to Stella CHARLES on Aug.25, Washington JAMES to Mariah ??? on June 11, Berry JONES to Tabitha WILEY on May 30, Henry WILLIAMS to Susan WILLIAMS on Sept.30, Virgil HILL to Peggy HILL on Sept.30, Isreal ROUSE to Adeline ??? on June 11, Lawrence ??? to Violet CARAWAY on May 6, Jerry SHULER to Levinia SHULER on Aug.27, Hardy JOHNSON to Elizabeth JOHNSON on Sept.5, Harry COLEMAN to Minny FLOWERS on Dec.8, John LEE to Sarah LEE on Oct.28, John GREEN to Mary Ann COWART on Dec.25, Prince Albert THOMAS to Sylvia BACHLOTTE on Dec.22, Alfred BROWN to Margaret THOMAS on Dec.26, Silas HATCH to Francis K. BRADLEY on Nov.20, Elbert CAMMERON to Martha STEPHENS on Dec.29, Levi BRINSON to Mary BROWN on July 1.

The following 1866 marriages were done by the authority of the Attorney General. May 6: Lawrence ???? to Violet CARAWAY: May 30: Berry JONES to Tabitha WILEY: June 11: Hiram ROUSE to Nancy DUNN, Washington JAMES to Mariah ????, Isreal ROUSE to Adeline ????. June 28: Bristol FOXWORTH to Elizabeth ???, Andrew/Benjamin WILLIAMS to Sibia ???, Stephen CASON to Julia, George GAIL to Bella ???, Robert MOORE to Charity ???, July 1: Tillis McKEEPER to Adom Benfaulin ???, Timothy WILLIAMS to Rosana WILSON, Jerry SNELL to Feba WILSON, Willington YOUNG to Hannah HAMS. July 4: Charles HULL/HALL to Silla ???, William BESSER to Moaucy ???, Sike POLITE to Dianna ???, John RIGGSBEE to Elizabeth ???, Richard WILLIAMS to Sarah ???, Joseph MANN to Rosa ???, Wm. INGERVILLE to Aimy ???, Joseph SNELL to Catherine ???, Jack HAINDEW to Charlotte ???, Pinkney READMAN to Jane ???, Robert BUTLER to Betsy ???, Sampson ALEXSON to Mary ???, Frank STOCKTON to Sarah ???, William MOBLEY to Lura ???, King STOCKTON to Lovenia ???,

Thomas WILLIAMS to Elizabeth ???. <u>July 20:</u> George WASHINGTON to Rebecca WASHINGTON. <u>Aug.25:</u> Austin ???? to Stella CHARLES. <u>Aug.26:</u> Peter GRAHAM to Julia MARTIN, Samuel MAUCEL to Keziah MAUCEL. <u>Aug.27:</u> Jerry SHULER to Levinia SHULER. <u>Sept.5:</u> Hardy JOHNSON to Elizabeth JOHNSON. <u>Sept.30:</u> Henry WILLIAMS to Susan WILLIAMS, Virgil HILL to Peggy HILL. <u>Nov.1:</u> Anthony RAWLS to Miley KEITH. <u>Dec.8:</u> Harry COLUMAN to Minny FLOWERS.

1867

Thomas N. BLOCK to Ellafaire HURST on Jan.23, James H. HARRIS to Sarah C. WATSON on Jan.10, Martin MOORE to Louisa ROBINSON on Jan.8, Stephen GOIN? to Henretta GLOVER on Jan.1, George WILLIS to Mary Ann SELPH on Jan.15, David McQUEEN to Margaret H. LANE on Jan.3, H.W. SUMMERFORD to Emma L. DREW on Jan.27, James McCOOK to Margaret BROOKS on Mar.3, Tamoline CATO to Emma BRIGG on Mar.5, Miller W. MIXON to Cereasey BODEFORD on Mar.4, Samuel H. HURST to Martha JOHNSON on Feb.17, John Z. Fetuer to Mary Ann WILSON on Jan.31, Wm.F. CARRAWAY to Merriza KING on Mar.14, Jesse GRAHAM to Louisa EASON on Mar.10, Benjamin T. BAILEY to Caroline HENDRICKS on Apr.4, Robert ROBINSON to Harriet LANDERS on Apr.13, Dr. John GRANT to Celestia R. McCLELLAN on May 30, Alexander WILSON to Martha PIPKINS on Apr.20, Thomas T. HILL to Elizabeth OWENS on Mar.19, William R. FULFORD m. Henrietta C. ROBERTSON on Apr.9, J.L. BOLES to S.H. ROBERTSON on Mar.27, Samuel W. HICKS to Anna H.J. MILLEY on May 22, David SIMMONS to Mariah JENKINS on May 26, John R. WILLIAMS to Cola B. HACKNEY on May 21, George MARTIN to Emaline MARTIN on May 20, John H. MICKLER to N.H. VAUPELL on May 20, Caesar BRYAN to Ocella WILLIAMS on June 30, John J. SAPP to Marietta BLACKWELL on Mar.14, Simon SUTTER to Mary BELL on July 19, John SMITH to Deania SUTTER on July 28, John J. HOLMES to Alice E. RILEY on Aug.8, Henry MEEKS to Nancy J. FULFORD on Sept.1, Green MEEKS to Ann E. FULFORD on Sept.1, George WALKER to Nancy JOHNSON on Sept.17, William W. GOODMAN to Synthia BRYAN on Oct.2, Hyder D. RIGSBY to Ellen J. McCLELLAN on Nov.5, John A. LEE to Caroline COWART on Nov.19, Samuel BARBER to Mary A. LEUSTE on Nov.25, 1867, Thomas BOONE to Eliza KENT on Nov.28, Seth M. DICKERSON to Jane CATO on Nov.19, Pliney MORGAN to Winifred GOFF on Dec.15, Charles SMITH to Jennie WILLIAMS on Dec.26, Earnest BERTON to Milly SMITH on Dec.26, J.L. LEUTING to Nancy McHANNON on Dec.17, William RILEY to Ann HARGROVE on Nov.10, Samuel RHODES to Rhoda DAVIS on Sept.5, Jesse JACKSON to Sophia McCALL on Oct.23, Isaac HART to Kate WILLIAMS on Nov.7, William H. McCLELLAN to Emma CHARLES on Oct.23, John SHORTER to Ann CARTER on Feb.9, George E. McCLELLAN to Mary HART on Dec.5, Johnston BRYANT to Josephine MONDIN on Jan.16.

1868

H.R. MILLS to Jane SMOKE on Feb.26, Morday BROWN to Epsey MITCHELL on Feb.10, Armistead BAILEY to Milly JONES on Apr.4, Joseph BRADLER to Josephine McPHERSON on Apr.29, January MURDOCK to Eliza URGUHART on May 6, Isaac WILLIAMS to Rebecca TAYLOR on July 4, Chadwick MARSH to Flora DeHAUN on Jan.27, Robert KENNEDY to Adeline TISON on July 21, Jesse HART to Nancy WILLIAMS on Dec.24, Emanuel RICE to Mollie H. BUCHANAN on Feb.22, Joshua WILLIAMS to Ellen WILSON on Nov.5, J.W. LEWIS to J.E. PERRY on Nov.25, William FULFORD to Adeline JAMESON on Dec.9, Perry ALLEN to Jane THOMAS on Dec.31, Wright CUNNINGHAM to Eliza SIMMONS on Sept.21, David TAYLOR to Marinda ROBINSON on Oct.11, Varda M. HOLLIMAN to Sue R. MILLER on Aug.29, Crawford WILLIAMS to Rhoda SMITH on Sept.15, Charles M. HODGKINS to Jane SALES on Nov.12, J.J.A. SUTTON to Sarah Jane BAILEY on Oct.26, Morris GAYLORD to Susan J. SCRIVEN on Nov.26, William J. HASTINGS to Susan SCARBOROUGH on Jan.23, Hamilton POLITE to Sylvia GIBBS on Feb.22, Joseph CAUSEY to Flora Ann BAILEY on Apr.17, Adam BOGGS to Mary WHITE on Apr.18, Abner R. CREEKMORE to Mary L. ALLISON on Jan.5, William T. BEACH to Julia E.V.SWAILS on May 14, Archibald RUSSELL to Ellen BLUE on July 4, Thomas C. WILLIAMS to Julia Ann HAWKINS on Dec.22, Samuel MARTIN to Virginia M. PEACOCK on Dec.3, York SHAFFER to Henrietta DUNKIN on Dec.25, Edmon SMITH to Susan HART on Feb.9, John W. GRANT to Lenia A. JOHNSON on Nov.20, Calvin PEACOCK to Ann IVEY on Dec.17, John W. GAMBLE to Carrie H. TAYLOR on Oct.13, John Wesley BROCK to Maria A. PARSHLEY on Oct.21, Peter JACKSON to Ann LATTAMORE on Oct.2, Robb W. BAILEY to Elizabeth BAILEY on Oct.26, C.A. RAMSEY to Faunin HOLLAND on Oct.13.

1869

Gabe SIMMONS to Candice SHAW on Jan.9, Richard HENDERSON to Mary HUNTER on Jan.13, George MAUKER to Carrie HARVEY on Feb.14, Thomas BRYAN to Emma GARDUN on Mar.4, E.C. SESSIONS to Mary A.R. MIMMS on Mar.28, William A. GARDINER to Tabitha A. POUCHER on Feb.28, Charles F. GARDINER to Sarah E. BOYETT on Feb.25, Louis CHAPEL to Francis WARDLAW on Mar.8, Charles LAWRENCE to Lu WILLIAMS on May 2, H.J. TAYLOR to Mary H. ROBERTS on Jan.3, Cherry CHESTNUT to Sarah A. RICKS on Apr.15, Littleton SMITH to Matilda GURGANUS on May 23, W.E. RAINS to Lucia A. WALKER on May 21, Albert STEWART to Julia ELLIS on Apr.1, Jarvis F. MARSHALL to Margaret SULLIVAN on Jan.9, James SMILEY to Rosella JOHNSON on Jan.9, John T. SHAW to Melvina SELLMAN on Oct.6, Rabon BLACK to Emmiliza HART on Nov.14, Albert STOCKTON to Tira POLITE on Aug.14, John GILLEY to Martha ATWELL on Sept.14, Lafton SHIPP to Caroline SMITH on Nov.21, John R. RIGGSBY to Merringa LAFTON on Oct.30, Pinkney GREEN to Elizabeth W. DEUT on Aug.29, M.J. MARTIN to Mollie ROUSSEAU on July 21, Solomon SULLIVAN to Sarah Ann GRANT on July 22, William H. HOLDER to Mary FETNER on Dec.26, Thomas MADDEN to Mrs. Delilah THOMPSON on Dec.21, William GATEWOOD to Lizzie MOSELY on Dec.30, Benjamin DAVIS to Lizzie GRAHAM on Jan.13, George MARSHALL to Jane WHITE on Jan.15, Jacob BETHEA to Lucy CUNNINGHAM on Jan.4, Marshall MIKELL to Adeline SMITH on Mar.13, Samuel ANDERSON to Amanda ANDERSON on Jan.2, Jackson THOMAS to Melvina JACKSON on Feb.27, William H. SLATE to Mrs. Tempy HIGDEN on Mar.21, David JONES to Mary Ann MILLS on Jan.21, Mr. Jeremiah to Savory LEAVIS on Jan.30, H.A. PARKER to Charity GOODBREAD on Apr.29, Thomas MOBLEY to Mrs. Sabrey HOGAN on May 22, William B. MICKLER to A.A. McPHERSON on Apr.17, Ernest BENTON to Mary HICKS on Jan.13, J.P. HARDY to E.L. BROCK on Feb.14, David KITE to Bella BAKER on Jan.6, Henry A. CARVER to Mary A. MAUREY on May 10, Anderson CONNER to Emeline CONNER on Oct.19, A.J. GIBBS to Emma BEVINS on Nov.4, C.L. WILLIAMS to Francis J. RAMSEY on Nov.4, Adison R. BAILEY to Ellinor L. PHILIPS on Sept.30, Abner SESSIONS to Martha J. BLACK on Nov.14, Edward BANKS to Harriet POLICO on Nov.19, Thomas LANGFORD to Anna GALOWAY on Oct.31, Dr.A.J.O. HALE to Mrs. L.W. KEITH on Dec.21, Kelly DEAN to Minton YOUNG on July 22, Richard GRAHAM to Eliza JACKSON on July 18, J.R. TAYLOR to Mary J. WILLIAMS on Dec.14, Joseph F. PUTNAM to A.F. WATERS on Dec.1, Seaborn JOHNSON to Rina JENKINS on Oct.10, Joseph B. BASTORS to Kizie GAYLORD on Nov.10, Martin BROWN to Agnes BEVILL on Dec.1, Isaac SHIVER to P.P. BROCK on Dec.23.

Cemeteries
Chapter 11

The Suwannee Democrat printed an interesting series on the now defunct town of Columbus. It was located on the site of the Suwannee River State Park. It was incorporated in 1841 and at its peak boasted a population of about 500 people.

COLUMBUS MAIN CEMETERY

The first cement block enclosure embraces 1) Mollie CANNON (b.1843, d.1890), 2) Jackson CANNON (b.1823, d.1906), 3) Jackson CANNON (b.June 20, 1877, d.Nov. 24, 1916). An inscription on his stone says "Woodsmen of the World Memorial...possibly the son of Mollie & Jackson Sr. 4) Baby CANNON (b.July 11, 1906, d.Dec.16, 1906). Inscription reads, "of Rosa & Jack Cannon Jr.". 5) Jearl CANNON (b.Feb.12, 1902, d.June 4, 1907)...also inscribed, "daughter of Rosa & Jack Cannon Jr.". 6) Rosa H. STOKES (b.Feb.22, 1884, d.Feb.15, 1973), 7) Rosa Cannon HARRIS (b.1910, d.1935).

The second section is encompassed by a metal fence and it houses, 1) Alice C. BARKLEY, wife of J.M. BARCLAY (b.Apr.1848?, d.1891), 2) Mary R. BARCLAY, wife of J.M. BARCLAY (b.Nov.10, 1849, d.Oct.20, 1885), 3) George Murray BARCLAY, son of J.M. & Mary R. BARCLAY (b.Aug.16, 1883, d.Nov.2, 1885), 4) Eugene McIVOR, wife of George A. McIvor, (b.Sept.7, 1867, d.Jan.21, 1892), 5) George A. McIVOR, a mason, (b.1857, d.Mar.14, 1896). 6) George Clark McIVOR, son of George A. & Eugene McIvor (b.Dec.18, 1881, d.Mar.3, 1889).

The third enclosure is of concrete block and houses 1) M.H. WIGGINS (d.May 24, 1870). There are 4 unmarked graves beside her. 2) Mary A. HARDEE, wife of Thomas E. Hardee (d.May 26, 1862) near Columbus, Fl. aged 60 years, 3) Sarah C. SPENCER, 2nd wife of J.B. Spencer who died at Sunnyside, FL., age 33 years and 14 days. She left a 7 month old son. NOTE: Her birth and death dates can only be understood if the next entry was her "7 month old son". If that is true, she was born on or near June 15, 1832 and died on or near July 1, 1865. 4) William Tison SPENCER, 3rd son of J.B. and Sarah C. Spencer (d.Aug.11, 1865 at Sunnyside, Fl. aged8 months and 17 days).

Toward the rear of the cemetery are the graves of 1) Regina G. BREVALDA, daughter of George & Emma Brevalda (b.Dec.26, 1877, d.Nov.18, 1885), 2) An unmarked metal marker is next to Regina's grave, 3) Thomas E. SWIFT, beloved husband of Amanda Swift (b.Mar.9, 1851, d.July 11, 1893). Mr. Swift's grave is enclosed in a metal fence.

There are 24 graves at this site. Life must have been difficult in this small town because the average life span was only 33 years. Only 3 lived beyond the age of 60, the rest were well under the age of 50.

The cemeteries that follow are all in the general vicinity of the now defunct Columbus. These will round out the families that lived in that area. The Suwannee County Genealogical Society has a listing of all the known cemeteries in Suwannee County.

DEAN CEMETERY

I was traipsing about the county looking for a cemetery... known or otherwise...and I found three. The first one I had looked for earlier but could not find was the Dean Cemetery. I found it this time...in the middle of the woods with a relatively new Sear's fence around it. The simplest way to find it is to take 90W to the dirt road on the right just before the inspection station...then turn around and take 90E about 300 yards (2/10 of a mile). Stop, get out of the car, and walk north (through the woods) to the grave site.

Those who are buried there are, 1)John T. ALEXANDER (b.1795, d.1878), 2) Justion Wilks ALEXANDER (b.1800, d.1880), 3) Charlie DEAN (b.1873, d.1874), 4) Pinkney DEAN (b.1879, d.1887), 5) Dorann DEAN (b.1869, d.1871), 6) Stonewall DEAN (b.& d.1863), 7) Charles DEAN (b.Mar.3, 1814, d.Dec.26, 1883), 8) James W. WILKS (b.1782, d.1868), 9) Rebecca Ann WILKS (b.1840, d.1875, 10) Bessie Eliza CLEMONS (b.1886, d.1887). This is one of several cemeteries in the now extinct town of Columbus, Florida.

The following two cemeteries are located on River Road...300 and 400 yards south of Route 90 respectively. River Road turns south off of 90. Both cemeteries have been designated as Negro cemeteries according to the Veteran's Graves Registration Project of 1941.

LEE CEMETERY

Those buried there are...1) Gladys LEWIS (b.June 10, 1913, d. May 18, 1991), 2) Curtis LEWIS (b.Nov.25, 1910, d.June 12, 1984), 3) unreadable, 4) Sarah B. LEWIS (b.Aug.28, 1907, d.Feb.25, 1973), 5) Lorenzo LEWIS (b.July 11, 1927, d.May 26, 1986), Pfc.,U.S.Army,WW2, 6) Several scattered unmarked wooden markers & one metal unmarked marker, 7) Katherine THOMAS (b.Apr. 19, 1923, d.Feb.12, 1987), 8) Mary LEWIS (b.May 11, 1911, d.Jan.16, 1992), 9) Clyde LEWIS (b.Jan.10, 1903, d.Nov.18, 1986) 10) Zola M. DOUGLAS (b.Dec.2, 1915, d.Aug.31, 1985), 11) Hinkey & Amie LEWIS (No dates. Iron posts with wooden nameplates attached), 12) Tom LEWIS Jr. (b.Oct.14, 1917, d.Jan.8, 1961) FL., Pvt.,U.S.Army, WW2), 13) Leon & Opey LEWIS (No dates. Iron posts with wooden nameplates attached), 14) P.E. LEWIS (b.Mar.13, 1900 d.June 8, 1972), 15) Marie B. LEWIS (b.May 15, 1881, d.Jan.25, 1985), 16) Arre LEWIS (b.May 8, 1896, d.Oct.3, 1908), 17) Ray Field JUDSON (b.Oct.2, 1933, d.Sept.1, 1981) Sgt.U.S.Army, 18) Jesse C. WILLIAMS (b.Feb.17, 1934, d.Feb.11, 1987), 19) Archer? WILLIAMS (b.1908, d.1918).

COLUMBUS NEGRO CEMETERY

This cemetery is located 100 yards further south on River Road. Those buried there are 1) Alberta RILEY (b.Sept.24, 1921, d.Aug.23, 1987), 2) Arthur Lee RILEY (b.1927, d.1981) Pvt.,U.S.Army, Korea, 3) Arthur Andrew LINTON (b.Mar.27, 1925, d.June 4, 1992), U.S.Army, WW2, 4) William B. HENRY (b.Oct.31, 1929, d.Mar.3, 1990), 5) Robert WRIGHT, pere (b.1814, d.1885), 6) Nancy WRIGHT (b.1817, d.1887), 7) Charles WRIGHT, fils (b.1843, d.1935), 8) Rebecca WRIGHT (b.1848, d.1912), 9) Mary Louise Wright POMPEY (b.Sept.11,1881, d.Dec.22, 1985), 10) James A. POMPEY (b.Aug.17, 1918, d.Mar.28, 1978), Pvt.,U.S.Army,WW2, 11) Inez P. TATUM (b.1914, d.1977), 12) Frances WRIGHT (b.Jan.15, 1894, d.Jan.22, 1976), 13) Rebecca WRIGHT (b.Apr.11, 1892, d.Jan.22, 1976), 14) Robert WRIGHT (b.Apr.11, 1890, d.Nov.11, 1971), Fl.Cpl.U.S.Army,WW1, 15) Vannie RILEY (b.July 17, 1888, d.Oct.23, 1977), 16) Elsie Riley SMITH (b.Dec.25, 1923, d.Sept.4, 1985), 17) Margaret W. MILLER (b.1878, d.1969).

CEMETERY LISTING OF THOSE BORN BEFORE 1850

PINE GROVE METHODIST CHURCH CEMETERY - We will list the name (with maiden name for the ladies where they are shown), and the year of birth & death, for each one. They are, Mary A. Raines PRIVETT, b.1836, d. 1916; James H. PRIVETT, b.1830, d.1900; John L. GRAMLING, b.1839, d.1920; Mary A. GRAMLING, b.1841, d.1906; William S. KEELING, b.1848, d.1936; Sarah HARRELL, b.1777, d.1860; William HARRELL, b.1822, d.1872; Attina Jane HARRELL, b.1822, d.1875; Sarah Rebecca Ann HARRELL, b.1842, d.1895; Mary Elnora HARRELL, b.1846 d.1875; Mary UMSTEAD, b.1807, d.1891; Rev.A. WRIGHT, b.1818, d. 1906; Martha A. WALLS, b.1836, d.1903; Andrew J. WALLS, b.1822, d.1902; John BAILEY, b.1811, d.1874; Sarah BAILEY, b.1814, d. 1898; Thomas CROSSGROVE, b.1811, d.1880; Susan PHILIPS, b.1837, d.1906; Jesse Y. BAILEY, b.1838, d.1912; L.L."Fate" BAILEY, b. 1848, d.1928; Mary A. Crossgrove BAILEY, b.1843, d.1916; Mary LUNDY, b.1840, d.1915; Louisa McNeil HUNTER, b.1850, d.1929; C. W.P. HOWELL, b.1837, d.1927; Frances McNEIL, b.1834, d.1933; Ellen GAY, b.1836, d.1918; Sapator HURT, b.1847, d.1908; Elizabeth HURT, b.1845, d.1875; John NORRIS, b.1828, d.1888; Louise M. DELEGAL, b.?, d.? (she had a child, T.D.Delegal, in 1862 so she must have been born before 1850); James Edgar LAWSON, b. 1848, d.1926; Annie J. ELLIOTT, b.1840, d.1905; Dred ELLIOTT, b.1837, d.1918; Hester Murry NORRIS, b.1842, d.1924; Harriot HENDRIX, b.1825, d.1892; James HENDRIX, b.1818?, d.1886; Mary E. UMSTEAD, b.1848, d.1924; George W. UMSTEAD, b.1827, d.1903; William D. RIGGS, b.1846, d.1903; Paul F. RIGGS, b.1848, d.1891; A.W. RIGGS, b.1812, d.1894; Mary RIGGS, b.1814, d.1883; W.A. GARDNER, b.1824, d.1901; Melissa H. TILLMAN, b.1841, d.1908; Louisa MEADOWS, b.1837, d.1904; Thomas T. KENADY, b.1833, d.1923; Alexander KENADY, b.1800, d.1886; Hollon KENNEDY, b.1811, d.1881; Capt. MICKLER, b.1812, d.1871; Sarah MICKLER, b.1807, d.1889; Peter Theodore MICKLER, b.1832, d.1900; Elizabeth Saxon MICKLER, b.1841, d.1872; Martha MICKLER, b.1815, d.1878; Joseph OLIVER, b.1763, d.1800; Jacob E. MICKLER, b.1834 d.1864; Louisa J. JOHNSON, b.1840, d.1867; John H. JOHNSON, b.1828, d.1898; Martha OLIVER, b.1833, d.1905; Alfred OLIVER, b.1823 d.1898; Elizabeth CORBETT, b. 1826, d.1889.

DEAN CEMETERY - John T. ALEXANDER, b.1795, d.1878; Justion Wilks ALEXANDER, b.1800, d.1880; Charles DEAN, b.1814, d.1883; James W. WILKS, b.1782, d.1868; Rebecca Ann WILKS, b.1840, d.1875.

LEE CEMETERY - Robert WRIGHT, b.1814, d.1885; Nancy WRIGHT, b.1817, d.1887; Charles WRIGHT, b.1843, d.1935; Rebecca WRIGHT, b.1848, d.1912.

COLUMBUS CEMETERY - M.H. WIGGINS (b.??, d.1870), Mary A. HARDEE (b.1802, d.1862), Alice C. BARCLAY (b.1848, d.1891), Mary R. BARCLAY (b.1849, d.1885), Mollie CANNON (b.1843, d.1890), Jackson CANNON (b.1823, d.1906).

GRANT CEMETERY - John H. GRANT (b.1841, d.1925), Nancy J. GRANT (b.1834, d.1892), Elminor E. ADAMS (b.1840, d.1924), J.M. ADAMS (b.1837, d.1911).

NEW HOPE METHODIST CEMETERY - Charlton HINES (b.1820, d.1856), John W. HINES (b.1822, d.1858), Joe F. (possibly Joab) BLACKMON (b.1835, d.1911), W.R. BEVAN (b.1832, d.1919), S.E. BEVAN (b.1832, d.1918), Elizabeth BEVAN (b.1837, d.1867), Emaline GIBBS (b.1846, d.1873), A.J. GIBBS (b.1847, d.1877), Christann HORNE (b.1843, d.??), Mary J. McDANIEL (1834, d.1910), T.T. McDANIEL (b.1821, d.1898), Eliza GIBBS (b.1840, d.1850), Elizabeth GIBBS (b.1814, d.1906), Thomas H. GIBBS (b. ?), d.1887), Johnny Mack SKEEN (b.1837, d.1939), John SKEEN (b.1826, d.1881), Mary SKEEN (b.1827, d.1904), J.D. DALRYMPLE (b.? , d.1876), Nancy F. DALRYMPLE (b.1846, d.1873), Alice G. KIRKPATRICK (b.1849, d.1885 Wife of Dr.Craven Lassiter), Mrs. M.A. MARTIN (b.1826, d.1869), Mrs. M.A. COBB (b.1828, d.1874), Mrs. A.D. DICKENSON (b.1803, d.1872), Rebecca E. McCORMICK (b.1825, d.1882), Callie A. SKEEN (b.1849, d.1897 Wife of Julius C. Skeen), George C. WHITE (b.1818, d.1905 Husband of Sarah F. White), Sarah F. WHITE (b.1824, d.1883), Joseph A. BOYD (b.1843 d.??), James WHITE (b.1846, d.1910), Ira DRAYTON (b.1850, d.1934), John Quincy SMITH (b.1835, d.1889), Elizabeth W. SMITH (1840, d.1908).

MIMS CEMETERY - John GOFF (b.1818, d.1883), ?? GOFF (b.1820, d.1860), Martha Jane SESSIONS (b.1841, d.1915), James MIMS (b.1785, d.1868), Mary MIMS (b.1812, d.1886), Nancy HART (b.1837, d.1898).

BRIDGES CEMETERY - James Frierson HUNT (b.??, d.1877), Caroline S. STOKES (b.1841, d.1910 Wife of Rev. James M. Stokes) Rev. James M. STOKES (b.1832, d.1876).

CHARLES CEMETERY - Rebecca CHARLES (b.1794, d.1852 Wife of

Reuben Charles).

GAMBLE CEMETERY - Henry P. GAMBLE (b.1839, d.1877), Mary F. GAMBLE (b.1843, d.1871).

MT.WILLING CEMETERY - Alfred WILLIAMS (b.1826, d.1918).

CLAYWOOD CEMETERY - Albert HOYE (b.1841, d.1910), Christmas HEMMING (b.1816, d.1920), Jane HEMMING (b.1844, d. 1923).

McCLELLAN CEMETERY - Emily Rosezella McCLELLAN (b.1849, d.1940), William H. McCLELLAN (b.1845, d.1914), B.J. WORRELL (b.1849, d.1915), Isabelle Sidney WORRELL (b.1842, d.1914), Philip E. LOWE (b.1835, d. 1892), Virginia T. LOWE (1844, d.1914), M. Clifford McCARDEL (b.1840, d.1877), Julia V. GOODBREAD (b.1833, d.1902), George E. McCLELLAN (b.1807, d.1866), S.S. McCLELLAN (b.1806, d.1860), C.J. McCLELLAN (b.1831, d.1833),T.T. McCLELLAN (b.1835, d.1836), G.R. McCLELLAN (b.1836, d.1843), Mary J. Ivey McLERAN (b.1838, d.1902), Jesse T. McLERAN (b.1832, d.1868), Rev. J.J. TAYLOR (b.1811, d.1862), Elizabeth TAYLOR (b.1812, d.1891), Robert C. MURDOCK (b.1836, d.1900), D.C.T. COLLINS (b.1832, d.1882), Pency I. COLLINS (b.1839, d.1899), William Clay MALLORY, M.D. (b.1836, d.1900), J.E. McDONALD (b.1841, d.1896), Mandola McDONALD (b.1839, d.1899), James T. NEELEY (b.1843, d.1912), Josephine M. NEELEY (b.1841, d.1919), John Henry TAYLOR (b.1835, d.1903), Joshua CUMMINS (b.1828, d.1900), Sarah PATTERSON (b.1846, d.1922), S.W. GARY (b.1837, d.1908), Mary A. PATTERSON (b.1830, d.1893), N.J. PATTERSON (b.1820, d.1890), Adolphus BROOKS (b.1849, d.1910), Mary Ann BROOKS (b.1849, d.1910), Susan Ann SPENCER (b.1823, d.1915), Hugh B. PATTERSON (b.1850, d.1886), Arabella PATTERSON (b.1843 in Camden Cty, Ga., d.1881), J.B. SPENCER (b.1816, d.1882), Brady L. MURDOCK (b.1843, d.1911), James F. MURDOCK (b.1842, d.1883).

HILDRETH CEMETERY - James PINKHAM (b.1820, d.1916), Talitha C. PINKHAM (b.1829, d.1892), Mary M. COLLINS (b.1847, d.1916.

ICHNETUCKNEE MEMORIAL CEMETERY - Maranda M. DAMPIER (b.1842, d.1904).

MT. GILEAD CEMETERY - Mrs. Kate HILTON (b.1847, d.1910) Charles F. O'HARA (b.1814, d.1885), Blanchie TISON (b.1828, d.1838), Henry TISON (b.1813, d.1885), Mary TISON (b.1837, d.1909), Sarah J. MERCER (b.1825, d.1890), Thomas R. MERCER (b.1809, d.1890), Emily MERCER (b.1842, d.1885), Elizabeth CANNON (b.1838, d.1906), W.A. McCOOK (b.1847, d.1911), Henry Jackson CANNON (b.1848, d.1925), Jane McCOOK (b.1850, d.1934), Phoeby CANNON (b.1830, d.1898), Annie PAGE (b.1849, d.1933), Dora Ann DEAN (b.1841, d.1938), Jeremiah B. DEAS (b.1828, d.1883), Mary Ann DEAS (b.1830, d.1888), Sarah A. JOHNSON (b.1819, d.1898), Elbert W. BLAND (b.1847, d.1933), S.M. DEAS (b.1832, d.1896), Zilphea DEAS (b.1839, d.1919), Sarah CLOW (b.1831, d.1908), Mary A. MARABLE (b.1825, d.1916), John A. MARABLE (b.1818, d.1900), I.R. HARDEE (b.1841, d.1914).

MARY BELLE CEMETERY - Mrs. Thomas G. BAXTER (b.1848, d.1919), Thomas G. BAXTER (No dates but served in Civil War), Ramsey SOLOMON (b.1845, d.1937), Caroline ROSIER (b.1840, d.1919), Rebecca M. JOWERS (b.1849, d.1922), J.H. JOWERS (b.1837, d.1914), Elisha WINBURN (b.1827, d.1901), Susan WINBURN (b.1831, d.1910), Mary G. BARROW (b.1849, d.1928), Joseph F. BARROW (b.1839, d.1904), Fannie E. GRIFFIN (b. b.1839, d.1934), Major Larkin L. GRIFFIN (b.1829, d.1910), E.D. GORNTOS (b.1817, d.1886), M.M. BLACKBURN (b.1826, d.1893), Julius A. ALLEN (b.1839, d.1893), Charlotte I. ALLEN (b.1844, d.1895), A.A. BLACKBURN (b.1814, d.1891), Ellen E. BLACKBURN (b. 1829, d.1901), Lucy Brantley HAWKINS (b.1831, d.1893), Bethelhugee H. H. HAWKINS (b.1823, d.1901), Epsie A. MORRIS (b.1840, d.1897), Robert J. MORRIS (b.1838, d.1911), James H. BURNETT (b. 1845, d.1926), William W. COATES (b.1842, d.1889), Mary E. COATES (b.1840, d.1909), James M. BRYAN (b.1813, d.1881), James R. LEWIS (b.1820, d.1889), Sarah Brinson ALLISON (b.1844, d.1877), Dr. William P. ALLISON (b.1821, d.1879), W.A. MARABLE (b.1849, d.1886), John W. ALLISON (b.1825, d.1906), Narcissa ALLISON (b. 1831, d.1902), William ALLISON (b.1794, d.1878), Mary F. Cress ALLISON (b.1798, d.1868), Moses EVANS (b.1811, d.1898), Adaline E. EVANS (b.1825, d.1901), W.H. SESSIONS (b.1847, d.1895), C.H. MARTIN (b.1849, d.1879), Sylvania CARROLL (b.1847, d.1885), Ella SESSIONS (b.1849, d.1909), John FRASER (b.1821, d.1890), Sophia FRASER (b.1821, d.1891), Savannah L. BLOUNT (b.1846, d.1883), Sydney BLOUNT (b.1830, d.1880), Elsie Ann BYNUM (b.or d. 1835), Dr. William Forsyth BYNUM (b.1832, d.1904), James R. BYNUM (b.@1830, d.???. Served in CSA), Lucy A. BYNUM (b.1833, d.1901. Married to James R. Bynum), A.D. HIGDEN (b.1822, d.1866), W.H. SLATE (b.1840, d.1886), Elvira KNIGHT (b.1826, d.1891), Amanda TAYLOR (b.1846, d.1917).

OAK GROVE CHURCH CEMETERY - Moriah SMITH (b.1835, d.1905), Mrs. Hunert DORSEY (b.1836, d.1900).

IVEY CEMETERY - Rev. William H. IVEY (b.1820, d.1868), Martha W. LANE (b.1842, d.1871), John Dorsey IVEY (b.1849, d.1883), Lydia Ann Long MARSHALL (b.1834, d.1876), Mary E. IRVINE (b.1840, d.1870), Hardy Conelius IVEY (b.1847, d.1864), Ann W. IVEY (b.1825, d.1891).

CEDAR GROVE CHURCH CEMETERY - Elizabeth Hall DAVIS (b.1849, d.1926), Joseph DUNHAM (b.1815, d.1887), Charles H. GROFF (b.1847, d.1886), Elizabeth A. GROFF (b.1848, d.1927), James Milledge HALL (b.1815, d.????), Sarah McClellan HALL (b.1820, d.????), Francis HALL (b.1846, d.????), Fleming HALL (b.1841, d.????),

ORANGE CHURCH CEMETERY - D.L. MATHIS (b.1833, d.1905), Winford MATHIS (b.1832, d.1925), Mrs. Fannie RILEY (b.1840, d.1925), Josephine MILLER (b.1840, d.1911), Elizabeth LANDEN (b.1809, d.1889), Lucy Landen HEWITT (b.1837, d.1909), Thomas P. LANDEN (b.1848, d.1895), John T. CLARK (b.1845, d.1928), Martha Elizabeth LANDEN (b.1848, d.1917), L.A. LANDEN (b.1845, d. 1927), Eliz SMITH (b.1841, d.1919), Martha E. Reed ROBINSON (b.1827, d.1889.

Wife of W.M. Robinson), G.W. CLARK (b.1834, d. 1915), Elizabeth LAMB (b.1838, d.1899), Susan Elisabetha Roberts PLATT (b.1842, d.1922), Esther Elizabeth Garnto ELLISON (b.1836, d.1915. Wife of Henry J. Ellison), William JOHNSON (b.1846, d.1936), Martha JONES (b.1830, d.1927. Wife of Gideon Jones), Gideon JONES (b.1838, d.1903. CSA), Lucinda WILLIAMS (b.1845, d. 1909), Charity Elizabeth WHATLEY (b.1847, d.1928), Lucy R. WHATLEY (b.1821, d.1905), Eliza Jane GOFF (b.1845, d.1924), Jehu GOFF (b.1848, d.1921).

MT. OLIVE BAPTIST - W.T. GARDNER (b.1846, d.1901), Sarah A. GARDNER (b.1834, d.1897), Margaret Wright Wood LEE (b.1840, d.1931), Hezekiah SMITH (b.1838, d.1910), Nancy W. SMITH (b.1843, d.1906), Martha Louisa ZIPPERER (b.1835, d.1925), T.J. ZIPPERER (b.1824, d.1915), Icy KNIGHTEN (b.1834, d.1906), Eliza RICHARDSON (b.1840, d.1917), Daniel Beantly? RICHARDSON (b. 1846, d.1933), Alicia P. SMALL (b.1850, d.1940), Nancy Connell LAW (b.1847, d.1929), S.B. LAW (b.1830, d.1905), J.H. BASS (b.@1830, d.@1920. Age 87 yrs), Mattie A. BASS (b.1843, d.1913), John Edward JONES (No dates. Served with McClellan & in CSA), R.E. CARROLL (b.1833, d.1905), Sarah E. CARROLL (b.1831, d.1904), William MIXON - b.1837, d.1905), V.W.A. HUTCHINSON (b.1840, d.1910), Mary E. HUTCHINSON (b.1844, d.1913), Sophie J. JOHNS (b.1846, d.1921).

ROCKY SINK BAPTIST CHURCH CEMETERY - Mary A. WOOLEY (b.1836, d.1925), Mary Bailey V. BROWN (b.1828, d.1914), Eugenia C. NEWLAN (b.1846, d.1922), Mary Jane NEWLAN (b.1847, d.1917), T.J. MITCHELL (b.1845, d.1909), Sarah Elizabeth MITCHELL (b.1845, d.1929), Sarah C. ROSS (b.1850, d.1929), Perry V. VOYLES (b.1823, d.1917).

JOHNSON CEMETERY - H.M. RICKERSON - (b.1810, d.1921).

DOWLING PARK CHURCH OF GOD CEMETERY - Rev.. William H. IVEY (b.1820, d.1868), Martha W. LANE (b.1842, d.1871), John Dorsey IVEY (b.1849, d.1883), Lydia Ann Marshall LONG (b.1834, d. 1876.), Mary E. Ivey IRVINE (b. 1840, d.1870), Hardy Cornelius IVEY (b.1847, d. 1864), Ann W. IVEY (b.1825, d.1891), John W. HON (b.1833, d. 1911), S. Jane RICE (b.1848, d.1911), B.A. PEEK (b.1848, d.1930), Col.W. IRVINE (b.1832, d.1882).

SCOTT CEMETERY - John R. SCOTT (b.1843, d.1904), Elizabeth Maynor SCOTT (b.1843, d.1908), Mary CANNON (b.1835, d. aft.1920).

SUWANNEE STATION - Rufus W. PHILLIPS (b.1830, d.1903), Anna R. PHILLIPS (b.1838, d.1897).

MT. OLIVE CHURCH OF CHRIST CEMETERY - John Henry CROSS (b.1849, d.1928), E.M.S. BLAIR (b.1847, d.1909), Nancy C.FLEMING (b.1838, d.1923), John C. OVERSTREET (b.1841, d.1921), Mary E. OVERSTREET (b.1840, d.1914), George W. O'HARA (b.1833, d.1910), A.M. HARRELL (b.1829, b.1910), Mary Jane LINDSEY (b.1835, d.1912), Sarah A. CLAYTON (b.1839, d. 1906), Corporal Milledge G. CLAYTON (b.1836, d.1903), Mrs. E.L. HARDEE (b.1843, b.1908), Martha E. MEEKS (b.1849 b.1916), Louise HARRELL (b.1811, d.1915), George W. DEMPSEY (b.1849 b.1921), William W. O'HARA (b.1847, d.1929).

ANTIOCH BAPTIST CHURCH (reputed to be the 2nd oldest church in the county) - John R. SESSIONS (b.1841 d.1888), F. KUNERT (b.1850 d.1913), Araminta A. ALLISON (b.1826 d.1902), George W. ALLISON (b.1822, d.1905), Mary L. CREEKMORE (b.1847, d.1946), A.R. CREEKMORE (b.1846, d.1898), Amanda Roberts BIRD (b.1836, d.1892), Sherrod BIRD (b.1823, d.1878), John W. LLOYD (b.1830, d.1902), Patience MILLS (b.1807, d.1868), A. MILLS (b.1814, d.1876), Martin V. MILLS (b.1847, d.1911), Charlton H. BRINSON (b.1843, d.1918), Martha A. BRINSON, (b.1847, d.1928), John W. BARNES (b.1846, d.1921), Cyprian BRINSON (b.1810, d.1875), Ann BRINSON (b.1818, d.1887), A.B. MORGAN (b.1845, d.1922), Roxiann Sapp MORGAN (b.1850, d.1927), James L. HADDOCK (b.1850, d.1934), David STAPLETON, Sr. (b.1837, d.1901), Eliza WOOD (b.1818, d.1886), Betti Wood LYONS (b.1849, d.1889), Mary J. MIKELL (b.1838, d.1908), James MIKELL (b.1834, d.1911), Allen WILLIAMS (b.1826, d.1891), John W. COATES (b.1830, d.1895), Eliza M. COATES (b.1836, d.1907), Miss C.S. MORRISON (b.1830, d.1916), Thomas W. FERGUSON (b.1836, d.1892), Maggie L. Wilson BURNETT (b.1819, d.1895), J.H. BURNETT (b.1814, d.1897), Henry CRAVENS (b.1849, d.1877), James BRANNON (b.1846, d.1873), Carrie G. DAVIS (b.1849, d.1874), Nancy BEVAN (b.1848, d.1906), G.W. BEVAN (b.1838, d.1909), Robert F. ALLISON (b.1831, b.1910), Laura J. ALLISON (b.1848, d.1898), Rev. A.J.FUTCH (b.1845, d.1933), Martha Lucille HANKINS (b.1847, d.1900).

VALHALLA CEMETERY - Wiley TISON, b.1812, d.1883; Jim POWELL, b.????, d.1860; Martha POWELL, b.????, d.1865, Isom DEESE, b.???? d.1878.

BRANNON CEMETERY - Benjamin U. BRANNON, b.????, d.???? (No dates, however he served in the Civil War. We also know his wife was born in 1838.

HARDEE CEMETERY - Cornelius HARDEE, b.1837, d.1900; Laura D. HARDEE, b.1845, d.1917.

DELAWARE A.M.E.CEMETERY - Lancaster STEWART, b.1824, d.1888; Vins FREEMAN, b.1834, d.1920.

MT. PLEASANT CEMETERY - James A. GRIFFIN (b.1836, d.1910,) Sallie E. GRIFFIN (b.1844, d.1889), Jacob Y. PURVIS (b.1822, d.1888), Alfred JERNIGAN (b.1816, d.1890), Emiline JERNIGAN (b.1843, d.1918), Mahaly A. HANCOCK (b.1825, d.1884), Simon HANCOCK (b.1824, d.1883), Mary V. CARVER (b.1842, d.1923), Winnie WOOD (b.1830, d.1900), Fannie HANCOCK (b.1832, d.1898), J.J. SEALEY (b.1843, d.1889), Aura Zenobia Rich SEALEY (b.1843, d.1920), Wyley ROBERTS (b.1808, d.1873), W.R. BELL (b.1842, d.1872), Mary P. BELL (b.1822, d.1881), Lemon P. ELLIS, (b.1845, d.1918), John W. TOMPKINS (b.1837, d.1909), Antonette O. TOMPKINS (b.1839, d.1910), Mary CHAMBLISS (b.1829, d.1892), Isaac E. OGDEN (b.1802, d.1861), Sarah R. OGDEN (b.1814, d.1885), Laura CHAMBLISS (b.1847, d.1878), M.E.COBB (b.1840, d.1907), T.J. COBB (b.1830, d.1896), Elizabeth FIELDING (b.1832, d.1902), Reed OGDEN (b.1849, d.1895), G.R. OGDEN (b.1839, d.1885), Elmira F. BRADDOCK (b.1848, d.1838), Henry BRADDOCK (b.1844, d.1924), James A. GRIFFIN (b.1836, d.1910), Tabitha HELTON (b.1817, d.1897), Washington HELTON (b.1806, d.1883), S.M. PARKER (b.1847, d.1936), Michael BROOKER (b.1810, d.1889), Jackson MORGAN (b.1815, d.1882), Robert L. ALLEN (b.1842, d.1882), Sallie L. HAWKINS (b.1843, d.1928), Jane HUTCHINGSON (b.1820, d.1885), Abel J. HUTCHINGSON (b.1814, d.1882), Sarah M. HART (b.1840, d.1926), Thomas W. HART (b.1840, d.1909), William C. CHAMBLISS (b.1837, d.1889), Laura CHAMBLISS (b.1847, d.1873), Henrietta D. BEADLER (b.1843, d.1869), W.S. RILEY (b.1849, d.1901), William SAVER (b.1838, d.1923).

CARVER CEMETERY - (NOTE: A lot of people were buried here including as many as as 50 slaves. There are no less than 34 unmarked graves.) The ones before 1850 that are marked are as follows: William CARVER (b. 1839, d.1885), Henry Wilson CARVER (No dates, but as a Civil War veteran, it is assumed he was born bef.1850), Feariba CARVER (b.1819, d.1877), Sampson CARVER (b.18?9, d.1894), Jesse P. STANSEL (b.1824, d.1872)

LITTLE RIVER CEMETERY - Zalpah Sandlin BRYAN (b.1843, d.1922), Nathan L. BRYAN (b.1839, d.1914), Joseph S. HOGANS, (b.1841, d.1899), Andrew J. GRESHAM Sr. (b.1819, d.1877), Zelia S. GRESHAM (b.1825, d.1910), Martha A. MILLS (b.1842, d.1920), Henry L. MILLS (b.1842, d.1901), John A. MILLS (b.1811, d.1892), John W. ROBERTSON (b.1815, d.1881), W. LEAK (b.1806, d.1874), E.K. GOFF (b.1846, d.1926), Jane D. HAMILTON (b.1836, d.1895), Abigill GAYLARD (b.1814, d.1882), Nathan R. GAYLARD (b.1820, d.1899), Samuel B. HAWKINS (b.1847, d.1853), David L. HAWKINS (b.1843, d.1853), Jane HAWKINS (b.1826, d.1883), Howell Sharp HAWKINS (b.1818, d.1887), Sophronia HAWKINS (b.1845, d.1897), Thomas H. HAWKINS (b.1845, d.1919), W.T. McLERAN (b.1825, d.1860), Rebecca McLERAN (b.1801, d.1855), Nevin McLERAN (b.1795, d.1852), Nancy V. GOFF (b.1832, d.1897), John GOFF (b.1828, d.1908), Daniel GAYLARD (b.1847, d.1912), James PARRISH (b.1840, d.1906), Doryann PARRISH (b.1842, d.1902), Mary VANN (b.1830, d.1907), and Homer TYSON (b.1830, d.1917).

EASTSIDE CITY CEMETERY - Mariah HOWARD (b.1843, d.1941), Nathaniel BROWN (b.1837, d. 1908), Rev. J.N. STOKES Sr. (b.1839, d.1908), Walter THOMAS (b.1831, d.????), Stephen MILLER (b.1832, d.1912), Maria MILLER (b.1825, d.1926).

HOUSTON CEMETERY - Charlie M. INGALLS (b.1845, d. 1914), Nellie C. INGALLS (b.1847, d.1916), Robert T. O'NEAL (b.1848, d.1905), Dr. W.M. HICKS (b.1838, d.1900), Ann HICKS (b.1836, d.1914), Dr. David Yearsley BLAIR (b.1830, d.1869), Sarah Ann WHITE (b.1844, d.1922), John Fletcher WHITE (b.1824, d.1901), Martha Faw WHITE (b.1826, d.1865), Dr. C.T. McMANNEN (b.1834, d.1907), Mary J. MORGAN (b.1838, d.1886), George W. ALLEN (b.1823, d.1876).

MT. BEULAH CEMETERY - H.M. STEVENS (b.1824, d.1921), Asa STEVENS (b.1822, d.1903), Eliza STRICKLAND (b.1812, d.1892), Mary J. BLUME (b.1822, d.1901), Henry M. BLUME (b.1830, d.1903), J.M.

ARRINGTON (b.1846, d.1925), Susan O. ARRINGTON (b.1848, d.1920), Naomi MOSELEY (b.1824, d.1896), Robert McCreary MOSELEY (b.1827, d.1899), Henry H. MOSELEY (b.1835, d.1896), Millie Ann MOSELEY (b.1835, d.1926), Angeline PARNELL (b.1833, d.1907), S.W. PARNELL (b.1815, d.1891), William S. NEWSOME (b.1849, d.1917), A.E. DANIELS (b.1823, d.1908), Adeline E. DANIELS (b.1841, d.1911), Mahaley Ussery BRANNON (b.1838, d.1906), Carolina C. STANSEL (b.1834, d.1904), Levicia HENDRICK (b.1842, d.1915), William H.C. HENDRICK (CSA soldier), Henry HOLTZCLAW (b.1844, d.1925), W.T. STANSEL (b.1849, d.1920), Mary J. MILLER (b.1837, d.1920),William M. MOSELEY (b.1849, d.1928).

NEW ZION CEMETERY - Mary Ann SCOTT (b.1848, d.1927), Mary WASHINGTON (b.1828, d.1940...112 years of age).

OAK GROVE MEMORIAL CEMETERY - John M. HALL (b.19848, d.1916), Pliason B. HALL (b.1844, d.1924), Robert A. IVEY (b.1847, d.1925), Sarah J. YOUNG (b. 1838. d.1907), Ephraim J. YOUNG (b.1831, d.1898), W.J. PETERSON (b.1849, d.1900), Ellen Jane PETERSON (b.1848, d.1898), Dr. William SIMPSON (b.1837, d.1891), James W. BRADLEY (b.1848, d.1924), Mrs. M.W. INGLISH (b.1840?, d.1915), M.W. INGLISH (b.1839, d.1897), Virginia MARTIN (b.1847, d.1903), Samuel M. MARTIN (b.1847, d.1922), J.N. STEPHENS (b.1833, s.1916), Harriet S. STEPHENS (b.1834, d.1911), Andrew Jackson CANNON (b.1840, d.1923), Mrs. A.M. DORSETT (b.1828, d.1902).

ADVENT CHRISTIAN CEMETERY - Rev. A. GORDON (b.1833, d.1921), Miss Annie STEWART (b.1845, d.1920), Miss Susan FLETCHER (b.1842, d.1918).

FRIENDSHIP CEMETERY - Mrs.Emily GREEN - (b.1840, d.1917), Thomas GREEN (b.1843, d.1900), Joseph A. WILLIAMS (b.1847, d.1883), Laura J. WREDE (b.1849, d.1926), Edward F. WREDE (b.1825, d.1899), Sanford BOND (b.1847, d.1912), Lucretia Ann WILLIAMS (b.1845, d.1913), William Paulhill WILLIAMS (b.1844, d.1920), Robert HOOKENSMITH (b.1829, d.1910), Andrew M. McCLELLAN (b.1810, d.1880), Christianna Watts McCLELLAN (b.1814, d.1890), Joshua McCLELLAN (b.1830, d.1954?), Robert HART (b.1848, d.1932), Margaret E. HART (b.1844, d.1910), Harriet QUIETTE (b.1831, d.1915), E.W. HURST (b.1810, d.1911), Georgia A. HURST (b.1842, d.1928).

BETHLEHEM CEMETERY - Grant BRINSON (b.1849, d.1935), Abraham PALMER? (b.1834, d.????).

CLAYLAND CEMETERY - William N. McLEOD (b.1802, d.1872), Mary Alday McLEOD (b.1811, d.1905), John BRIM (b.1832, d.1925), Nancy BRIM (b.1841, d.1925).

HOUSTON CEMETERY - Josephine JOHNSON (b.1849, d.1922), Isaac ALEXANDER (b.1840, d.1914).

IDA GROVE CEMETERY - W.M. SUMNER (b.1846, d.1909), Balzora SUMNER (b.1844, d.1921).

LAKE BUTLER CEMETERY - Albert STOCKTON (b.1832, d.????).

LEONA MEMORIAL CEMETERY - Elizabeth A. BLACKMON (b.1844, d.1931), William BLACKMON (b.1847, d.1925), Richard A. HOWELL (b.1830, d.1907), Lucy A. NEWSON (b.1830, d.1911), Mrs. R.J. BLACK (b.1834, d.1926), James B. BLACK (b.1828, d.1896).

MACEDONIA CEMETERY - Emmerline BAILEY (b.1841, d.1917), Thomas BAILEY (b.1846, d.1897), Jane CARROLL (b.1827, d.1894), Matilda CARROLL (b.1827, d.1885), Briton CARROLL (b.1838, d.1893), Mary Ann BRANNAN (b.1845, d.1918), W.F. BRANNAN (b.1842, d.1904), Adaline Baxter HART (b.1814, d.1880), Robert A. REID (b.1843, d.1897), Rev. M.W. MIXSON (b.1814, d.1874), Mrs. Mattie HURST (b.1849, d.1917), J.T. HURST (b.1848, d.1916), Paralee GREEN (b.1836, d.1875), T.T. HURST (b.1831, d.1902), Nancy Jowers CARROLL (b.1820, d.1885), Annie Jowers NEVEILS (b.1841, d.1917), William A. NEVEILS (b.1844, d.1920), Mary Jowers HOBBS (b.1845, d.????).

MT. PISGAH CEMETERY - G.R. KIRKLAND (b.1835, d.1916), Sarah A. KIRKLAND (b.1832, d.1922), ?. ?. ROBERTS (b.1844, d.1931), Mary Jane JOHNS (b.1846, d.1930), Harriet Johns ROBERTS (b.1839, d.1927), Mrs. H.M. CARVER (b.1849, d.1894), T.J. WILLIAMS (b.1822, d.1909), Mary Amanda WILLIAMS (b.1834, d.1883), Mary Jane TAYLOR (b.1847, d.1934), Joseph K. TAYLOR (b.1836, d.1909), G.F. GARDNER (b.1845, d.1914), William R. DAUGHTRY (b.1846, d.1937), Sallie DAUGHTRY (b.1849, d.1921), James DAUGHTRY (b.1810, d.1897), Susie Harrell HARPER (b.1831, d.1915), Rebecca LONG (b.1823, d.1901), Angeline L. BADEN (b.1843, d.1923), J.S. BADEN (b.1840, d.1903), Eliza HERNDON (b.1841, d.1914), W.M. WARREN (b.1841, d.1902), John J. HOLMES (b.1847, d.1924), Mariah HOLMES (b.1849, d.1920).

NEW HARMONY CEMETERY - Caroline MOSES (b.1846, d.1924), John P. HOWLAND (b.1847, d.1930), Thomas J. McCALL (b.1837, d.1912), G.B. COLE (b.1824, d.1901), Mary M.E. THOMPSON (b.1842, d.1925), Isabella D. IVEY (b.1838, d.1883), Jasper N. IVEY (b.1827, d.1889), Elizabeth CLARK (b.1831, d.1906), William Wycliffe ROGERS (b.1822, d.1889), Lavinia A. ROGERS (b.1839, d.1917), Sarah A. GAMBLE (b.1807, d.1896), J.N. GAMBLE (b.1842, d.1921), Eliza A. GAMBLE (b.1842, d.1903), L.A. YOUNG (b.1825, d.1893), Cornelia H. YOUNG (b.1830, d.1924), Alfred SURRENCY (b.1840, d.1900), Sarah SURRENCY (b.1844, d.1920), Emma C. WHITMAN (b.1842, d.1890), Amanda BALLENTINE (b.1812, d.1881), Mrs. GAMBLE (b.1846, d.1922...mother of William), Annis ADAMS (b.1834, d.1917), George W. HERRING (b.1849, d.1922).

PINE LEVEL CEMETERY - Marcus D. BUSH (b.1842, d.1944).

PLEASANT HILL CEMETERY - Alexander LEE (b.1843, d.1921), Samantha STARLING (b.1828, d.1919), Lizzie A. KNAPP (b.1843, d.1920), Robert A. JENKINS (b.1848, d.1901), J.A.M. NOBLES (b.1835, d.1909), William P. NOBLES (No dates. CSA soldier & husband of J.A.M.Nobles, presumably born bef.1850), William H. HILLHOUSE (b.1844, d.1909), Susan N. HILLHOUSE (b.1848, d.1936),

B.D. HARRELL (b.1836, d.1916).

PHILADELPHIA CEMETERY - Eliza B. MILLS (b.1835, d.1903), Ada G. MILLS (b.1837, d.1906), Johnnie Mitchell JOHNSON (b.1809, d.1895), Nancy HINGSON (b.1820, d.1889), James H. JENKINS (b.1832, d.1909), John O. ROSS (b.1846, d.1929), Roxie Ann ROSS (b.1842, d.1900), Jane R. HINGSON (b.1843, d.1939), John R. HINGSON (b.1842, d.1895), Susan F. WALKER (b.1849, d.1910), Eliza JOHNAN (b.1830, d.1892), F.M. THOMAS (b.1832, d.1911), George H. ROSS (b.1849, d.1895), R.J. LANIER (b.1819, d.1900), Emmaline LANIER (b.1833, d.1916), Mahalam BOATRIGHT (b.1848, d.1917), Ama Huel BOATRIGHT (b.1825, d.1900), A.M. FRIER (b.1843, d.1910), Levi H. CHESHIRE (b.1849, d.1913), Sarah H. CHESHIRE (b.1849, d.1914), Robert G. CLARY (b.1849, d.1929), Luvenia RANKIN (b.1836, d.1922), Asa G. RANKIN (b.1839, d.1920), Mary STRICKLAND (b.1831, d.1901), Julia C. HERRING (b.1849, d.1929), William W. HERRING (b.1843, d.1927).

BEULAH BAPTIST CHURCH CEMETERY - William T. RICHARDSON (b.1842, d.1919), J.E. BAXTER (b.1817, d.1913), Mary Tidwell BAXTER (b.1823, d.1922), M. ALBRITTON (b.1839, d.1919), Levi STARLING (b.1838, d.1926), Patrick CARROLL (b.1836, d.1916).

CRAWFORD LAKE CEMETERY - Myra BELL (b.1829, d.1911), Welthy Ann DOWNING (b.1849, d.1919), John Ruben STANFORD (b.1846, d.1916), Elsie E. ROWDEN (b.1838, d.1911), Mary A. DeSHAZO (b.1843, d.1936), Elizabeth A. BLANTON (b.1831, d.1916), David T. BLANTON (b.1825, d.1909).

McALPIN ADVENT CHRISTIAN CEMETERY - Cynthia Jane Roberts GRIFFIN (b.1844, d.1913), J.J. BONNELL (b.1846, d.1926), Mary A. BONNELL (b.1844, d.1934), Joseph D. RAGAN (b.1838, d.1919).

SCOTT CEMETERY - Elizabeth Maynar SCOTT (b.1843, d.1908), John R. SCOTT (b.1843, d.1907).

WARNER FARM CEMETERY - F.M. WARNER (b.1825, d.1894).

LIVE OAK CEMETERY - James M. BARCLAY (b.1849, d.1920), Rev. Robert M. EVANS (b.1847, d.1924), M.C. MILLS (b.1832, d.1910), Oliver LYON (b.1821, d.1908), George A. LYON (b.1849, d.1912), Lecretia Devall WILSON (b.1837, d.1934), Rev. J.A. KIMMONS (b.1824, d.1905), Henrietta Phillips CLARK (b.1838, d.1902), Elizabeth Putnam PORTER (b.1827, d.1907), John Wesley SPERRING (b.1833, d.1914), Sarah Ann SPERRING (b.1832, d.1924), John W. CAMPBELL (b.1830, d.1910), William McDANIEL (b.1835, d.1906), Martha McDANIEL (b.1843, d.1924), John F. McCLELLAN (b.1830, d.1884), Susan Frances McCLELLAN (b.1842, d.1924), Rev. Curtis GRUBB (b.1849, d.1930), Urich D. HIGGINS (b.1847, d.1909), John H. COCKCROFT (b.1838, d.1913), Thomas C. BRADFORD (b.1841, d.1915), Presley G. AMBROSE (b.1848, d.1928), Louise T. AMBROSE (b.1849, d.1935), Mary S. BACHE (b.1836, d.1925), A. WILSON (b.1846, d.1934), Mattie WILSON (b.1840, d.1923), Lillian Pinkney LUCAS (b.1849, d.1926), John W. ROBERTSON (b.1815, d.1881), Sarah Ann Whitehurst ROBERTSON (b.1821, d.1896), Robert F. STRANG (b.1848, d.1904), Mary B. BLAIR (b.1827, d.1907), Mary Ann Barnett DOWLING (b.1846, d.1930), George Dallas DOWLING (b.1846, d.1905), Silas T. OVERSTREET (b.1830, d.1905), Carrie KNOX (b.1840, d.1903), Michael C. BURNS (b.1825, d.1904), Mary E. BURNS (b.1838, d.1906), Dr. W.S. AIRTH (b.1849, d.1900), Jane D. McARTHER (b.1848, d.1935), Elijah McARTHER (b.1848, d.1921), W.B. MICKLER (b.1844, d.1913), William D. HANKINS (b.1845, d.1925), Caroline Weaver HANKINS (b.1847, d.1937), Rev. Thomas Joseph PHILLIPS (b.1842, d.1909), Daniel W. TEDDER (b.1832, d.1911), Mary Ann M. TEDDER (b.1843, d.1922), Sallie MORRIS (b.1800, d.1903), Emma HAIR (b.1848, d.1934), David C. HARVARD (b.1848, d.1926), Charles N. HILDRETH (b.1842, d.1934), Daniel Munn McALPIN (b.1844, d.1893), Amanda C. BEVAN (b.1841, d.1915), George W. TOWNSEND (b.1848, d.1924), Sarah J. WILLIAMS (b.1839, d.1912), Elizabeth CANTRELL (b.1839, d.1917), John PARSHLEY (b.1813, d.1868), Lewis DOWLING (b.1848, d.1909), Mahaly DOWLING (b.1815, d.1910), H.F. DEXTER (b.1848, d.1907), Henry Mussy JOHNSON (b.1836, d.1909), Katherine Phillips JOHNSON (b.1837, d.1936), Samuel Pope MAYS (b.1845, d.1913).

UNION CEMETERY - Benjamin Franklin McCOLISTER (b.1848, d.1919), Mattie HALL (b.1848, d.1919), Arabelle HATCHER (b.1838, d.1926), John HATCHER (b.1832, d.1909), A.W. JACKSON (b.1836, d.1899), John N. BARNETT (b.1835, d.1916), Julia A. BARNETT (b.1839, d.1914), Ozias Wesley McCORMICK (b.1833, d.1911), James T. CRAWFORD (b.1833, d.1919), Susan M. ERNEST (b.1820, d.1896), Andrew J. AGEE (b.1836, d.1921), Susan F. AGEE (b.1843, d.1908).

SANTA FE CEMETERY - W.J. CROSIER (b.1835, d.1914), Lucy CROSIER (b.1846, d.1920), J.W. BRADSHAW (b.1848, d.1922), M.M. CORLEY (b.1849, d.1918), John D. DALE (b.1833, d.1901), Nancy A. MILTON (b.1835, d.1900), Henry R. MILTON (b.1821, d.1900), Mrs. Emily SCOTT (b.1840, d.1902), Anna Marla DeHART (b.1815, d.1887), Benjamin A. SMITHIE (b.1849, d.1894), John A. GILLEY (b.1846, d.1920), Annie E. LANIER (b.1831, d.1890), John BIBBY (b.1843, d.1925), Martha A. BIBBY (b.1849, d.1934), J.H. LACQUEY (b.1833, d.1887), Mary Westfall COLLINS (b.1848, d.1923).

WELLBORN CEMETERY - Carrie CUSHMAN (b.1845, d.1929), James J. CONNELL (b.1846, d..1931), A.W. MIZELLE (b.1845, d.1913), Thomas F. HARRISON (b.1849, d.1923), William A. TISON (b.1845, d.1922), Lucinda KEEFE (b.1827, d.1906), G.B. WALTER (b.1832, d.1921), E.A. WALTER (b.1834, d.1907), Rev. J.R. SAVAGE (b.1829 in N.Y., d.1903), Smithy BROCK (b.1838, d.1916), Martin BROCK (b.1846, d.1905), Emma J. RIVERS (b.1845, d.1924), D.J. RIVERS (b.1847, d.1928).

GODBOLD-WILLIAMS CEMETERY - James D. GODBOLD (b.1825, d.????), Susan C. GODBOLD (b.1827, d.1891), James S. GODBOLD (No dates. Served in CSA in Civil War. Probable pre-1850 birth).

CHAMBERS FAMILY CEMETERY - Martha O. CHAMBERS (b.1829, d.1900), Rev. Kinsey CHAMBERS (b.1814, d.1889), Asa A. STEWART (b.1813, d.1880), Carrie DUPREE (b.1840, d.1901).

MOUNT ZION CEMETERY - Henry NOEGEL (b.1828, d.1903), Mary NOEGEL (b.1840, d.1908), Apalonia BAUER (b.1813, d.1884), Sarah A.E. MILLER (b.1827, d.1907), Samuel Jordan WOODS (b.1848, d.1912), Mary A. WALDRON (b.1843, d.1911).

MISCELLANEOUS ARTICLES
Chapter 12

STATE AND COUNTY CHANGES

I was skimming through some materials recently and ran into an interesting statement. The statement read, "From 1728 to as late as 1863, a person born or living in Virginia could have actually been living in Illinois (1781-1818), Indiana (1787-1816), Kentucky or Maryland (1775-1792), North Carolina (1728-1779), Ohio (1778-1803), Pennsylvania (1752-1786), Tennessee (1760-1803), or West Virginia (1769-1863). How could this be? Very easily. Until these states became states they were part of Virginia. If your ancestor was living in any of the above areas during the specified dates...the records would be found in the Virginia Archives in Richmond...not in the states mentioned.

The same idea holds true in our Suwannee County. A person living in the area that is now Suwannee County could find records in St. John's county (1822-1824), Alachua county (1824-1832) or Columbia county (1832-1858). If your great-grandparents (depending on your age) were living in Live Oak area in 1850...their records would be found in Columbia County since 1832...or Alachua County during the years 1824-1832...or St.John's County during 1822-1824. If they lived here before 1821, their records would probably be found in St. Augustine or Pensacola (both Spanish settlements before Florida became a United States territory.

An individual could have lived in the Suwannee County area during 1800-1860 and be counted a resident of a foreign country and 5 Florida counties during that time...1) Spain (pre-1800 to 1821), 2) St.John's County (1821-1822), 3) Duval County (1822-1824), 4) Alachua County (1824-1832), and 5) Columbia County (1832-1858). Suwannee became a county on December 21, 1858. In 1845, when Florida graduated from being a "Territory" to become a bonafide "State", only 66,000 people lived in Florida...including slaves! When Suwannee became a county the population was 2,302 individuals...1,467 whites and 835 slaves.

HELPFUL INFORMATION SOURCES

Is your research leading you to points north...places like the Carolina's or Virginia, the following sources may be able to help by providing books/information relevant to that area. A little known source for Virginia (especially the southwest quarter of the state is the Bassett Public Library, Rt.7, Box 250, Bassett, Va. 24055. Its a small library, but it has a lot of info and the workers are quite helpful. Drop them a line. The Iberian Publishing Co. located in Athens, Ga. at 548 Cedar Creek Drive has excellent source materials. Again, it is small but has some very significant offerings. A company that specializes in Virginia books and maps is Heritage Books, Inc., 1540-E Pointer

Ridge Place, Bowie, MD 20716. Another small company that deals with most of the states is Heritage Papers, P.O. Box 7776, Athens GA 30604-7776.

I have found a listing of available books on Florida. Some may prove helpful. I will list them here. "Florida Territory in 1844" by E.C. Anderson, "Travels of William Bartram from 1773-1778" (traveled through North Florida), "Battey & Company" (contains biographical data on early settlers of Florida & Georgia), "Fort Mellon: 1837-1842" by A.E. Francke (deals with 2nd Seminole War), "Who Was Who in Florida" by H.S. Marks (brief biographies of early settlers from early 1800's to 1972), "Florida During the Territorial Days 1821-1845" by S.W. Martin, "The Georgia-Florida Frontier" by R.K. Murdoch (from 1793-1796), "Florida Map @1825" from Hinton Pub. (Shows county lines and roads, etc.), "American Centennial Newspapers from Florida" (@1876. Microfilm. Arranged alphabetically by city and title), and "Florida State Censuses 1825-1945" comes on 14 microfiche.

NOTES FROM "THE AMERICAN SIBERIAN"

In 1891 J.C. POWELL wrote of the lives of those involved in the Florida Prison System in a place called Padlock, Florida during the years 1876-1890. Padlock was about 5 miles south of Live Oak, Florida...not too far from Sing Sing...another prison camp about 4 miles from Padlock. Florida was a rough countryside in those days...thick forests, swamplands, diseases, alligators, wild animals, Indians, etc. The following names were found in the writing. They include both prisoners and guards among others. They were, Noble HAWKINS of Nassau County, FL., Major H.A. WISE, a merchant in Live Oak, Green CHEERS of Leon County, FL., W.F. POWELL, J.C.'s brother who was in charge of the prison, Robert and Eugene WEAVER, prisoners from the north, Cy WILLIAMS, a Negro prisoner, John PONDE, a murderer from Bradford County, George TURNER, a guard, FREEMAN, McPHERSON & PERRY, prisoners, Louis FENNISON, a trustee, Rodger WAH, commissary man, Henry STEVENS, a trustee, John ROBERTS & William REVEL, two farm boys serving 1 year. Later they went to Waycross, Ga. Buck HARDER, backwoodsman, Joseph ALSTON, a guard, FRY, HURST, Cyrus COOKS, Sol LOVE, prisoners, HURST, a guard (no relation to the above mentioned prisoner named HURST), McINTYRE, a guard, Peter REDDICK and George GOMEZ, prisoners, WATSON, a Negro preacher from Madison County, FL. serving time for stealing cotton, Thomas JUMP, a backwoodsman from Hernando County, FL., Simon MOODY, a Negro from Bradford County, FL., CLOW, a druggist, James PETERSON, a thief sent from Gainesville, FL., Jim JOHNSON, Columbus SEE, John G. LIPPFORD, and William WILLIAMS, convicts, W.J. HILLMAN, Captain of one of the convict camps, Henry DUNCAN, a Negro Assistant Cook, Miss Lizzie POWELL, wife of J.C. POWELL who came from South Georgia, John STEELE, a deputy sheriff, Mrs. REDDING, a rape victim, Jack BAKER, a convict, Georgianna ABBOTT, a female convict, George SMITH, a convict The following are all turpentine contractors...E.B. BAILEY, from Monticello,

FL., J.A. CRAWFORD, from Columbia County, FL., R.A. WILLIAMS and C.K. DUTTON, from Suwannee County, FL., and J.W. WEST, from Hamilton County, FL. W.W. WILLINGHAM, convicted of killing two men...a man named ROCKNER and his brother-in-law...a man named McLAUGHLIN, Robert ROWLEY, a convict from Pensacola, Daniel BLACKBURN, a Floridian, Jack TREPPARD, a convict from Louisville, a Mr. PLANT of the Plant Investment Co., E.D. OWENS of New York, Captain FITZGERALD, Mr. HILDRETH of Live Oak, FL., Henry SIMMONS, a convict, Henry HOWELL, a guard, Dr. HAWKINS, the prison doctor, Charles JOURDAN, a convict, Arthur GLEATON, a guard, Will DARE, a convict whose true name was discovered to be William PORTER, brother of the Mayor of Nashville, TN. His mother was Mrs. Mary PORTER of Nashville, TN. Charles KELLY, a convict from the north, John McCARTY, from County of Cork, Ireland, Tom HEALEY, a guard, Handsome KEENE, a woman convict, Mr. WILDER, a convict runner, Marietta WILLIAMS, a female Negro convict who turned out to be a man in disguise, Mr. W.T. HILLMAN, W.P. POWELL's assistant, Edward BELL, Alice FRANKLIN, female convict, LANIER, a guard, Silas B. CARTER, pardoned convict, Mr. MILLS, a guard, William BRYANT, William TYNER, and John ANDERSON, convicts, REED, a guard, Allan DAVIS, trustee, RAYFORD, a citizen of an area just north of Valdosta, Ga., SESSIONS, sheriff of Live Oak, FL., Charles SPRINGER and Sol SIMONS, convicts, John EVANS, a mulatto, RODGERS, a guard, W.B. PHILLIPS, a guard, John JACOBS, James GOINGS, and William ALEXANDER, convicts, Col./Judge WHITE, Frank JOHNSON, convict, Louis RICHARD, guard, Tony TUCKER, convict, JONAKER, Richard EVANS, sheriff & city marshall of Pensacola, FL., Calvin GRIFFIN, Bill NEWLAND, guard, William FILER, trustee, T.J. LEVERETT, guard, Thomas NETTLES, PRINCE, brother-in-law of Thomas NETTLES, a shingle maker, Jesse SIMPKINS, a one-armed trustee from Madison County, FL., GILCHRIST, guard, Dave WALKER, negro convict, R.A. MILLS, guard, Alexander LEGE and Nathan SHELL, convicts, John Key WEST, trustee, Dick EVANS, convict who was a police officer, Gus POTTSDAMER, city marshall of Lake City, FL., HENRY, a sheriff, William HADLEY, Walter SHAVERS, convict, Captain HENDERSON, a guard from Cedartown, Ga., H.S. HAINES, general superintendent of the S.F.& W. Railroad, Jason MOORE, a sub-foreman who died, William RICH, guard, Jack POWELL & W.A. DURDEN, both found guilty of murder. DURDEN was POWELL's stepfather. He lived near Ochesa on the Appalachicola River, Jack FORRESTER, a sub-foreman from Cedartown, Ga., J.W. BAKER, a judge, Mr. DRAIN, a railroad agent, Marcellos FERNANDEZ, Maud FOSTER, woman convict from New York, Jim OTA, Smith OLIVER, a convict who murdered fellow prisoner Horace STALSWORTH, Thomas NIX, settled in Randolph County, Ga., John JACOBS, negro outlaw, Pump CRUTCHFIELD, a sheriff, Col. HART, Beverly LEWIS, convict, Horace STALSWORTH, convict from Pensacola who was murdered by Smith OLIVER, Jackson COX and Joseph WILLIAMS, convicts, Bill HARRISON, Live Oak resident, Hardy HAYS, James McDANIELS from Washington, D.C. and John KELLY from St. Augustine...both convicts, Sol PHILLIPS, guard, HEWITT, FENNISON, & GREEN, convict cooks, "Doc" MONTAGUE, life convict, Frank MANNING, Harvey TODD, Alexander GADSEN, Henry WILLIAMS, and Samuel JOHNSON, convicts, Mr. ROLLINS, an old settler, George

BALL, convict from Pensacola, FL., Captain Charles P. JOLLY, T.J. LEVERETT, William BRYANT & Daniel BASS, horsetraders. Convicted of murdering a man named MOORE from Georgia.

CAROLINA GLEANINGS

"Carolina Gleanings" is a periodical concerning folks in the South Carolina region in the early days. The edition of that periodical is underlined. The date in parenthesis after the name is the birth date of the individual. (Spring, 1989) Moses HENDRICKS Sr.(1760), Moses HENDRICKS Jr. (1793), William Robert GAFFORD (1790), George MOCK (@1720), John HOLLAND (1778), Benjamin KIRKLAND (1794), Richard BAKER (@1718), Joseph HACKNEY (1778), (December 1990) John STEWART (@1760). The following were involved in land transactions in and around 1790 in Rutherford County, S.C.; David DICKEY (Surveyor), William GILBERT, John HOLLAND, James GLASGOW, Willoughby WILLIAMS, John BRYAN, Phil HAWKINS, Daniel THATCHER, Robert MILLER, Abner NASH, Jonathan HAMPTON, September 1990 Samuel WOODRUFF (1763), Silas WHITE (@1790), Cornelius KEITH (1715), Aaron ADKINS (1789), Robert TINDALL (1737), Connely WALKER (@1797), Sandiver V. DAVENPORT (1853), Charles HARRIS (1776), Jane CANNON (1788), John PYLE (1869), June 1990 Jesse MOTES (1772), Hogan MOTES (1807), Rev.Jesse MOTES (1795), Pressley MOTES (1821), Capt.Tandy WALKER (1812), Fall 1988 Charles LYNCH (1736), Jesse SPARKS (@1785), Thomas JONES (@1745), William GRESHAM (1775), James NORRELL Sr. (@1730), Spring 1988 Richard ROBINSON (1751), William YOUMANS Jr. (1805), William LYNCH (1742), Fall 1986) John CALDWELL (1758), John RICHEY (@1750), George WILSON (1752), Richard WRIGHT (Husband of Lucy. He was born around 1750), Ann JACKSON (1809), Samuel TURNER (1804), Oscar Walter HALL (1855), William DOZIER (1842), Charles W. KILLINGSWORTH (1882), John Samuel ADAMS (1856), Spring 1986 John B. BROGDON (1815), David FOX (1720), Jacob Harold KERR (1859), John McDOWELL (1763 in Ireland), William McDOWELL, 1789, John H. BURNETT (1858), David Lewis ANDERSON (1764). The following are wills made between 1836-9..David ANDERSON, Hugh LEEMAN, Sarah SIMPSON, Mary COLE, Barnett ROBERTSON, William REED, John McCOY Sr., John WAIT, James BLAKELY, William GOODWIN, Even BEAL, Rebecca SWAN, David BELL, Milly ALLEN, Seth P. POOL, Martha McCLINTOCK, Abraham RIDDLESPERGER, William PITTS, Ellis CHEEK, Edward JONES, Jane HAMILTON, William DUNLAP, Elijah WATSON, Robert McNEESE, John CUMMINGS, Bryant LEAK, John CALHOUN, Fall 1985 Wyatt SMITH (1740), James MATTISON (1762), Caleb SMITH (bef.1790), George EICHELBERGER (bef.1731), Spring 1985 David Marlin POSEY (1830), C.M. WILSON (1859), Fall 1989 Jefferson STRINGER (1811), James Williamson MILLER (1818), Moses Columbus WINCHESTER (1847), March 1990 John RAMAGE (@1730), Pendleton ISBELL (1806), John JOWERS (1755), Daniel POLK (1787), Nathan PITTS (1838).

Many of our Florida people came from South Carolina...to Georgia...to here!

COLUMBIA CTY & WELLBORN GLEANINGS

I have read an interesting book entitled "A History of Columbia County" by Edward F. Keuchel. I mentioned this work in an earlier writing. For the first 80 pages it has information that is relative to the area that became Suwannee County...remember that until 1858, we were a part of Columbia County. Several short biographical sketches are shown plus many little known facts concerning the rest. It would be worth your time to secure this book (possibly by inter-library loan). I am going to list the names of those who are mentioned in the first 80 pages. D.J. AULD, BEDENBAUGH family, Mary Minus BIDDLE, Arch Fred BLAKEY, J. BLUE, B.C. BRANNING, Wilson BROOKS, BROWN family, Robert BROWN, John BRYAN, Samuel BURNETT, E.C. CABELL, William CASON, Reuben CHARLES, Asa CLARK, Robert B. CLAYTON, Charles H.B. COLLINS, Daniel Newnan CONE, William CONE, William H. CONE, C.M. COOPER, John J. DAVIS, Burnett and Simeon DELL, Thomas DEXTER, Joseph DICKS, Martin P. DOBY, Douglas DORSEY, DOUGLAS family, Jemima DOUGLAS, William T. DOUGLAS, Cole DOWLING, Joseph DYALL, Henry EDWARDS, James EDWARDS, G.W. ELLIS, Thomas ELLIS, FEAGLE family, John FRINK, GILLETT family, George GILLITTO, Jacob T. GOODBREAD, Jane GOODBREAD, John Starling GOODBREAD, Elizabeth HAGAN, Jacob HALBROOK, Guy HAMILTON, Esther Bernice HAYWORTH, Allen HISTON, Kate IVES, Lancaster JAMISON, Elizabeth JOHNS, Samuel JOHNSON, Charles LANMAN, Abel LOPER, John K. MAHON, Alexander MARTIN, Lewis MATTAIR, George E. McCLELLAN, Lucy McLEOD, David MIZELL, E.F. MONTGOMERY, Warren MOORE, Daniel NEWNAN, James NIBLACK, William NIBLACK, John D. O'STEEN, James O'STEEN, Sarah O'STEEN, Allen PARRISH, John PEOPLES, POWELL family, James PREVATT, Noel RAULERSON, William M. REED, David RIDGEWAY, Abraham I. ROBERTS, John W. ROBERTS, Zachariah Randall ROBERTS, William B. ROSS, SHEALY family, M. Whit SMITH, James SPARKMAN, Jacob SUMMERALL, Jacob SUMMERLIN, Jordan SWINDLE, Charleton W. TEBEAU, John TIFFINS, TILLIS family, TOLBERT family, Daniel TREZVANT, William VANZANT, Bryan VANZANT, Garrett VANZANT, Theophilus WEEKS, WELLS family, WILLIAMSON family, Claude Augustus WILSON, WITT family, and J.S. WOOD.

Early Passports from Georgia

The following is from the book "Passports Issued By Governors of Georgia"...to points south and west. The names in these "passports" compare to common names in north Florida. These passports date from 1785 through 1820. I will list the name, county and/or city in Georgia, and year the passport was issued. When a destination is shown, I will also list that.

1) Moses SPENCER, Wilkes, 1785 (served in Revolutionary War), 2) John TARVIN, Augusta, 1789 (resident among Creek Indians), 3) James SMITH, Liberty, 1793 (to Creek nation to search for stolen Negroes), 4) Samuel KING, Liberty, 1793 (to travel with #3), 5) Solomon BOYKIN and Malachi ODUM, Burke, 1803, 6) Lt.Col.John DAVIES, James LESTER, Samuel BIRD, Simeon LOWREY, David ROBINSON, William BELL, Capt.Jams WELCH, Richard HINES,

Green BELL, Francis WARD, Capt. Thomas BURKE, Thomas ALLDAY, Coroner...supporters for #5, Burke, 1803, 7) Travis THIGPEN, Jefferson, 1803, 8) Andrew McDUGALL, Washington, 1803, 9) Jared EDWIN, David BLACKSHEAR, Francis BOYKIN, Lt.Col. John RUTHERFORD, Jesse B. GARDNER, Major John HOWARD, Washington, 1803 (supporters of #8), 10) Jacob RAY and William COLEMAN, Wilkes, 1803 to Bigby Cty), 11) Ayres HOLLOWDAY, Lincoln, 1803 (to Mississippi Territory), 12) William JOHNS, Wilkes, 1803 (to Mississippi Territory) 13) Benjamin COLEMAN, Burke?, 1803 (to Bigby Cty), 14) James ROUNDTREE, James WHITE, and Alexander STRINGER, Burke, 1803 (through Creek Nation), 15) William IVY and Laben CASON, Montgomery, 1803, 16) William McCALL, Bullock, 1803, Isaac LEWIS, Jefferson, 1803 (to Northern states), 17) James JACKSON of Barnwell District, S.C., 1803 (to Mississippi), 18) Edward & Richard STORY, Warren, 1803, 19) Elijah GRANADE, Green HILL, Edmond HAYS, John LANDRUM Jr, John LANDRUM Sr, and Joseph SMITH, 1803 (all to Tombigby or Dunbigbe through the Creek Nation), 20) Absolem BOWLER, Columbia, 1803.

Unless shown otherwise these folks went to Louisianna. They are, 1) George McFALLS (Clarke Cty, 1804), 2) Isaac JACKSON, Stephen & Ellington EVANS, and Samuel BUTLER (1804 to points west), 3) James SCARLET (Hancock Cty, 1804), 4) John CARTER & Col. Larkin CLEVELAND (Augusta, 1804), 5) George SMITH (Burke Cty, 1804), 6) Isaac BUSH (Barnwell Dist.of S.C., 1804), 7) James TILLMAN (Burke Cty, 1804), 8) Jonathan Surmon & Frances COLEMAN (Barnwell Dist.of S.C.,1804), 9) George & Enoch WALKER (Burke Cty, 1804), 10) Moses & John PARKER (Jackson Cty, 1804 to Natchez), 11) Daniel BEALL (Franklin Cty, 1804 thru Cherokee Country), 12) Travis THIGPEN (1804 thru Creek Nation), 13) Capt. Micajah LITTLE (1804 for trade with Creek or Cherokee Nations), 14) Henry W. EVANS & Benjamin WILLIAMS (1804, no destination given), 15) Moses KEATING (a mullato man, 1804, to Natchez), 16) John GEORGE (Barnwell Dist.of S.C., 1804), 17) George HERBERT (1804 to Natchez), 18) Robert BURNES (1804 to Mississippi), 19), John RANDON & William HOLLINGER (1804, back to Georgia thru Creek Nation...passed Fort Wilkins on June 2, 1804), 20) James NESSMITH (born & raised in Burke & Scriven Cty, 1804, no dest.given) 21) Jacob FREEMAN (Screven Cty, 1804, no dest.given), 22) James MARTIN (1804 thru Creek Nation), 23) Isaac DUBOSE, son Peter, & son-in-law Frances BAKER (1804, to westward country), 24) William ALEXANDER (Burke Cty, 1804 to Tom Bigbey), 25) John PEEK, Senator of Columbia Cty, 1804, thru Creek Nation), 26) Joseph THOMAS (1804, to Natchez), 27) Joseph LANDRUM (Warren Cty, 1804, to Natchez), 28) Joseph BREED Jr. (Warren Cty, 1804).

Scottish Immigrants

I would like to give notice to the many Scottish names that have been settlers in this part of the world. I will list some common names with some background regarding heritage. 1) MacALPIN...son of Alpin, descended from Kenneth MacALPINE, an early ancestor of the Scottish kings, 2) MacAULEY...son of Auley, grandson of Auley, brother of Maldowan, Earl of Lennox, 3) MacLELLAN...son of Lellan, descended from David MacLellan, 1217, 4) MacDONALD...son of Donald, descended from Angus MacDonald whose father, Reginald, was the son of Somerled, Thane of Argyll, 5) MacKAY...son of the champion (meaning of name), descended from Ymore, son of Donald of Strathnavern, a descendent of Achonacher (an ancestor of the Forbes family), who came from Ireland about the end of the 12th century, 6) MacLEOD...son of Leod, descended from Malcolm, son of Termod MacLeod from David II, 7) MacNEIL...son of Neil descended from Anradan, son of Gillebride, king of the isles in the 12th century, 8) AIRTH...from the village of Airth in Stirlingshire, descended from Sir William de Airth from Robert Bruce, 9) CARMICHAEL...from the barony of Carmichael in Lanarkshire, descended from William de Carmichael. Sir John Carmichael of Carmichael accompanied Archibald, Earl of Douglas to the assistance of Charles VI of France. He distinguished himself in the battle of Beauge by dismounting the English general, the Duke of Clarence, 10) DALRYMPLE...from the barony of Dalrymple in Ayrshire, descended from Adam de Dalrymple descended from Alexander III, 11) GRAY...from the castle of Croy in Picardy descended from Sir Andrew Gray, Lord of Longforgan in Perthshire, from Robert Bruce, through Anchestil de Croy who came into England with the Conqueror from Fulbert, Great Chamberlain to Robert of Normandy. There are many other Scottish names in this book dated 1862.

WELLBORN, FLORIDA TIDBITS

Ms. Elizabeth Bothwell ELWOOD of Key Biscayne, FL. is descended from some very early settlers in the Wellborn area. Her grandmother descended from Thomas Lockhart WILLIAMS (a planter). Her grandmother also listed her brothers as W.W. WILLIAMS and J. WILLIAMS (also planters). Her grandmother married Dr. Thomas Wells BOTHWELL in 1886. Mrs. ELWOOD also sent me an article clipped from the February 28, 1990 edition of the Suwannee Democrat written by Jinny WILSON which show that in 1841 Wellborn was called Little River. I had also discovered that George E. McCLELLAN had served as postmaster of Little River's post office for a number of years. It was also interesting to notice that Wellborn derived its name from Louis WELLBORN, a surveyor for the East-West railroad which was built in 1858. For his efforts he was awarded 162 acres of land. Wellborn received its present name in 1860 and for some time did well as a community. Unfortunately, the depression of the early 1930's took its toll and the town charter was abolished. Wellborn still has a goodly number of residents and a long and interesting history to be proud of.

HISTORICAL HELPS

Allow me to spend some time sharing valid information concerning how settlers arrived at their destinations. I remember discovering my wife's immigrant who came to this country in the late 1700's. I found him living in Frying Pan Creek, Pittsylvania County, Virginia through a courthouse marriage record. The big question was "How in the world did he ever end up there?"...and more importantly, "Why?". You may wonder something like this about some of your ancestors. We'll be sharing ideas for you to help you in your quest. Is your family history taking you back to 1790 and earlier? If so you need to have some idea of the activities of history and the time in which these events took place. I would like to list these events by date adding some explanation as deemed necessary. 1607 - Founding of Virginia; 1619 - First American legislative assembly meets at Jamestown; 1620 - Arrival of Mayflower with its 100+ English settlers (one needs to read the book "Saints & Strangers" on this subject); 1623 - New Netherland (later consisting of the areas of New York, New Jersey, and Delaware) settlement by Dutch West Indies Company; 1630-40 - Puritan migration to New England; 1631 - Founding of Maryland; 1649 - Arrival of first Jewish immigrants to New Amsterdam (later named New York); 1660 - Emigration from England discouraged. Population of colonies was 52,000; 1664 - New Netherland taken over by England; 1682 - Arrival of William Penn; 1683 - First German settlers arrive in Pennsylvania; 1685 - Revocation of Edict of Nantes (an edict giving political equality to the Huguenots (any French Protestant in 1600-1700's)); 1697 - Slave trade expands. 275,000 inhabitants in colonies; 1709 - German Palatines begin their exodus to America; 1717 - English parliament authorizes transportation of convicts to the colonies; 1718 - Beginning of a large scale immigration of the Scotch-Irish; 1720 - Redemptioner trade becomes systematized (a "redemptioner" was a person in Colonial Days who paid for his passage from Europe to the colonies by being a bond-servant for a stipulated period of time); 1727 - Immigrants to Pennsylvania required to swear allegiance to the crown; 1730 - Southern migration of some German and Scotch-Irish immigrants; 1733 - Founding of Georgia; 1740 - Alien immigrants to colonies are made British citizens by an act of parliament; 1751755 - Acadians expelled from Nova Scotia (in 1604-1713 a group of French settlers found in Nova Scotia and in a parish of Louisianna; 1775 - English immigration suspended; 1775-1783 - The Revolutionary War; 1790 - First official census recording 3,227,000 inhabitants in America.

CONVICTS AND REBELS

I would like to share some thoughts on "Indentured Servants", and "Convicts and Rebels". A large part of our country was settled by people in these categories. Indentured servants were generally poor individuals and families who, in the hope of bettering their lot in life, committed their lives as servants of merchants and other wealthy people to pioneer the new world. They usually agreed to serve their benefactors for a period of 4 to 7 years. Passage to the colonies was assured and during this time they received only a place to live, food to eat, and clothing. The majority farmed the lands of their patrons and at the end of their tenure they received "two suits of clothing, two hoes, and an axe, and a small grant of land upon which to start their new lives. Still others, desiring to come to America, would seek passage without money. In these cases, ship captains would agree to take them on condition that they would allow themselves to be auctioned off on arrival...the captain keeping the profit for their fare. Even though life was hard, sometimes almost unbearable for these early pioneers, they felt it was worth it...and many of us owe our heritage to them.

Throughout the 1700's there was an enormous need for laborers as this new country was developing. One source was that of convicts and political rebels. Criminals and rebels were exiled to this land by the boatloads. They were assigned where the need was the greatest. The ports of entry for these outcasts were primarily Virginia, Georgia, and Maryland. Interestingly enough, good records were kept of these individuals. However, these records are scattered throughout many books and periodicals. A great deal of research (which is expensive in today's economy) is needed to discover information of these individuals. Many of these names were recorded in the "Gentleman's Magazine" which can be found through the auspices of the Mormon Church Genealogical Society. Not all "convicts" were violent or dangerous. Punishments in England were quite severe...and for crimes that were insignificant. For example, the death penalty was imposed for such crimes as stealing a sheep, sending threatening letters, or by not responding to the queries of one's superiors. Many of these individuals became model citizens in this country. Regarding the so-called "rebels"...many of these exiled persons went on to become great men in this new society. John Bradshaw once said, "Rebellion towards tyrants is obedience to God"...and many of England's early leaders were indeed tyrants. During the times of the colonies the European nations (especially England and Scotland) were suffering greatly through religious uprisings. Persecutions abounded towards those who disagreed with the allegiance of the kings and queens. Thus...exile!!!

INDEX

Note: This index includes two columns...1) last name, and 2) page number. The researcher will have to look up each surname in order to discover which one(s) are important to his/her lineage.

ABBOTT	118	AULD	121
ADAMS	33,61,72,76,84, 87,89,95,99,106, 113,120	AUSTIN	46,98
		AVANT	89
ADKINS	120	BACHE	114
AGEE	84,115	BACON	46
AIRTH	61,81,115,123	BADEN	38,84,113
ALBRITTON	57,114	BAILEY	39,45,46,75,79,81, 84,87,89,93,98-102 105,113,119
ALDEN	57		
ALDERMAN	89,93	BAIN	57
ALDREDGE	68	BAINS	43
ALEXANDER	22,45,104,106, 112,119,122	BAISDEN	31,34,54,62,72,75, 96,99
ALEXSON	99	BAKER	35,38,45,59,76,79, 89,93,95,102,118- 120,122
ALFORD	75,96		
ALLDAY	96		
ALLEN	33,38,39,43,45,46, 48,58,73,74,76,77, 81,84,94,95,98,101 108,111,120	BALDWIN	99
		BALL	120
		BALLENTINE	52,54,81,113
		BALZ	83
ALLENSTEN	43	BANGS	83
ALLENDER	83	BANKS	48,65,77,102
ALLISON	38,39,46,54,58,71, 73,78,79,81,83,84, 87,89,93-96,98,99, 101,108,110	BARBER	17,27,35,43,44,89, 100
		BARCLAY	66,103,106,114
		BARCO	42,43
ALPORT	63	BARFIELD	81
ALSTON	118	BARKLEY	38,39
ALTMAN	38,46	BARNES	45,46,72,73,76,79, 80,84,93,97,99,110
ALVEREZ	43		
AMBROSE	114	BARNETT	39,57,84,87,115
AMERSON	73,74,84,87,89,93, 98	BARRETT	68,81
		BARROW	74,84,87,108
AMISON	45	BARRS	41
AMONS	38	BARTLEY	45
ANDERSON	38,40,89,99,101, 118-120	BARTRAM	118
		BASINGER	83
ANDREW	43	BASS	35,45,46,57,73,84, 97,109,120
ANDREWS	34		
ANGUS	84	BASTORS	102
ANSLEY	89	BATCHLOTTE	99
ARCHER	84	BATES	35
ARMISTEAD	78	BATEY	45,118
ARNOLD	32,60	BATTLE	45
ARRINGTON	84,112	BAUER	116
ATKINSON	76	BAXTER	38,55,84,108,114
ATWATER	65	BEACH	84,87,101
ATWELL	63,81,101	BEADLER	111
AUCHINCLOSS	60	BEAL	44,120,122

BEDENBAUGH	121	BLOXHAM	55
BEGGS	93	BLUE	35,40,43,70,73-75, 79,89,93,101,121
BELL	35,37-39,46,58,60, 72,74,84,89,97,100 110,114,119,120, 121	BLUME	66,70-71,79,84,111
		BLUNT	37-38
		BOATWRIGHT	38,46,61,69,75,77, 84,87,93,97,114
BELTON	48,83	BODEFORD	100
BELVIN	45	BOGGS	101
BEMBRY	84	BOLAND	66
BENDS	62	BOLEN	93
BENGHEIME	72	BOLER	81
BENJAMIN	46,99	BOLES	94,100
BENNETT	3,22,43,67,81,89	BOND	84,87,112
BENTON	45,101	BONDEN	83
BERRY	45,76,84	BONDS	38,46,84,87,98
BERTRAM	83	BONE	44
BESSER	99	BONNELL	66,84,87,114
BETHEA	31,51,81,101	BOONE	100
BEVAN	39,51,66,76,79,84 106,110,115	BOOZER	65
		BORDEN	14
BEVANS	76,98	BORROUGHS	78,93
BEVILL	102	BOSTON	67,73
BEVIN	46,89,102	BOTHWELL	123
BEVINS	102	BOURKE	83
BEXLEY	35	BOWDEN	99
BIBBY	115	BOWEN	83
BIDDLE	121	BOWLEN	81
BIGBY	122	BOWLER	89,122
BIGGARSTAFF	84	BOYCE	83
BIRD	40,46,49,54,63,72, 73,84,93,94,110, 122	BOYD	38,44,76,84,106
		BOYEN	83
BIVANS	76	BOYER	48,89
BIVENS	89	BOYETT	38,48,72,74,84,97, 101
BIVIN	46	BOYKIN	122
BIVINS	93	BOYT	73,93
BIXLER	65	BOZEMAN	78,79
BLACK	46,57,83,87,97, 101,102,113	BRADDOCK	84
		BRADFORD	46,114
BLACKBURN	35,40,42,52,54-56, 58,79,89,94-96,108 119	BRADLER	45,100
		BRADLEY	42,81,89,99,112
		BRADSHAW	115
BLACKMAN	39,53,73-75,79,81, 84,87,94,97,98	BRADY	66,83
		BRANHAM	39
BLACKMON	45,64,81,106,113	BRANNAN	44,45,69,73,81,84, 85,87,89,93,98,113
BLACKSHEAR	39,122		
BLACKWELL	64,95,100	BRANNEN	74,76,78,79
BLAIR	93,109,111,115	BRANNING	73,121
BLAKELY	97,120	BRANNON	110,112
BLAKEY	121	BRANTLEY	28
BLAND	84,107	BRAZELL	112
BLANTON	67,84,87,114	BREED	122
BLOOM	45,74,79,93	BREEN	58
BLOUNT	43,48,53,63,78,79, 108	BREVALDA	103

BRIDGES	57,66,85,,95,96	BUTLER	37,38,44-46,65,69, 99,122
BRIGG	100		
BRIM	39,85,87	BYNUM	38,54-56,60,64,71, 72,78,81,85,89,93, 94,95,108
BRINKLEY	35,39,89,93		
BRINSON	37-40,51,57,63,72, 73,75,78,79,81,85, 89,94-99,110,112		
		BYRD	35,38,39,76-79,81, 89
BRISON	54		
BRITTON	43		
BROCK	39,46,59,65,74,78, 79,85,87,89,93,98, 101,102,115	CABEL	121
		CAIN	79,83,90,95,97
		CALDWELL	77,120
BROGDON	120	CALHOUN	81,120
BRONSON	46	CALL	84
BROOKER	111	CALLAHAN	82,93
BROOKINS	40,81	CALLAWAY	93
BROOKS	43,44,46,77,81,100 107,121	CALWELL	76
		CAMAL	84
BROOME	42,59,64,66,68	CAMERON	99
BROWER	83	CAMPBELL	58,84,87,114
BROWMAN	43	CANNON	38,44,45,77,85,103 106,107,109,112, 120
BROWN	38,44-46,48,54,60, 62-65,72-74,84,89, 96,99,100,102,109, 111,121		
		CANTRELL	115
		CARL	35
BROWNING	43	CARLISLE	46
BRUINTON	46	CARMICHAEL	123
BRUNSON	35,39	CARNES	84
BRUNSWIG	54	CARPENTER	83
BRYAN	21,35,38,40,43,48, 68,70-72,76,77,85, 89,93,100,101,108, 111,120,121	CARVER	35,39,40,42,45,46, 49,51,53,56,70,72- 81,90,93,96,98,99
		CARROLL	46,58,85,87,108-9, 113,114
BRYANT	35,43,45,74,79,89, 100,119,120	CARRUTH	32,35,39,45,46,49- 52,73-75,77,80,89, 90,93,96,98
BRYCKE	72		
BRYDE	73		
BRYSON	62,63,65,81,95	CARSON	82,94
BUCHANAN	48,101	CARTER	35,38,43,44,62,64, 65,73,76,78,87,89, 96,98,100,119,122
BUFF	76		
BUGG	45,76,78,79,93		
BULKLEY	73	CARVER	30,32,35,39,42,49, 66,70,71,74,77,81, 85,89,90,93,97,102 110,111,113
BULLARD	81		
BUNKER	50		
BURKE	83,99,122		
BURNETT	39,55,85,98,108, 110,120,121	CASON	35,39,44,46,81,89, 93,99,121,122
BURNS	87,115,122	CATE	45,61
BURNSED	44	CATES	46,84
BURROUGHS	73,75,78	CATHEY	44,72,93
BURTCHALL	39	CATO	35,37,71-74,76,77, 79,80,100
BURTON	83,100		
BURWELL	60	CHAIRS	98
BUSH	64,85,113,122	CHALKER	85
BUSHMAN	83	CHAMBERS	39,52,85,89,115

CHAMBLISS	71,77,79,85,110,111
CHANCEY	62
CHANDLER	67
CHAPEL	101
CHAPMAN	35,83
CHARLES	23-25,35,38,40,89,98-100,106,107,121
CHASTAIN	75,90,93
CHEEK	38,120
CHEERS	118
CHERRY	45,76
CHESHIRE	73,114
CHESTNUT	101
CHEWING	75
CHILDS	83
CHIPPIER	54
CHURCH	89,93
CIVILS	38
CLARELY	76
CLARIDAY	85
CLARIDGE	83
CLARK	35,38,41,43,46,48,55,57,58,62,74,75,78,83-85,87,97,98,108,109,113,114,121
CLARY	114
CLAYTON	35,48,57,85,87,109,121
CLEMONS	39,63,73,76,90,104
CLEMENTS	35,39,42,55,73,75,
CLENDENING	84
CLEVELAND	122
CLIFFORD	84
CLIFTON	44,97
CLINE	72,93
CLONTS	53-55
CLOUNTS	96
CLOW	107,118
CLUTE	42
COATES	38,39,46,49,70,72,73,75,78,80,81,85,90,93,97,98,108,110
COBB	53,56,85,106,110
COCKCROFT	114
COKELY	98
COFFEE	66,93
COKER	80
COLDHAM	46
COLE	39,41,58,73,113,120
COLEMAN	44,99,100,122
COLLIER	48,73
COLLINS	27,38,44,58,70,73,75,80,81,107,115,121
COLSON	48,81
COLT	41
COMBS	41,43,63
COMER	48,68
COMPTON	46
CONE	35,44,89,95,121
CONEWALL	39
CONNELL	85,115
CONNOR	39,46,52,53,58-69,81,95,96,102
COOK	41,44,83
COOKS	118
COOPER	35,83,121
COPELEY	46
CORBETT	81,82,96,106
CORBIN	35,43
CORLEY	115
CORNWALL	48
COTTLE	43
COULTER	83
COUSINS	35,69,73,77,80,89,96
COWARD	43,44
COWERT	41,43,99,100
COX	119
CRAIG	83
CRAVENS	110
CRAWFORD	39,57,69,73,76,77,79,85,87,89,91,115,119
CRAWLEY	38,87
CREEKMORE	48,59,70,73,77,81,82,85,87,101,110
CREWS	42,44,45
CROFT	85
CROSBY	43
CROSIER	87,115
CROSS	109
CROSSGROVE	83,105
CROUSE	43
CROW	76
CROWSON	81
CRUTCHFIELD	119
CSORAN?	81
CUMASKY	83
CUMMINGS	120
CUMMINS	107
CUNNINGHAM	46,84,101
CUREY	43
CURL	42,46,74,77,80,90,97,98
CURNEY	83

CURRY	25,35,46	DENSLER	48,94,98
CUSHMAN	115	DENT	81,101
CUTTS	73,93	DESHAZO	114
		DEVAL	67
		DEVORE	84
DADE	84	DEXTER	35,37,39,40,42,53, 56,57,59,61,63,69-74,77,80,81,90,91, 93,115,121
DALE	115		
DALRYMPLE	45,90,97,106,123		
DALTON	83		
DAMPIER	107	DIAS	44
DANGERFIELD	43	DICKENS	58
DANIEL	43,70	DICKENSON	106
DANIELS	41,43,59,77,83,97,112	DICKERSON	41,100
		DICKEY	120
DARBY	66	DICKS	121
DARE	119	DICKSON	45,73,77,90
DASHER	66	DIGGERS	41
DAUGHERTY	85	DINOR	74
DAUGHTRY	37,72	DIVINE	38
DAUSEY	101	DIXSON	38,68,87
DAVENPORT	77,78	DOBY	121
DAVIES	122	DODGE	83
DAVIS	35,38,43,46-48,51, 55,68,74-78,82,83, 85,90,100,101,108, 110,119,121	DONAVAN	84
		DORMAN	35,56,57,62,85,90,95
		DORSETT	112
DAWSON	38	DORSEY	28,29,46,98,108,121
DAY	78		
DAZLER	54	DOUGHTY	84
DEAKLE	39,90	DOULITTLE	98
DEAN	35,37,38,42,45,48, 74,85,89,90,102, 104,106,107	DOUGLAS	41,61,72,93,104,121
		DOWANCE	41
DEAS	40,45,85,107	DOWLESS	45,76
DEBUSK	41	DOWLING	43,63,65,115,121
DECOURSNEY	83	DOWNING	98,114
DEES	32,35,39,43,47,48, 52,65,69,71,73,76, 79-82,87,90,93,97-99	DOWNES	84
		DOZIER	35,120
		DRAIN	119
		DRAYTON	106
DEGRAF	83	DREW	98,100
DEHAM	72	DRAWDY	38
DEHART	115	DRIGGERS	76
DEHAWN	100	DRISLAN?	82
DELANEY	43	DRIVER	35,98
DELEGAL	35,38,40,45,46,55, 74,78,81,82,85,90, 99,105	DRUSLER	98
		DRYDEN	43
		DUBOIS	90,94,122
DELIONS	46	DUCKER	87
DELL	121	DUERR	35
DEMERE	90	DUFFIELD	57
DEMERY	73	DUNCAN	72,93,118
DEMFRO	75	DUNHAM	108
DEMPSEY	81,109	DUNFEE	61
DENARD	48,98	DUNKIN	101

DUNLAP	83	FETEUR	99
DUNLOP	120	FETNER	101
DUNN	49,69,70,77,83,90, 98,99	FEWOX	42
		FIELD	39
DUNSTEN	77	FIELDING	71,81,82,85,87,96, 110
DUPREE	45,77,80,90,97,115		
DURDEN	97,119	FIELDS	22,38,47,80,83,98
DURRELL	72	FIGG	47,99
DURRENCE	42	FILER	119
DUTTON	38,39,60,89,119	FILLMORE	38
DUVALL	47,85	FINLAYSON	39
DYALL	25,26,35,42-44,73, 74,79,80,90,91,98, 121	FISH	82,94
		FISHER	35,40,54,82
		FITCHETT	44
DZIALENSKI	93	FITZGERALD	119
		FITZPATRICK	42
		FLANNAGAN	83
EADY	75	FLEMING	45,68,109
EARNEST	39,115	FLETCHER	44,61,68,73,79,85, 90,112
EASON	100		
ECCLES	40,93	FLOWERS	99,100
EDDINS	48	FLOYD	38,45,47,48
EDWARD	121	FOARD	97
EDWARDS	35,40,48,72,76,90, 93	FOLK	84
		FOOTMAN	78
		FORCE	93
EDWIN	122	FORD	75,84,93
EICHELBERGER	120	FORREST	47
ELLIOTT	39,45,48,64,72,77, 78,81,85,87,97,105	FORRESTER	119
		FORSON	47,97
ELLIS	35,42-45,71,73,75, 76,80,85,95,96,101 110,121	FORT	38,48,82,93
		FORTH	47
		FOSTER	35,38-40,45,72,73, 76,79,80,84,85,87, 90,94,119
ELLISON	87,109		
ELSBEE	68		
ELWOOD	123	FOX	120
ENGALLS	58	FOXWORTH	99
ENGLISH	75	FOWLE(R)	14
EPSEY	87	FRANCIS	80
EVANS	35,56,78,108,114, 119,122	FRANCKE	118
		FRANKLIN	99,119
EVERETT	35,64	FREDERICK	38
EVERS	35,39,45,70,71,73, 76,79,90,93,98	FRASER	39,57,58,63,82,83, 108
		FREEMAN	110,118,122
		FRICKS?	76
FAGAN	39	FRIER	39,44,114
FAGG	55	FRIEZE	43
FAIRCHILD	72	FRINK	44,72,73,75,76,78, 97,121
FARLEY	83		
FARNELL	39	FRY	40,82,90,118
FAULKER	38	FRYER	35,65
FEAGLE	121	FULCHER	38
FENNISON	118,119	FULCHEIR	47
FERGUSON	85,87,110	FULCUM	47
FERNANDEZ	119		

FULFORD	48,100,101	GLEATON	119
FULGUNE	37	GLENN	47,50,84
FULLER	84	GLISSON	44,76
FULLERTON	83	GLOVER	48,72,77,90,100
FUNDERBURK	75	GODBOLD	35,39,74,90,115
FUQUAY	56,89,98	GODBOLT	40
FUTCH	43,85,87,110	GODFREY	43,50
		GODWIN	35,37,43,47
		GOENS	48
GAIL	38	GOFF	38,39,44,46,47,55,
GAINER	47		56,78,80-82,85,89,
GAINEY	44,59		90,93,94,97,98,100
GAINOR	38		106,109,111
GALE	48	GOIN	100
GALLAGHER	62,85	GOINGS	119
GALLAWAY	102	GOLDSMITH	45
GAMBLE	48,52,54,81,82,85,	GOLESBY	43
	89,107,113	GOLPHIN	46
GARDENER	90,101	GOMETO?	65
GARDINER	57,73,74,83	GOMEZ	118
GARDNER	39,45,46,53,76,85,	GOODBREAD	26,39,44,71,73,74,
	89,93,96,99,105,		81,90,94,98,101,
	109,113,122		107,121
GARDUN	101	GOODMAN	38,39,47,49,75,98,
GARFIELD	45		100
GARNER	41,42	GOODSON	70
GARRETT	63	GOODWIN	120
GARTON	44	GORDEN	84,112
GARY	58,59,82,87,95,107	GORNTO	89,108
GASKINS	35,42	GOSHONO	81
GASSET	56	GOSHORN	82
GATEWOOD	101	GOSS	95
GAULDING	47	GOULD	56
GAY	105	GRAHAM	38,45,61,71,72,77,
GAYLARD	45,70,71,79,80,111		78,84,90,95,99-102
GAYLORD	38,67,85,90,101,102	GRAMLIN	85,105
GEORGE	55,77,122	GRANADE	122
GERRY	73,74,76	GRANT	38,69,72,83,85,96,
GIBBS	35,45-47,56,74,75,		100,101,106
	80,85,87,90,93,94,	GRANTHAM	47,53,74
	97,101,102,106	GRAY	39,45,68,123
GIBSON	44	GREEN	43-46,62,65,66,70-
GILBERT	120		74,76,78,79-83,85,
GILCHRIST	119		89,93-95,97,99,101
GILES	45		112,113,119
GILITTO	121	GREENE	87,90
GILKYSON	68	GRESHAM	46,77,82,85,94,111
GILL	48,69,93		120
GILLEN	65	GRIFFIN	39,47,52,59,66,68,
GILLESPIE	35,72		75,85,87,97,108,
GILLETT	35,39,43,83,121		110,119
GILLIAM	55	GRIFFITH	83
GILLIE	39,101,115	GRIGGS	78,84
GILLIS	62,67	GRIMES	46,99
GLASGOW	120	GRIMSLEY	32,51,52

GROFF	108	HARGROVE	98,100
GROOMS	84	HARPER	87,113
GROOVER	62	HARRELL	35,38,39,46,47,56, 67,70,72-74,82,85, 87,90,93,98,105, 109,114
GROSE	45		
GROYNER	70		
GRUBB	114		
GUFFERE	85		
GUFFEY	80,98	HARRINGTON	97
GUNTER	75	HARRIS	38,39,46,47,52,55, 74-76,79,80,95,100 103,120
GURGANUS	35,77,101		
GURNEY	44		
GWYNN	47	HARRISON	72,78,99,115,119
		HARROD	75
		HART	26,27,35,47,50,72- 74,76-78,80,85,90, 93,100,101,106, 111-113,119
HACKETT	83		
HACKNEY	39,49,50,56,59,66, 70,73-75,90,93,94, 97,100,120		
		HARVARD	115
		HARVEY	37,44,48,54,85,101
HADDOCK	56,73,77,110	HASTINGS	101
HADLEY	77,119	HARVILL	41
HAGAN	55,81,121	HARWOOD	80
HAINDEW	99	HASEL	44
HAINES	119	HASSTIEN	39
HAIL	53	HASTINGS	74
HAIR	35,42-44,52,53,90, 115	HATCH	76,99
		HATCHER	85,115
HAISTEN	45,90	HATELY	73,75,78
HALBROOK	121	HAUGHTON	63
HALE	102	HAVENS	35
HALL	35,39,45,47,48,51, 58,68,71,73,75,81, 82,84,85,87,89,90, 98,99,108,112,115, 120	HAWKINS	26-28,32,35,36,38, 39,40,42,46,56,60, 61,64,70,79-83,89, 90,95,97,98,101, 108,111,120
HALLMAN	81	HAY	47
HALTER	83	HAYNES	78
HAMBY	54,58,59	HAYS	93,97,119,122
HAMILTON	46,98,111,120,121	HAYWORTH	121
HAMLIN	66	HEALEY	119
HAMMS	98,99	HECK	83
HAMMOND	57	HEDDING	45
HAMPTON	49,120	HEDGECOCK	97
HANCOCK	35,39,43,44,90,	HEIMER	84
HANKEL	93	HELTON	38,85,90,111
HANKINS	38,54,67,110,115	HELVENSTON	62,63,68
HANNOCK	98	HEMMING	59,65,67,107
HARDEE	39,47,61-64,70,74, 78-80,90,93,98,102 103,106,107,109,110	HENDEE	66
		HENDERSON	39,47,66,81-83,94
		HENDRICKS	39,73,76,79,80,85, 90,100,105,112,120
HARDEN	68		
HARDER	118	HENDRIX	46
HARDGREE	47	HENNINGTON	43
HARDING	84	HENLEY	53
HARE	45	HENRY	46,78,105,119
HARGRAVES	35	HENY	90

HERBERT	122	HON	109
HERNDON	42,55,78,81,113	HOOD	83
HEROD	70	HOOKENSMITH	112
HERRIN	93	HOOKER	36
HERRING	22,39,48,80,85,89, 113,114	HOOPER	40
		HOPKINS	84
HEWITT	79,108,119	HORNE	65,84,106
HICKS	43,44,46,50,73,74, 77,78,85,95,97,100 102,111	HORTON	39
		HOTCHKISS	84
		HOUGH	39
HIERS	98	HOUGHENS	73
HIGDON	37,47,78,85,98,99, 101,108	HOUGHINGTON	79
		HOWARD	36,38,51,59,60,83, 111,122
HIGGS	32		
HIGGINS	114	HOWE	55
HIGH	38,96	HOWELL	22,39,47,73,75,77, 78,80,85,98,99,105 113,119
HILDRETH	115,119		
HILL	22,35,39,43,46,47, 51,69-71,75,76,78- 80,83,84,97-100, 122		
		HOWINGTON	93
		HOWLAND	85,89,113
		HOYE	107
HILLHOUSE	85,114	HOYLE	38,63
HILLMAN	63,118	HUGGINS	46,52,73
HILTON	39,107	HUGHES	46,68,82
HINES	39,40,44,73,78,90, 91,106,121	HULL	28,36,38-40,43,70, 72-74,76-80,82,90, 94,95,96,98,99
HINGSON	89,114		
HINSON	22,23,85	HUMPHRIES	38,46,63,64
HINTON	35,121	HUNNICUT	38
HOBBS	57,113	HUNT	40,55,72,76,81,106
HOCKER	62	HUNTER	43,66,75,77,80,90, 93,97,101,105
HODGE	83,90		
HODGES	35,38,39,45,58,60, 62,73,74,76,82	HURLEY	83
		HURLYHIGH	84
HODGKINS	101	HURST	36-40,46,47,57,76, 80,81.85,90,100, 112,113,118
HOEY	57		
HOGAN	85,101		
HOGANS	43,87,111	HURT	36,38,46,73,76,77, 85,95,105
HOLDER	43,101		
HOLLAND	35,46,47,73,74,81, 83,89,93,99,101, 120	HUTCHERSON	38,70
		HUTCHINGSON	71,74,75,87,90,111
		HUTCHINSON	52,85,109
HOLLIMAN	39.46,70,87,101	HUTTON	39
HOLLINGER	122	HYDE	83
HOLLOMAN	35,74,90,98		
HOLLOWAY	38,122		
HOLLY	58	IDLETT	68
HOLLYMAN	79	INGALLS	111
HOLMAN	31	INGERVILLE	38,39,46,50,70,71, 74-77,79-81,90,93, 99
HOLMES	35,42,45,46,64,83, 93,100,113		
		INGLISH	112
HOLSENDORF	37,47	INGRAM	38,76
HOLSTEN	87	IRVIN	37,82,90
HOLTZCLAW	56,85,112	IRVINE	36,39,40,47,48,52,
HOMER	59		

	74,77,78,80-82,94,		120
	108,109	JUDSON	104
IRWIN	39,53,54,82,98	JUMP	118
ISBELL	120		
IVES	36,43,59,65,73,121		
IVEY	36-38,43,44,47,48,	KEATING	122
	54,63,65,70,73,76,	KEATS	83
	77,81,82,90,96,98,	KEEFE	115
	101,108,109,112,	KEELING	105
	113,122	KEEN	36,43,76,93,119
		KEIRNS	83
		KEITH	36,38,73,75,76,78-
JACKSON	37,38,46-48,59,73,		80,85,90,94,98-100
	78,84,85,87,100-2,		102,120
	115,120,122	KELLER	77
JACOB	48	KELLY	48,119
JACOBS	81,119	KENDRICK	42
JACOBUS	83	KENDRICKS	36
JAMES	76,93,99	KENNEDY	44,45,53,85,87,100
JAMISON	76,101,121		105
JARVERS	72	KENNERLIN	58
JEFFERS	84,99	KENNY	83,84
JEFFERSON	59	KENNON	46,99
JEFFREY	47	KENT	100
JEFFS	83	KEPLER	83
JEFFUS	47	KERR	120
JENKINS	36,41,47,68,75,85,	KEUCHEL	121
	87,89,97,99,102,	KEY	63,82
	113,114	KIKE?	46
JENNINGS	38	KILLINGSWORTH	120
JERKINS	42	KIMMERLIN	63
JERNIGAN	110	KIMMONS	62,67,114
JERVIS	57	KING	22,47,73,95,96,100
JEWELL	83		121
JIMMERSON	48	KINGSBERRY	55
JOHNAN	114	KINKERLY	84
JOHNS	36,39,42,43,67,85,	KINNEY	57
	87,90,93,94,99,109	KINSEY	81,90
	113,121,122	KIRK	54
JOHNSON	36-40,42,44,46,47,	KIRKLAND	85,89,113,120
	50,53,55,59,60,63,	KIRKPATRICK	106
	65-67,69-74,76,78-	KITE	85,102
	81,83,85,90,93,94,	KNAPP	113
	97-102,106,107,109	KNARR	83
	112,114,115,118-21	KNEELAND	84
JOHNSTON	38,43,44	KNIGHT	72,80,93,96,108
JOINER	44	KNIGHTEN	109
JOLLY	122	KNOWLTON	84
JONAKER	119	KNOX	115
JONES	37,38,42-44,46,47,	KUNERT	110
	66,72,78,82,84,85,	KUPMAN	54
	93,96,98-101,109,		
	120		
JORDAN	36,73,81,119	LAFTON	101
JOWERS	38,39,74,85,87,108	LADD	93

LAMB	36,39,41,47,63,64, 85,89,109		104,108,119,122
LAME	84	LIGHT	43
LANDERS	71,100	LINDSEY	47,57,90,109
LANDING	85,87	LINKOUS	14
LANDON	108	LINTON	73,105
LANDRUM	122	LINZA	98
LANE	36,43,46,47,63,66, 69,70,76-80,84,90, 91,94,97,98,100, 108,109	LIPCOMB	37,40
		LIPPFORD	118
		LISLE	48,72,78
		LISTER	99
		LISTON	46
LANG	73,76,77,81,84,97	LITTLE	38,122
LANGFORD	36,39,72,79,80,93, 102	LIVELY	39
		LIVINGSTON	22,36,38,41,47,93
LANGSTON	75	LLOYD	39,46,47,75,78,80, 85,89,90,97,110
LANGWOOD	38,47		
LANIER	36,44,55,69,85,89, 114,115,119	LOFTIN	43
		LONDON	38
LANMAN	121	LONG	40,43,44,59,65,67, 81,82,85,90,91,109 113
LAQUAY	38,115		
LASSITER	51,73,79,80,96,106		
LASHLEY	98	LONGLE	42
LATHROPE	72	LONGMIRE	55
LATIMER	76,101	LONIS	53
LAUGHLIN	83	LONSOME	47
LAUER	98	LOPER	121
LAW	85,89,109	LOTT	39
LAWRENCE	47,97,101	LOUD	41
LAWSON	36,46,73,74,85,93, 94,105	LOVE	118
		LOVETT	67
LEAK	83	LOVIS	83
LEALMAN	40,71,73-78,90,94	LOWE	36,40,43,58,85,87, 90,94,107
LEAVIS	101		
LEE	36,39,40,45,48,64, 65,70,71,73,77,85, 87,89,90,99,100, 109,113	LOWRY	122
		LUCAS	59,114
		LUNDY	47,62,98,105
		LUTHER	74,83
LEEMAN	120	LUTTERLOH	69,77,90,93,94
LEGE	119	LUTTERTON	39
LEGGETT	47,87	LYLE	85
LELMAN	37	LYMAN	71
LEMON	84	LYNCH	120
LESLIE	68,69	LYON	78,110,114
LESTER	122	LYONS	46,71,72,78,97
LETHAN	66		
LETSOUN	57		
LEUSTE	100	MACHET	43
LEUTING	100	MACK	47
LEVERANT	120	MADDEN	81,101
LEVERETT	119	MADISON	42
LEVINGSTON	36	MAHON	121
LEVY	48,78	MAIN	68
LEWIS	36,39,40,43,47,57, 60,70,73,74,76,78, 80,82,85,90,101,	MAITLAND	83
		MALLETT	36
		MALLORY	60,64,65,82,87,107

MANDRELL	39,46	McCOLLISTER	86,115
MANKER	48	McCOLLUM	38,46,51,67,71,90,97
MANN	44,99		
MANNING	36,42,79,119	McCONIKE	39
MANSEL	90	McCONNELL	49
MAPLES	42	McCOOK	100,107
MARABLE	82,83,107,108	McCORMACK	86,90
MARCUM	43	McCORMICK	36,38,81,87,106,115
MARION	42,73		
MARKHAM	43,84	McCOY	86,120
MARSH	100	McCULLER	65
MARSHALL	43,47,81,101,108	McCULLERS	86
MARTAIN	90,91	McDANIEL	48,57,86,87,95,98,106,114,119
MARTIN	36,40,62,85,87,93,95,96,99-101,106,108,112,118,121-2	McDONALD	72,81,83,86,89,107,123
MASINGALE	78	McDONNELL	39
MATHIS	55,75,85,87,108	McDOWELL	120
MATTAIR	28,29,36,37,40,42,47,50,71,73,74,78-80,82,90,93,94,121	McDUGALL	122
		McELVIN	49
		McFALLS	122
MATTHEWS	44	McGEE	47,99
MATTISON	84,120	McGEHEE	40,89,90
MAUCEL	99,100	McGLASHAN	54
MAUKER	101	McGOWAN	44
MAURRY	102	McGRAW	83
MAXWELL	67	McGUIRE	39
MAY	42	McHANNON	100
MAYS	42,93,115	McINNIS	48,79
McALPIN	59,96,115,122	McINTOSH	36,38,48,54,82,89
McARTHUR	115	McINTYRE	118
McAULEY	29,36,40,50,52,73,74,76,77,79,80,90,95,123	McIVOR	98,103
		McKAY	38,123
		McKEAVY	84
McBRIDE	36,90	McKEEFER	98
McCALL	36,72,74,79,80,86,87,90,95,100,113,122	McKEEPER	99
		McKEEVER	46,47
		McKENZIE	76
McCANN	84	McKINNAN	47
McCARDELL	47,81,98,107	McKINNEY	43,93
McCARTNEY	83	McKINNIS	47
McCARTY	41,119	McKINSEY	90
McCASKILL	70,80,82,90	McLAUGHLIN	60,84,119
McCASKIN	90	McLAURIN	97
McCLELLAN	29-31,36-40,42,43,45,46,49,50,54,64,67,69,70,72-80,83,86,90,91,95,96,100,107,112,114,121,123	McLEAN	73
		McLENNON	44
		McLEOD	55,66,75,77,78,86,95,96,112,121,123
		McLERAN	31,36,39,49-51,59,70,74-77,82,90,95,107,111
McCLELLAND	66		
McCLENNON	44	McLEROY	52
McCLINTOCK	120	McMANNEN	53,86,111
McCLOUD	73	McMEE	83
McCLURE	56	McMILLAN	76

138

McNEESE	120	MOLPHUS	43
McNEIL	36,39,46,73,77,79,80,90,93,94,105	MONDIN	100
		MONK	93
McPHERSON	71,75,90,101,102,118	MONROE	84
		MONTAGUE	55,119
McQUEEN	39,67,77,100	MONTGOMERY	84,121
McWIGGIN	83	MOODY	44,81,83,118
MEADOWS	105	MOORE	40,43,59,60,66,67,70-73,75,76,78,79,81,90,93,99,100,119-121
MECKEN	98		
MEE	83		
MEEKS	38,46-48,70,72-75,79-81,85,87,90,93,97,100,109,	MOORS	71
		MORANT	68
		MORDSEN?	58
MELLON	83,99	MOREE	80
MENKIN	54	MORGAN	36,43,46,47,62,80,82,86,93,99,100,110,111
MERCER	38,83,107		
MERCHAND	46		
MERCHANT	38		
MERRICK	84	MORRIS	108,115
MESSER	81	MORRISON	41,110
MICKLER	31,36,39,40,42,45,46,63,73-77,79,81,83,87,100,101,105,106,115	MORSE	80
		MOSELEY	36,38-40,46-48,52-54,56-60,64,70,77,78,81,82,86,89,90,95,96,101,112
MIKELL	47,85,87,101,110		
MILES	98	MOSES	113
MILLANS	47	MOTE	75
MILLER	36,44,46-48,65,69,74,78,85,101,105,108,111,112,116,120	MOTES	43,120
		MOTLEY	36
		MOTON	47,99
		MUDGE	83
MILLEY	100	MULCAHEY	84
MILLS	37-39,46,47,69,70,72,80,81,85,86,87,90,100,101,110,111,114,119,	MULLER	48
		MULVALHAL	83
		MURDOCK	31,36,39,45,75,77,86,87,90,100,107,118
MILTON	62,98,115		
MIMMS	36,47,49,70,72,73,77,79,80,82,89,90,93-95,97,98,101,106	MURPHY	40,46,80,81,86
		MURRAY	38,54,66,68
		MUSTELL	84
MINTON	84		
MITCHELL	36,38,39,47,60,86,87,93,94,97,98,100,109	NALEY	67
		NASH	120
		NEELEY	83,86,87,107
MIXON	70,77,82,86,99,100	NELSON	64,68,79,98
MIXSON	53,90,93,94,109,113	NESMITH	122
		NETTLES	119
MIZELL	46,86,87,115,121	NEVEILS	113
MOAH?	97	NEWBURN	36
MOAT	73	NEWELL	83
MOBLEY	36,45,47,95,96,99,101	NEWLAN	86,109
		NEWLAND	55,95,96,98,119
MOCK	120	NEWMAN	46,51,68,71,72,75,77,78,80,87,90,95,
MOFFET	53		

	97,121
NEWSOME	26,98,112
NEWSON	113
NEWTON	44
NIBLACK	43,44,75,77,95,121
NICHOLAS	83
NILES	70
NIX	119
NIXON	46,82
NOBLE	84
NOBLES	32,47,48,82,86,87,99,113
NOEGEL	116
NORRILL	93,120
NORRIS	49,105
NORTON	83
NORWOOD	39
NUNEZ	44
NUTTER	81
O'DONIEL	38
O'HARA	38,57,86,107,109
O'NEAL	62,81,111
O'NEIL	36,42,86,93
OATES	72,76,80,90
ODUM	47,71,79,80,120
OGDEN	86,110,111
OGLESBY	76
OLLIFF	39,40,58,60,73,80,93
OLIVER	38,81,106,119
OMANS	58
OSBURN	43
OSTEEN	36,41,43,75,82,89,121
OTA	119
OVERSTREET	41,47,48,52,57,64,75,77,79-81,86,87,89,90,96,98,109,115
OWENS	73,75,80,86,87,90,100,119
PACE	93
PAGE	38,53,81,82,107
PAINTER	87
PALMER	72,77
PALMORE	93,94,112
PARDON	84
PARIS	67
PARKER	36,43,48,50,63,66,67,70-74,78-80,86,89,90,93,94,95,99,101,111,122
PARNELL	62,86,112
PARRAMORE	36,39,89
PARRISH	42-44,81,82,86,87,89,94,111,121
PARSHLEY	47,58-60,82,101,115
PARSONS	86
PASCHAL	72,75,77
PATRICK	38
PATTERSON	38,107
PATTON	56,83
PAYNE	44
PEACOCK	36-40,48,62,66,71,72,74-81,90,93,96,101
PEARCE	44
PEARSON	36
PEED	38,90
PEEK	38,109,122
PELHAM	43
PELLAM	98
PELOT	36,40,53
PENNYPACKER	68
PEOPLES	44,121
PEPPERDAY	66
PERNANCE	53
PERRY	47,83,101,118
PERSONS	66
PETERS	67
PETERSON	36,38,42,44,48,71,75,82,90,99,112,118
PETOLLE	43
PETTIWAY	93
PHILLIPS	47,56,67,72,83,84,87,96,102,105,109,115,119
PICKARD	64,65
PIERCE	43
PINKHAM	38,65,107
PIPKIN	36,75,80,90
PIPKINS	73,100
PIRTLE	39
PITTS	120
PLANT	119
PLATT	36,38,39,41-43,47,64,86,90,93,97,109
PLEASANT	74
PLOWDEN	90,91
POLITE	38,46,47,99,101
POLK	36,38,41,71,73,74,80,90,93,120
POMPEY	105

PONCHIER	36,39,40,46,73,74,76,78,80,87,90,93
PONDE	118
PONDERGAST	53
POOL	120
POPPELL	89
PORTER	61,114,119
POSEY	120
POSTELL	70,90
POTSDAMER	64,95,119
POUCHER	97,101
POWELL	32,36,39,42,44,49,51,52,71,74-76,79,81,90,110,118,119,121
POWERS	78
PRESTON	52
PREVATT	41,43,44,93,121
PRICE	47
PRINCE	45,119
PRIVETT	56,86,87,105
PRIZER	68
PROCTOR	83
PURVIS	97,110
PURVIANCE	56,75,90,93
PUTNAM	102
PYLE	120
QUARTERMAN	98,99
QUICK	97
QUIETTE	48,87,112
QUINCE	73,93
QUINN	84,97
RADFORD	65
RAFFERTY	83
RAGAN	86,87,114
RAINEY	70
RAINS	101
RAMAGE	120
RAMSEY	99,101,102
RAMSOUR?	93
RANDALL	84
RANDAN	122
RANDOLPH	47
RANKIN	86,87,114
RAULERSON	43,44,96,121
RAUSE	38
RAWLINS	37,86
RAWLS	36,40,47,71,75,90,93,98-100
RAY	67,122
RAYFORD	119
REDDICK	47,118
REDDING	36,39,41,48,80,81,94,118
REDMAN	45,99
REED	36,46,73,77,86,96,112,119-121
REES	61,63,68,96
REGISTER	65,67,68
REID	38,86,87,95,98,113
RENFROW	43
RENTZ	36
REVEL	118
REVELLS	39,86
REYNOLDS	54
RHODES	100
RICE	39,48,51-54,77,90,96,101,109,119
RICHARD	119
RICHARDSON	41,86,109,114
RICHEY	120
RICKERSON	38,109
RICKS	101
RIDDLESPERGER	120
RIDOUT	86
RIDGEWAY	41,121
RIGDON	81
RIGGS	39,105
RIGGSBEE	45,49,50,59,70,74,81,90,99-101
RILEY	67,71,79,83,99,100,105,108,111
RIVERS	48,65,115
RIXFORD	59,84,86
ROAD	72
ROBBERDS	90
ROBBINS	59
ROBERSON	98
ROBERTS	36,38,41-45,73,77,79-82,87,89,90,94,96,97,101,110,113,118,121
ROBERTSON	37,39,41,47,48,61,67,81-83,86,90,94,97,100,111,114,115,120
ROBINSON	36,37,39,40,55,57,62,64,65,94,95,100,101,108,109,120,121
ROBISON	48
ROCKNER	119
RODGERS	51,119
ROEBUCK	75,93,97
ROGERS	50,72,76,86,95,97,113

ROLAND	36,90	SELF	97
ROLLINS	38,48,120	SELLERS	38,81
ROONEY	83	SELMAN	36,101
ROSIER	108	SELPH	41,45,100
ROSS	36,38,42,43,48,50, 63,71,78,86,95,96, 109,114,121	SENNAN	84
		SESSIONS	38,39,45,46,56,58, 63,74,76,77,82,86, 87,89,91,93,94-96, 101,102,106,108, 110,119
ROSSEAU	36,39,40,42,51,73, 74,76,80,90,95,96, 98		
ROTHCHILD	72	SEWN?	40
ROUNDTREE	75,122	SHAFFER	48,93
ROUSE	41,46,47,98,99	SHANNON	46
ROUSSAN	101	SHARPE	27,28,32,37,83,84
ROWDEN	114	SHAVERS	119
ROWLAND	36,40,42,71	SHAW	82,84,101
ROWLEY	119	SHEALY	121
RUNER	84	SHEARECKER	83
RUSHING	44	SHEEFFILIN	93
RUSSELL	84,101	SHEFFIELD	37,39,40,72,75,91, 93
RUSSEN	40		
RUTHERFORD	122	SHELDON	61
RUTLEDGE	43	SHELFER	86,87
RYAN	83	SHELL	119
		SHELTON	73,90
		SHEPPARD	38,39,48,74,77,86
		SHERWOOD	55,68
SADLER	41	SHIP	47,101
SALES	101	SHIVER	102
SALMOND	41	SHORTER	100
SALTER	43	SHULER	99,100
SANDERLING	44	SHUMARD	84
SANDERS	48,78,80,91	SILAS	47,70
SAPP	43,45,62,86,89,99	SIMMONS	42,46,75,78,83,91, 97,100,101,119
SARLES	84		
SAUCER	86	SIMMS	45,93
SAUNDERS	72,93,94	SIMPKINS	119
SAVAGE	39,42,47,73,77	SIMPSON	14,38,82,86,94,112 120
SAVER	111		
SAVIN	83	SIONS	47
SAWYER	91	SIPPLE	41
SCARBOROUGH	39,43,79,101	SISTRUNK	37,42,89
SCARLETT	122	SKEEN	38,39,47,53,57,63, 73,78,80,91,106
SCHAFFER	84,101		
SCHAFFNER	68	SKELTON	87
SCHNEIDER	62,83	SLADE	41,43
SCOTT	38,44,46,57,73,82, 86,87,89,93,98,99, 109,112,114,115	SLATE	82,95,101,108
		SLATEN	39
		SLOAN	89
SCRANTON	47	SMALL	109
SCRIVEN	101	SMILEY	37,72,73,76,98,99, 101
SEALEY	74,87,110		
SEALMAN	50,93	SMITH	32,37,41-49,52,54, 63,65,68,73,75-78, 81,82,86,87,90,93,
SEARS	36,66,90		
SEE	118		

142

	94,96-101,105,106, 108,109,118,118-121	STRICKLAND	38,43,89,111,114
		STRINGER	120.122
		STRINGFELLOW	98
SMITHIE	115	STULMAN	84
SMITHSON	37,64,65,96	SULLIVAN	47,66,86,101
SMOKE	100	SUMMER	67
SMYTH	83	SUMMERALL	44,121
SNEAD	46	SUMMERFORD	100
SNELL	72-74,80,90,94,95,99	SUMMERLAND	91
		SUMMERLIN	43,89,95,121
SNIDER	86	SUMNER	112
SNODGRASS	76,77,80,91	SURAT	43
SOLOMON	108	SURRENCY	86,113
SOWELL	46	SUTTON	41,46,100,101
SPARKMAN	41-43,75,121	SWAILS	81,82,101
SPARKS	120	SWAN	120
SPEAR	37,81	SWASEY	68
SPEARS	91	SWEAT	87
SPEIR	50,71,74,75,79,80,98	SWEATMAN	84
		SWEET	41
SPENCER	37,39,48,72,76,81, 82,84,94,103,107, 121	SWETT	43,44
		SWIFT	103
		SWINDALL	41,121
SPERRING	67,68,81,114	SWINNEY	44
SPRINGER	119	SYKES	37,83
STAFFORD	44,83,87,93,97,98		
STALLSWORTH	119		
STANFORD	87,114	TABB	47
STANLEY	38	TALBERT	63
STANSEL	45,67,86,87,91,111 112	TARVES?	60
		TARVIN	121
STANTON	61	TATUM	43,87,91,105
STAPLETON	47,86,110	TAVEL	47
STARLING	38,84,86,87,89,113 114	TAYLOR	31,37-39,42,45,47, 49,51-53,56,58,59, 70-77,81,83,86,89, 91,98-102,107,108, 113
STEADWELL	74		
STEBBINS	47,53,54,56,95		
STEELE	50,93,118		
STEPHENS	44,47,48,60,75,81, 86,89,91,99,112	TEBEAU	121
		TEDDER	45,52,65,71,72,74-78,80,86,87,91,93, 115
STEVENS	86,89,111,118		
STEWART	37-40,43,44,46,47, 63,73,75-80,83,84, 86,87,89,90,98,101 110,112,115,120		
		TELFORD	38,48,54,77
		THATCHALL	84
		THATCHER	120
STINSON	47	THEIS	84
STOCKTON	45,46,86,99,101, 113	THIGPEN	122
		THOMAS	37,43-47,49,73,74, 76,84,86,93,99,101 104,111,114,122
STOKELEY	37,39		
STOKES	45,54,87,103,106, 111		
		THOMPSON	37-39,43,44,73,75, 77,78,83,84,86,91, 93,98,101,113
STONE	61,77		
STORRS	23		
STORY	89,122	THOMSON	51
STRANG	115	THORNHILL	38,47

THORNTON	83	URSEY	86
THRALLS	96		
TIDWELL	39		
TIER	43		
TIFFINS	121	VAILING	84
TILLIS	37,39,40,42,43,70, 73,74,76,77,80,89, 91,93,97,98,121	VANN	38,87,89,111
		VARNES	43
		VAYLES	86
TILLMAN	47,62,99,105,122	VICKERS	43,44
TIMMERMON	82	VILLALONGA	73
TIMMONS	47	VINZANT	43,79,96,121
TINDALL	120	VAUPELL	100
TISON	30,35,40,43,86,101 107,110,115	VOREEZS	44
		VOYLES	109
TISORD	37	VREELAND	84
TODD	72,119		
TOLBERT	121		
TOLE	57	WADE	47
TOMLINSON	86	WADSWORTH	37,43,66,77
TOMPKINS	38,64,75,78,80,86, 91,110	WAGNER	84
		WAH	118
TOOL	84	WAIT	120
TOWNER	57	WALDRON	116
TOWNSEND	43,44,70,78,115	WALKER	38,39,42-44,47,48, 71,73,78-80,84,89, 91,94,97,98,100, 101,114,119,120, 122
TRAPP	68		
TREADWELL	73,99		
TREAT	84		
TREPPARD	119		
TREZVANT	72-74,93,121	WALLACE	46,47,98
TRIMMOUS	50	WALLER	42
TRIP	38	WALLS	62,86,105
TRIPLETT	51,91	WALSTON	76,86
TRUBUCK	75	WALTERS	55,115
TRUIT	76,97	WALTON	48,60,87
TRYVANT	42	WANDELL	83
TUCK	84	WARD	43,47,81,122
TUCKER	44,89,119	WARDLAW	93,101
TULLIS	42,46	WARNER	114
TUMMAND?	65	WARREN	86,113
TUNNO	93	WARRICK	73,74,78
TURNER	38,41,48,70,78,86, 87,91,118,120	WASHBURN	60
		WASHINGTON	37,38,64,68,77,91, 99,100,112
TUTEN	42,46	WATSON	39,47,48,51,62,70-72,74,75,79,80,86, 91,93,97,100,118, 120
TUTORS	78		
TYLER	48		
TYNER	37,57,91,119		
TYSON	39,45,47,111		
		WATERS	102
		WATTERS	43
ULM	86	WATTS	29,37,41
UMSTEAD	86,96,105	WAYNE	42
UNDERHILL	44	WEAVER	118
UNDERWOOD	43,93,95	WEBB	37,42
URGUHART	37,45,72-74,78,91, 93,96,97,99,100	WEDELL	67
		WEEKS	37,42-44,47,121

WEIGHT	38	WISHARD	77,93
WELCH	84,121	WITT	121
WELLS	39,45,67,84,121	WOLFE	59,60,64
WESHING	84	WOOD	27,37,39,42,43,46,47,58,63,73,76,77,79,89,91,93,110,121
WESLEY	47,81		
WESSON	73		
WEST	41,47,66,67,78,119		
WESTBURY	37	WOODRUFF	84,120
WESTER	44	WOODS	74,116
WHALEY	86,87	WOODWARD	37
WHATLEY	109	WOOLEY	109
WHEELER	87	WORCESTER	83
WHETSEL	61	WORDLAW	67
WHIDDON	44,89	WORRELL	107
WHITE	38,39,41,46,47,51,53,56,59,61,63,82,83,86,87,89,95,101 106,111,119,120,122	WORTHINGTON	43,44
		WORUFF?	98
		WREDE	73,77,86,112
		WRIGHT	41,43,47,60,76,77,79,81-84,86,91,94,105,106,120
WHITEHURST	37,42		
WHITFIELD	37,40,70	WYCHE	66,89
WHITMAN	113	wYLEY	91
WICKHAM	41	WYNN	46
WIGGINS	38,43,44,47,55,56,103,106	WYSE	48,54,81
WIGHTMAN	48		
WILBURN	68		
WILCOX	68	YARBOROUGH	73,91,93
WILDER	46,71,73,77,119	YEARICK	84
WILEY	42,70,71,75,76,78,97,99	YLVENTON	44
		YORK	69,83,84
WILKERSON	44	YOUMANS	120
WILKINS	47,77	YOUNG	38,46,48,49,54,75,77,81,84,86,95,99,102,112,113
WILKINSON	43,60,68,69,89		
WILKS	104,106		
WILLIAMS	37-48,56,58,61,63-65,67,73-76,81-84,86,87,89,91,93,94,97-102,104,107,109 110,112,113,115,118-120,122,123		
		ZEIGLER	84
		ZERBENDINE	44
		ZIPPERER	37,39,40,41,72,91,94,97,109
WILLIAMSON	121		
WILLINGHAM	44,119	ZOW	38,45
WILLIS	99		
WILSON	42,44,45,47,57,67,72,78,83,98-101,114,120		
WIMBERLY	78		
WINBURN	38,47,108		
WINCHESTER	120		
WINCY	38		
WINEGORD	44		
WINN	39,89		
WINSON	63		
WISE	39,71,93,118		

www.ingramcontent.com/pod-product-compliance
Lightning Source LLC
Chambersburg PA
CBHW080404170426
43193CB00016B/2803